PRIZE ESSAYS

OF THE

AMERICAN HISTORICAL ASSOCIATION

———

1910

THE NEGRO IN PENNSYLVANIA

SLAVERY—SERVITUDE—FREEDOM

1639–1861

BY

EDWARD RAYMOND TURNER, Ph. D.,
PROFESSOR OF HISTORY IN THE UNIVERSITY OF MICHIGAN

NEGRO UNIVERSITIES PRESS
NEW YORK

Originally published in 1911
by American Historical Assocaition

Reprinted 1969 by
Negro Universities Press
A DIVISION OF GREENWOOD PUBLISHING CORP.
NEW YORK

SBN 8371-2045-4

To

My Father
CHARLES TURNER

AND TO

My Mother
ROSALIND FLYNN TURNER

This Book
IS DEDICATED IN
Loving Remembrance

PREFACE.

THIS work was undertaken for the purpose of obtaining exact information about the status of the negro in some section of the United States. Pennsylvania was chosen because of the great store of material available for such a study. An attempt has been made to give a complete account of the legal, social, and economic history of the Pennsylvania negro in his rise from slavery to freedom. The study ends with 1861.

Among the more important things revealed by the investigation are the following:

(1) Slavery in Pennsylvania, as regards its legal origin, was probably a divergence from servitude.

(2) This slavery was a development—very different at different times.

(3) As a race movement the rise of the negro from one status to another was gradual—he passed from slavery through intermediate stages of servitude to freedom.

(4) The gradual rise continued after he became free, for he was not yet upon a plane of equality with the white man. There was civil inequality until 1780; political inferiority until 1870.

(5) Under favorable conditions the social and economic improvement of the negro was considerable.

(6) A strong race prejudice developed among the white people after most of the negroes were free.

(7) The suffrage was never granted to the negroes in Pennsylvania before the Civil War.

(8) The friends of the negro were the Quakers, the abolitionists, and the anti-slavery advocates.

(9) Abolitionism preceded anti-slavery, and was less violent.

(10) Along with dislike for the negro developed a strong hostility to slavery, which was manifested in opposition to the extension of Southern slavery, and in encouragement given to fugitive slaves.

Effort has been made to consult all material bearing upon the subject, and many secondary works have been used. As a rule, however, lack of space has made it impossible to cite them, so that the several thousand references are almost exclusively to sources. The preparation of this work has entailed a search through some 3,000 printed volumes, more than 10,000 pamphlets, and probably 50,000 pages of manuscript.

The work was written at the suggestion of Professor James Curtis Ballagh of the Johns Hopkins University, whose unrivalled knowledge of all things relating to the legal development of American slavery was at all times at my service. From Professor John Martin Vincent of the Johns Hopkins I had helpful and kindly guidance, while for that sympathetic assistance and stimulating criticism which mean so much to the beginner, I am indebted to Professor Charles McLean Andrews, now of Yale University.

It is a pleasure to recall the courtesy shown me while I was carrying on my researches. I am under obligations to Dr. John W. Jordan, Mr. Ernest Spofford, and Miss Wiley, of the Historical Society of Pennsylvania, to Mr. Bunford Samuel of the Ridgway Library, to Mr. Thomas Lynch Montgomery of the State Library at Harrisburg, and to Mr. Luther R. Kelker of the Division of Public Records in the same place. At the American Philosophical Society, the Library Company of Philadelphia, the Philadelphia Law Library, and the Peabody Library in Baltimore, I received numerous favors. The accumulations of the local historical societies were most graciously placed at my disposal, and in many cases I was allowed to inspect private collections, particularly that of Mr. Gilbert Cope of West Chester.

While I was writing my book I received helpful criticism from scholars who had studied various aspects of the subject. Among others I must mention Ex-Governor Samuel W. Pennypacker of Pennsylvania, President Isaac Sharpless of Haverford College, Professor Albert Bushnell Hart of Harvard University, and Dr. William Roy Smith of Bryn Mawr College.

Last of all it is a pleasure to acknowledge the particular obligations under which I am to my friend, Mr. Albert Cook Myers of Moylan, Pennsylvania. Not only did he help and encourage me at every stage of my task, but with rare generosity he put at my disposal all of his own collections and his vast knowledge of the location of the sources for Pennsylvania history. At his suggestion and through his recommendation I used manuscripts which I could not have obtained otherwise. Not a few of the facts contained in my book were furnished by him directly.

EDWARD RAYMOND TURNER.

ANN ARBOR, MICHIGAN.

CONTENTS.

(xi)

CHAPTER I.

The Introduction of Negroes into Pennsylvania.

THERE were negroes in the region around the Delaware river before Pennsylvania was founded, in the days of the Dutch and the Swedes. As early as 1639 mention is made of a convict sentenced to be taken to South River to serve among the blacks there.[1] In 1644 Anthony, a negro, is spoken of in the service of Governor Printz at Tinicum, making hay for the cattle, and accompanying the governor on his pleasure yacht.[2] In 1657 Vice-director Alricks was accused of using the Company's oxen and negroes. Five years later Vice-director Beekman desired Governor Stuyvesant to send him a company of blacks. In 1664 negroes were wanted to work on the lowlands along the Delaware. A contract was to be made for fifty, which the West India Company would furnish.[3] In the same year, when the

---

[1] Breviate. Dutch Records, no. 2, fol. 5. In 2 *Pennsylvania Archives*, XVI, 234. *Cf.* Hazard, *Annals of Pennsylvania*, 49. The " Proposed Freedoms and Exemptions for New Netherland," 1640, say, " The Company shall exert itself to provide the Patroons and Colonists, on their order with as many Blacks as possible " . . . 2 *Pa. Arch.*, V, 74.

[2] C. T. Odhner. " The Founding of New Sweden, 1637-1642 ", translated by G. B. Keen in *Pennsylvania Magazine of History and Biography*, III, 277.

[3] Hazard, *Annals of Pennsylvania*, 331; O'Callaghan, *Documents relative to the Colonial History of the State of New York*, II, 213, 214. The Report of the Board of Accounts on New Netherland, Dec. 15, 1644, had spoken of the need of negroes, the economy of their labor, and had recommended the importation of large numbers. 2 *Pa. Arch.*, V, 88. See also Davis, *History of Bucks County*, 793.

English captured New Amstel, afterward New Castle, the place was plundered, and a number of negroes were confiscated and sold. From Peter Alricks several were taken; of these eleven were restored to him.[4] At least a few were living on the shores of the Delaware River in 1677.[5] A year later an emissary was sent by the justices of New Castle to request most urgently permission to import negroes from Maryland.[6]

Thus negroes had been brought into the country before Pennsylvania was founded. Immediately after Penn's coming there is record of them in his first counties. They were certainly present in Philadelphia County in 1684, and in Chester in 1687.[7] Penn himself noticed them in his charter to the Free Society of Traders. In 1702 they were spoken of as numerous.[8] By that time merchants of Philadelphia made the im-

---

[4] 2 Pa. Arch., XVI, 255, 256; Hazard, Annals of Pennsylvania, 372. Sir Robert Carr, writing to Colonel Nicholls, Oct. 13, 1664, says, " I have already sent into Merryland some Neegars wᶜʰ did belong to the late Governor att his plantation above " . . . 2 Pa. Arch., V, 578.

[5] The Records of the Court of New Castle give a list of the " Names of the Tijdable prsons Living in this Courts Jurisdiction " in which occur " three negros ": " 1 negro woman of Mr. Moll ", " 1 neger of Mr. Alrichs ", " Sam Hedge and neger ". Book A, 197-201. Quoted in Pa. Mag., III, 352-354. For the active trade in negroes at this time cf. MS. Board of Trade Journals, II, 307.

[6] " Wth out wch wee cannot subsist " . . . MS. New Castle Court Records, Liber A, 406. Hazard, Annals, 456.

[7] " Ik hebbe geen vaste Dienstbode, als een Neger die ik gekocht heb." Missive van Cornelis Bom, Geschreven uit de Stadt Philadelphia, etc., 3. (Oct. 12, 1684). " Man hat hier auch Zwartzen oder Mohren zu Schlaven in der Arbeit." Letter, probably of Hermans Op den Graeff, Germantown, Feb. 12, 1684, in Sachse, Letters relating to the Settlement of Germantown, 25. Cf. also MS. in American Philosophical Society's collection, quoted in Pa. Mag., VII, 106: " Lacey Cocke hath A negroe " . . . , " Pattrick Robbinson--Robert neverbeegood his negor sarvant " . . . " The Defendts negros " are mentioned in a suit for damages in 1687. See MS. Court Records of Penna. and Chester Co., 1681-1688, p. 72.

[8] MS. Ancient Records of Philadelphia, 28 7th mo., 1702.

portation of negroes a regular part of their business.[9] Thenceforth they are a noticeable factor in the life of the colony.

While there was an active demand for negroes, there was, nevertheless, almost from the first, strong opposition to importing them. This is evident from the fact that during the colonial period the Assembly of Pennsylvania passed a long series of acts imposing restrictions upon the traffic. In 1700 a maximum duty of twenty shillings was imposed on each negro imported. Five years later this duty was doubled.[10] By that time there had arisen a strong adverse sentiment, due partly to economic causes, since the white workmen complained that their wages were lowered by negro competition, and partly to fear aroused by an insurrection of slaves in New York.[11] Accordingly in 1712 the Assembly very boldly passed an act to prevent importation, seeking to accomplish this purpose by making the duty twenty pounds a head. The law was immediately repealed in England, the Crown not being disposed to tolerate such independent action, nor willing to allow interference with the African Company's trade.[12] Either the local feeling was too strong, or the requirements were less, since in spite of this failure there was for a while a falling off in the

[9] MS. William Trent's Ledger, 156. For numerous references to negroes brought from Barbadoes, see MS. Booke of acctts Relating to the Barquentine *Constant Ailse* Andw: Dykes mastr: from March 25th 1700 (— 1702). (Pa. State Lib.)

[10] *Statutes at Large of Pennsylvania* (edited by J. T. Mitchell and Henry Flanders), II, 107. *Ibid.*, II, 285. The act of 1705-1706 was repeated in 1710-1711. *Ibid.*, II, 383. Cf. *Colonial Records of Pennsylvania*, II, 529, 530.

[11] *Votes and Proceedings of the House of Representatives of the Province of Pennsylvania*, I, pt. II, 132. *Stat. at L.*, II, 433.

[12] MS. Board of Trade Papers, Proprieties, IX, Q, 39, 42. *Stat. at L.*, II, 543, 544.

number imported.[13]   A more moderate duty of five
pounds was imposed in 1715, but again the English
authorities interposed, repealing it in 1719. Meanwhile
an act to continue this duty had been passed in 1717-
1718, but apparently it was not submitted to the Crown.
In 1720-1721 the five pound duty was again imposed,
this act also not being submitted. In 1722 the duty was
repeated, and once more the law expired by limitation
before it was sent up for approval.[14]

Up to this time restrictive legislation had been largely
frustrated. It had encountered not only the disapproval
of certain classes in Pennsylvania, but the powerful
opposition of the African Company, which could count
on the decisive interposition of the Lords of Trade.[15]
The Assembly accordingly submitted the acts long after
they had been passed, and made new laws before the
old ones had been disallowed.[16] Nevertheless the number

[13] Jonathan Dickinson, a merchant of Philadelphia, writing to a cor-
respondent in Jamaica, 4th month, 1715, says, " I must entreat you to
send me no more negroes for sale, for our people don't care to buy. They
are generally against any coming into the country." I have been unable
to find this letter. Watson, who quotes it (*Annals of Philadelphia*, II,
264), says, " Vide the Logan MSS." *Cf.* also a letter of George Tiller
of Kingston, Jamaica, to Dickinson, 1712. MS. Logan Papers, VIII, 47.

[14] *Stat. at L.*, III, 117, 118; MS. Board of Trade Papers, Prop., X, 2,
Q, 159; *Stat. at L.*, III, 465; *Col. Rec.*, III, 38, 144, 171. During this
period negroes were being imported through the custom-house at the
rate of about one hundred and fifty a year. *Cf. Votes and Proceedings*,
II, 251.

[15] In 1727 the iron-masters of Pennsylvania petitioned for the entire
removal of the duty, labor being so scarce. *Votes and Proceedings*, 1726-
1742, p. 31. The attitude of the English authorities is explained in a
report of Richard Jackson, March 2, 1774, on one of the Pennsylvania
impost acts. " The Increase of Duty on Negroes in this Law is Mani-
festly inconsistent with the Policy adopted by your Lordships and your
Predecessors for the sake of encouraging the African Trade " . . . Board
of Trade Papers, Prop., XXIII, Z, 54.

[16] *Votes and Proceedings*, II, 152; *Col. Rec.*, II, 572, 573; 1 *Pa. Arch.*,
I, 160-162; *Votes and Proceedings*, 1766, pp. 45, 46. For a complaint
against this practice *cf.* " Copy of a Representat⁰ of the Board of Trade
upon some pennsylvania Laws " (1713-1714). MS. Board of Trade Papers,
Plantations General, IX, K, 35.

of blacks in the colony had steadily increased, and in 1721 was estimated to be somewhere between twenty-five hundred and five thousand.[17] The wrath of the white laborers was correspondingly increased, and in this year they presented to the Assembly a petition asking for a law to prevent the hiring of blacks. The Assembly resolved that such a law would be injurious to the public and unjust to those who owned negroes and hired them out, but the restrictions on importing them were maintained.[18] In 1725-1726 the five pound duty was imposed again, and in the same year five pounds extra was placed upon every convict negro brought into the colony. This became law by lapse of time.[19]

In 1729 the duty was reduced to two pounds. This duty continued in force for a generation, satisfactory partly because the opposition to importing negroes seems to have been less strong, partly because white servants proved to be cheaper and more adapted to industrial demands.[20] The newspaper advertisements announce the arrival of many more cargoes of servants than of negroes; this notwithstanding the fact that white servants frequently ran away, often to enlist in the wars. Referring to this fact a message from the Assembly to the governor says that while the King has seemed to desire the importation of servants rather than of negroes,

[17] O'Callaghan, *N. Y. Col. Docs.*, V, 604.
[18] *Votes and Proceedings*, II, 347.
[19] *Stat. at L.*, IV, 52-56, 60; *Col. Rec.*, III, 247, 248, 250.
[20] *Stat. at L.*, IV, 123-128; *Col. Rec.*, III, 359; Smith, *History of Delaware County*, 261. For a while, no doubt, there was a considerable influx. Ralph Sandiford says (1730), " We have *negroes* flocking in upon us since the duty on them is reduced to 40 shillings per head." *Mystery of Iniquity*, (2d ed.), 5. Many of these were smuggled in from New Jersey, where there was no duty from 1721 to 1767. Cooley, *A Study of Slavery in New Jersey*, 15, 16.

yet the enlistment acts make such property so precarious, that it seems to depend on the will of the servant
and the pleasure of the officer.[21] Nevertheless the number of negroes brought in steadily dwindled. By 1750
importation had nearly ceased.[22]

A few years later the great efforts made in the last
French and Indian War caused loud complaints again
about enlisting servants. It was feared that people
would be driven to the necessity of providing themselves
with negro slaves, as property in them seemed more
secure. This is probably just what occurred, for the
increase of negroes is said to have been alarming.[23] As
a result restrictive legislation was tried again in 1761,
when the duty was made ten pounds. The law was
carried only after considerable effort. While the bill
was in the hands of the governor a petition was sent to
him, signed by twenty-four merchants of Philadelphia,
who set forth the scarcity and high price of labor, and
their need of slaves. After two months' contest the bill
was passed. One provision of the act was that a new
settler need not pay the duty if he did not sell his slave
within eighteen months.[24] In 1768 this act was renewed.

[21] Cargoes of servants are advertised in the *American Weekly Mercury*,
the *Pennsylvania Packet*, and the *Pennsylvania Gazette*, *passim*. As to
enlistment of servants *cf. Mercury, Gazette*, Aug. 7, 1740; *Col. Rec.*, IV,
437. Complaint about this had been made as early as 1711. *Votes and
Proceedings*, II, 101, 103.

[22] Smith, *History of Delaware County*, 261; Peter Kalm, *Travels into
North America*, etc., (1748), I, 391.

[23] *Col. Rec.*, VII, 37, 38.

[24] *Stat. at L.*, VI, 104-110; *Votes and Proceedings*, 1761, pp. 25, 29, 33,
38, 39, 40, 41, 52, 55, 63; *Col. Rec.*, VIII, 575, 576. "The Petition of
Divers Merchants of the City of Philadelphia, To The Honble James
Hamilton Esqr. Lieut. Governor of the Province of Pennsylvania, Humbly Sheweth, That We the Subscribers . . . have seen for some time past,
the many inconveniencys the Inhabitants have suffer'd, for want of Labourers, and Artificers, by Numbers being Inlisted for His Majestys

In 1773 it was made perpetual, the former law having been found to be of great public utility; but the duty was raised to twenty pounds. Once more the act became law by lapse of time.[25]

The act of 1773 was the last one which the Assembly passed to limit the importation of negroes. Not only was the duty sufficiently high, now, but its presence was hardly needed.[26] A silent but powerful movement was overthrowing slavery in Pennsylvania; and in a short time the outbreak of the Revolutionary War brought the traffic to an end. Shortly thereafter, in 1780, the state did what England had never permitted while she held authority: forbade the importation of slaves entirely.[27]

The real reason for the passage of these laws is not always clear. They may have been passed either to keep negroes out,[28] or to raise revenue for the govern-

Service and near a total stop to the importation of German and other white Servants, have for some time encouraged the importation of Negros, . . . that an advantage may be gain'd by the Introduction of Slaves, wch will likewise be a means of reduceing the exorbitant Price of Labour, and in all Probability bring our staple Commoditys to their usual Prices." MS. Provincial Papers, XXV, March 1, 1761.

[26] *Stat. at L.*, VII, 158, 159; VIII, 330-332; *Col. Rec.*, IX, 400, 401, 443, ff.; X, 72, 77. The Board of Trade Journals, LXXXII, 47, (May 5, 1774), say that their lordships had some discourse with Dr. Franklin " upon the objections . . . to . . . *imposing Duties amounting to a prohibition upon the Importation of Negroes.*"

[26] *Cf.* MS. Provincial Papers, XXXII, January, 1775.

[27] *Stat. at L.*, X, 72, 73. It was forbidden by implication rather than specific regulation. It had been foreseen that an act for gradual abolition entailed stopping the importation of negroes. *Pa. Packet*, Nov. 28, 1778; 1 *Pa. Arch.*, VII, 79.

[28] Professor E. P. Cheyney in an article written some years ago (" The Condition of Labor in Early Pennsylvania, I. Slavery," in *The Manufacturer*, Feb. 2, 1891, p. 8) considers these laws to have been restrictive in purpose, and gives three causes for their passage, in the following order of importance: (a) dread of slave insurrections, (b) opposition of the free laboring classes to slave competition, (c) conscientious objections. I

8   THE NEGRO IN PENNSYLVANIA

ment.²⁹ An analysis of the laws themselves seems to
show that both of these purposes were constantly in
mind.³⁰ When, however, they are taken in connection
with matters which they themselves do not mention,
namely, the predominance of the Quakers in the colonial
Assembly together with the abhorrence which they felt
for the slave-trade and later for slavery itself,³¹ it be-

---

cannot think that this is correct. (a) seems to have been the impelling
motive only in connection with the law of 1712, and seems rarely to have
been thought of. It was urged in 1740, 1741, and 1742, when efforts were
being made to pass a militia law in Pennsylvania, but it attracted little
attention. *Cf.* MS. Board of Trade Papers, Prop., XV, T: 54, 57, 60.

²⁹ In a MS. entitled "William Penn's Memorial to the Lords of Trade
relating to several laws passed in Pensilvania," assigned to the year 1690
in the collection of the Historical Society of Pennsylvania, but probably
belonging to a later period, is the following: " These . . . Acts . . . to Raise
money . . . to defray publick Exigences in such manner as after a Mature
deliberaĉon they thought would not be burthensom particularly in the Act
for laying a Duty on Negroes " . . . MS. Pa. Miscellaneous Papers, 1653-
1724, p. 24.

³⁰ 1700. 20 shillings for negroes over sixteen years of age, 6 for those
under sixteen. No cause given. Apparently (terms of the act) *revenue.*—
1705-1706. 40 shillings—a draw-back of one half if the negro be re-
exported within six months. Apparently *revenue.*—1710. 40 shillings—
excepting those imported by immigrants for their own use, and not sold
within a year. Almost certainly (preamble) *revenue.*—1712. 20 pounds.
The causes were a dread of insurrection because of the negro uprising
in New York, and the Indians' dislike of the importation of Indian
slaves. Purpose undoubtedly *restriction.*—1715. 5 pounds. Apparently
(character of the provisions) *restriction* and *revenue.*—1717-1718. 5
pounds. To continue the preceding. *Restriction* and *revenue.*—1720-
1721. 5 pounds. To continue the preceding. *Revenue* (preamble) and
restriction.—1722. 5 pounds. To continue provisions of previous acts.
Revenue and *restriction.*—1725-1726. 5 pounds. *Revenue* and *restriction.*—1729. 2 pounds. Reduction made probably because since 1712 none
of the laws had been allowed to stand for any length of time, and because
there had been much smuggling. *Revenue* and *restriction.*—1761. 10
pounds. No cause given for the increase. *Restriction* and *revenue.*—
1768. Preceding continued—" of public utility." *Restriction* and *revenue.*—1773. Preceding made perpetual—" of great public utility "—
but duty raised to 20 pounds. *Restriction. Cf. Stat. at L.,* II, 107, 285,
383, 433; III, 117, 159, 238, 275; IV, 52, 123; VI, 104; VII, 158; VIII,
330.

³¹ See below, chapters IV and V.

comes probable that the predominant motive was restriction.[32] It is also probable that while the obtaining of revenue was the obvious motive in many of these acts, yet revenue was so raised precisely because Pennsylvania desired to keep negroes out; that imported slaves were taxed largely for reasons similar to those which caused the Stuarts to tax colonial tobacco, and which lead modern governments to tax spirituous liquors and opium. It may be added that Pennsylvania always held, both in colonial times and afterwards, that England forced slavery upon her. That there was much justice in this complaint the failure of the earlier legislation goes far to sustain.[33]

The negroes imported were brought sometimes in cargoes, more often a few at a time. They came mostly from the West Indies, many being purchased in Barbadoes, Jamaica, Antigua, and St. Christophers.[34] As a

[32] " Man hat besonders in Pensylvanien den Grundsatz angenommen ihre Einführung so viel möglich abzuhalten " . . . *Achenwall's in Göttingen über Nordamerika und über dasige Grosbritannische Colonien aus mündlichen Nachrichten des Herrn Dr. Franklins . . . Anmerkungen*, 24, 25. (About 1760).

[33] *Stat. at L.*, X, 67, 68; I *Pa. Arch.*, I, 306. *Cf.* Mr. Woodward's speech, Jan. 19, 1838, *Proceedings and Debates of the Convention of the Commonwealth of Pennsylvania, to Propose Amendments to the Constitution*, etc., X, 16, 17.

[34] " Aus Pennsylvanien . . . fahren gen Barbadoes, Jamaica und Antego. Von dar bringen sie zurück . . . Negros." Daniel Falkner, *Curieuse Nachricht von Pennsylvania in Norden-America*, etc., (1702), 192. For a negro woman from Jamaica (1715), see MS. Court Papers, Philadelphia County, 1619-1732. Also numerous advertisements in the newspapers. *Mercury*, Apr. 17, 1729, (Barbadoes); July 31, 1729, (Bermuda); July 23, 1730, (St. Christophers); Jan. 21, 1739, (Antigua). Oldmixon, speaking of Pennsylvania, says, " Negroes sell here . . . very well; but not by the Ship Loadings, as they have sometimes done at Maryland and Virginia." (1741.) *British Empire in America*, etc., (2d ed.), I, 316. *Cf.* however the following: " A PARCEL of likely Negro Boys and Girls just arrived in the Sloop Charming Sally . . . to be sold . . . for ready Money, Flour or Wheat " . . . Advt. in *Pa. Gazette*, Sept. 4, 1740. For a consignment of seventy see MS. Provincial Papers, XXVII, Apr. 26, 1766.

rule they were imported by the merchants of Philadelphia, and, being received in exchange for grain, flour,
lumber, and staves, helped to make up the balance of
trade between Philadelphia and the islands.[85] A few
seem to have been obtained directly from Africa. When
so brought, however, they were found to be unable to
endure the winter cold in Pennsylvania, so that it was
considered preferable to buy the second generation in
the West Indies, after they had become acclimated.[86]
Some were brought from other colonies on the main-
land, particularly those to the south. At times Pennsylvania herself exported a few to other places.[87] The
prices paid in the colony naturally fluctuated from time
to time in accordance with supply and demand, and
varied within certain limits according to the age and
personal qualities of each negro. The usual price for
an adult seems to have been somewhere near forty
pounds.[88]

[85] *Cf.* MS. William Trent's Ledger, "Negroes" (1703-1708). Isaac
Norris, Letter Book, 75, 76 (1732). For a statement of profit and loss
on two imported negroes, see *ibid.,* 77. In this case Isaac Norris acted as
a broker, charging five per cent. For the wheat and flour trade with
Barbadoes, see *A Letter from Doctor More . . . Relating to the . . .
Province of Pennsilvania,* 5. (1686).

[86] Some were probably brought from Africa by pirates. *Cf.* MS. Board
of Trade Papers, Prop., III, 285, 286; IV, 369; V, 408. The hazard
involved in the purchase of negroes is revealed in the following: " Accot
of Negroes Dr to Tho. Willen £17: 10 for a New Negro Man . . . £15 and
50 Sh. more if he live to the Spring " . . . MS. James Logan's Account
Book, 91, (1714). As to the effect of cold weather upon negroes, Isaac
Norris, writing to Jonathan Dickinson in 1703, says, . . . " they're So
Chilly they Can hardly Stir frō the fire and Wee have Early beginning
for a hard Wintr." MS. Letter Book, 1702-1704, p. 109. In 1748 Kalm
says, . . . " the toes and fingers of the former " (negroes) " are frequently
frozen." *Travels,* I, 392.

[87] *Mercury,* Sept. 26, 1723. MS. Penn Papers, Accounts (unbound),
27 3d mo., 1741. Also *Calendar of State Papers, America and West
Indies, 1697-1698,* p. 390; *Col. Rec.,* IV, 515; *Pa. Mag.,* XXVII, 320.

[88] A Report of the Royal African Company, Nov. 2, 1680, purports to

As to the number of negroes in Pennsylvania at different times during the colonial period almost any estimate is at best conjecture. Not only are there few official reports, but these reports, in the absence of any definite census, are of little value.[39] Apparently one of the best estimates was that made in 1721, which stated the number of blacks at anywhere between 2,500 and 5,000.[40] In 1751 it was at least widely believed that

show the first cost: " That the Negros cost them the first price 5li: and 4li: 15s. the freight, besides 25li p cent which they lose by the usual mortality of the Negros." MS. Board of Trade Journals, III, 229. The selling price had been considered immoderate four years previous. *Ibid.*, I, 236. In 1723 Peter Baynton sold " a negroe man named Jemy . . . 30 £." Loose sheet in Peter Baynton's Ledger. In 1729 a negro twenty-five years old brought 35 pounds in Chester County. MS. Chester County Papers, 89. The Moravians of Bethlehem purchased a negress in 1748 for 70 pounds. *Pa. Mag.*, XXII, 503. Peter Kalm (1748) says that a full grown negro cost from 40 pounds to 100 pounds; a child of two or three years, 8 pounds to 14 pounds. *Travels*, I, 393, 394. Mittelberger (1750) says 200 to 350 florins (33 to 58 pounds). *Journey to Pennsylvania in the Year 1750*, etc., 106. Franklin (1751) in a very careful estimate thought that the price would average about 30 pounds. *Works* (ed. Sparks), II, 314. Acrelius (about 1759) says 30 to 40 pounds. *Description of . . . New Sweden*, etc. (translation of W. M. Reynolds, 1874, in *Memoirs of the Historical Society of Pennsylvania*, XI), p. 168. A negro iron-worker brought 50 pounds at Bethlehem in 1760. *Pa. Mag.*, XXII, 503. In 1790 Edward Shippen writes of a slave who cost him 100 pounds. *Ibid.*, VII, 31. It is probable that the value of a slave was roughly about three times that of a white servant. *Cf. Votes and Proceedings* (1764), V, 308.

[39] In 1708 the Board of Trade requested the governor of Pennsylvania that very definite information on a variety of subjects relating to the negro be transmitted thereafter half yearly. Were these records available they would be worth more than all the remaining information. *Cf.* MS. Provincial Papers, I, April 15, 1708; 1 *Pa. Arch.*, I, 152, 153.

[40] *N. Y. Col. Docs.*, V, 604. As to the necessity for allowing so large a margin in these figures *cf.* the following. " The number of the whites are said to be Sixty Thousand, and of the Black about five Thousand." Col. Hart's Answer, etc., MS. Board of Trade Papers, Prop., XI, R: 7. (1720). " The number of People in this Province may be computed to above 40,000 Souls amongst whom we have scarce any Blacks except a few Household Servants in the City of Philadelphia " . . . Letter of Sir William Keith, *ibid.*, XI, R: 42. (1722). Another communication gave the true state of the case, if not the exact numbers. " This Government has not hitherto had Occasion to use any methods that can furnish us

there were in Philadelphia 6,000, and it is asserted that
the total number in Pennsylvania including the Lower
Counties was 11,000.[41] It is probable that the same number was not much exceeded in Pennsylvania proper at
any time before 1790. In these estimates no attempt was
made to distinguish the free from the slaves. The number of slaves, it is true, was very near the total at both
these periods, but after the middle of the century it began dwindling as the number of negro servants and free
men increased. In 1780 a careful estimate placed the
slaves at 6,000.[42] According to the Federal census of
1790 the number of negroes in Pennsylvania was
10,274.[43]

Of these negroes the great majority throughout the
slavery period were located in the southeastern part of
Pennsylvania, in and around Philadelphia. There were
many in Bucks, Chester, Lancaster, Montgomery, and
York counties. There were negroes near the site of

with an exact Estimate, but as near as can at present be guessed there
may be about *Forty five thousand* Souls of *Whites* and *four thousand*
Blacks." Major Gordon's answer to Queries, *ibid.*, XIII, S: 34. (1730-
1731).

[41] William Douglass, *A Summary, Historical and Political,* . . . *of the
British Settlements in North-America*, etc. (ed. 1755), II, 324; Abiel
Holmes, *American Annals*, etc., II, 187; Bancroft, *History of the United
States* (author's last revision), II, 391.

[42] Letter in *Pa. Packet*, Jan 1, 1780. This made allowance for the numerous runaways during the British occupation of Philadelphia. Also *ibid.*,
Dec. 25, 1779; 1 *Pa. Arch.*, XI, 74, 75. For a higher estimate, 10,000, for
1780 but made in 1795, see MS. Collection of the Records of the Pa.
Society for the Abolition of Slavery, etc., IV, 111.

[43] Slaves, 3,737; free, 6,537. Other enumerations occur, but are evidently without value. Oldmixon (1741), 3,600. *British Empire in
America*, I, 321. Burke (1758), about 6,000. *An Account of the Euro-
pean Settlements in America*, II, 204. Abbé Raynal (1766), 30,000. *A
Philosophical and Political History of the British Settlements* . . . *in North
America* (tr. 1776), I, 163. A communication to the Earl of Dartmouth
(1773), 2,000. MS. Provincial Papers, Jan. 1775; 1 *Pa. Arch.*, IV, 597.
Smyth (1782), over 100,000. *A Tour in the United States of America*,
etc., II, 309.

Columbia by 1726. John Harris had slaves by the Susquehanna as early as 1733. In 1759 Hugh Mercer wrote from the vicinity of Pittsburg asking for two negro girls and a boy. The tax-lists and local accounts reveal their presence in many other places.[44] Doubtless a few might be traced wherever white people settled permanently. In general it may be said that they were owned in the English, Welsh, and Scotch-Irish communities. The Germans as a rule held no slaves.

Where negroes were owned they were for the most part evenly distributed, there being few large holdings. In rare instances a considerable number is recorded as belonging to one man, and the iron-masters generally had several. The tax-lists, however, indicate that the average holding was one or two, except in Philadelphia among the wealthier classes where it was double that number.[45]

The character of slavery in Pennsylvania was in many respects unique, but in no way was this so true as in connection with the number of negroes held. Generally speaking, the farther south a section lay the more

[44] MS. (Samuel Wright), A Journal of Our Rem(oval) from Chester and Darby (to) Conestogo . . . 1726, copied by A. C. Myers; Morgan, *Annals of Harrisburg*, 9-11; *Col. Rec.*, VIII, 305, 306. Tax-lists printed in 3 *Pa. Arch.* Also Davis, *Hist. of Bucks Co.*, 793; Futhey and Cope, *Hist. of Chester Co.*, 423 425; Ellis and Evans, *Hist. of Lancaster Co.*, 301; Gibson, *Hist. of York Co.*, 498; Bean, *Hist. of Montgomery Co.*, 302; Lytle, *Hist. of Huntingdon Co.*, 182; Blackman, *Hist. of Susquehanna Co.*, 72; Creigh, *Hist. of Washington Co.*, 362; Bausman, *Hist. of Beaver Co.*, I, 152, 153; Linn, *Annals of Buffalo Valley*, 66-74; Peck, *Wyoming; its History*, etc., 240.

[45] MS. Assessment Books, Chester Co., 1765, p. 197; 1768, p. 326; 1780, p. 95; MS. Assessment Book, Phila. Co., 1769. As early as 1688 Henry Jones of Moyamensing had thirteen negroes. MS. Phila. Wills, Book A, 84. An undated MS. entitled " A List of my Negroes " shows that Jonathan Dickinson had thirty-two. Dickinson Papers, unclassified. An owner in York County is said to have had one hundred and fifty. 3 *Pa. Arch.*, XXI, 71. This is probably a misprint.

slaves did it possess. Thus there were fewer in New
England than in the middle colonies; there were fewer
there than in the South. But to this rule Pennsylvania
was an exception, for it had fewer negroes than New
Jersey, and not half so many as New York.[46] This was
due to two sets of causes: the first, ethical; the second,
economic. The first of these are easily understood.
They resulted from the character of many of the people
who settled Pennsylvania, their dislike for slavery, and
their refusal to hold slaves. The second are not so
easily traceable, but were doubtless more powerful in
their influence, for they were owing to the character of
Pennsylvania's industrial growth.

The plantation system, which is most favorable to the
increase of slavery, never appeared in Pennsylvania.
During the whole of the eighteenth century the activ-
ities of the colony developed along two lines not favorable to negro labor: small farming, and manufacturing
and commerce.[47] The small farms were almost always
held by people who were too poor to purchase slaves, at
least for a long while, and the kind of farming was not
such as to make slavery particularly profitable. In commerce no large number of negroes was ever employed,
while manufacturing demanded a higher grade of labor
than slaves could give. It is true that in some cases
where there was an approach to the factory system, and
where the work was rough and needed little skill, slaves
could answer every purpose. For this reason at the old

---

[46] In 1790 the numbers were as follows: New York, 21,324 slaves, 4,654
free, total 25,978; New Jersey, 11,423 slaves, 4,402 free, total 15,825;
Pennsylvania, 3,737 slaves, 6,537 free, total 10,274.

[47] On Pennsylvania's amazing commercial and industrial activity see
Anderson, *Historical and Chronological Deductions of the Origin of Commerce*, etc. (1762), III, 75-77.

ironworks negroes were in demand.[48]   As a rule, however, this was not the case.   It was because of its industrial character that Pennsylvania was peculiarly the
colony of indentured white servants.

Furthermore, ethical and economic influences inter-
acted with subtle and powerful force.   Barring all other
considerations, the cost of a slave was a considerable
item, not to be afforded by a struggling settler; hence
slavery never attained magnitude on the frontier.   Before 1700 Pennsylvania was all frontier; hence it had
very few negroes.   In the period from 1700 to about
1750 the country between the Delaware and the Susquehanna was filled up, and the early conditions largely disappeared.   It was then that the greatest number of
negroes was introduced.   In the period between the
middle of the century and the Revolution this older
country became well developed and prosperous; farms
became larger and better cultivated; there were numerous respectable manufacturers and wealthy merchants.
These men could easily afford to have slaves, and large
importations might have been expected; but there was
no great influx of negroes.   Economic conditions were
favorable, but ethical influences worked strongly against
it.   In this eastern half of Pennsylvania two racial elements predominated: the Germans and the English
Quakers.   The Germans had abstained from slave-
holding from the first;[49] the Quakers were now coming
to abhor it.[50]   The same play of causes was seen again in
the " old West."   After 1750 in the mountains and val-
leys beyond the Susquehanna the earlier frontier condi-

[48] See below, p. 41.
[49] See below, chapters IV and V.
[50] See below, *ibid.*

tions were lived over again. Here the settlers were largely Scotch-Irish, and had no dislike for slavery, but as yet the conditions of their life did not favor it. When finally western Pennsylvania passed out of the frontier stage, and its inhabitants could purchase negroes, the days of slavery in Pennsylvania were nearly over.[51] For all of these reasons from first to last Pennsylvania's slave population remained small.

[51] Nevertheless slavery took root in the western counties, and lingered there longer than anywhere else in Pennsylvania.

CHAPTER II.

Legal Status of the Slave.

THE legal origin of slavery [1] in Pennsylvania is not easy to discover, for the statute of 1700, which seems to have recognized slavery there, is, like similar statutes in some of the other American colonies, very indirect and uncertain in its wording. Before this time, it is true, there occur instances where negroes were held for life, so that undoubtedly there was *de facto* slavery; but by what authority it existed, or how it began, is not clear. It may have grown up to meet the necessities of a new country. It may have been an inheritance from earlier colonists. More probably still, it developed by diverging from temporary servitude which, in the case of white servants at least, flourished among the earliest English settlers in the region.

It is probable that slavery existed among the Dutch of New Netherland, and possibly among the Swedes along the Delaware.[2] In 1664 their settlements passed under English authority. To regulate them the so-called "Duke of York's Laws" were promulgated. Meanwhile around the estuary of the Delaware English colonists were settling with their negroes. In 1676, five

[1] Throughout this work the fundamental distinction between the words "slave" and "servant," as used in the text, is that "slave" denotes a person held for life, "servant" a person held for a term of years only.

[2] *Cf.* O'Callaghan, *Voyages of the Slavers St. John and Arms of Amsterdam*, etc., 100, for a bill of sale, 1646. Sprinchorn, *Kolonien Nya Sveriges Historia*, 217.

years before Penn set out for his territories, the Duke's laws seem to have been obeyed in part of the Delaware River country.[a] In these laws servants for life are explicitly mentioned. In them it is also ordained that no Christian shall be held in bond slavery or villenage.[b] This latter may be a tacit permission to hold heathen negroes as slaves.

Not much can be based upon the Duke of York's laws since their meaning upon this latter point is doubtful. Moreover, when Penn founded his colony they were superseded after a short time by laws enacted in Pennsylvania assemblies. In the years following at first no act was passed recognizing slavery, but that some slaves were held there is apparent. Numerous little pieces of evidence may be accumulated indicating that there were negroes who were not being held as servants for a term of years, nor does anything appear to indicate that this was looked upon as illegal.[c] In 1685 William Penn,

[a] MS. Record of the Court at Upland in Penn., Sept. 25, 1676.

[b] "No Christian shall be kept in Bondslavery villenage or Captivity, Except Such who shall be Judged thereunto by Authority, or such as willingly have sould, or shall sell themselves," . . . *Laws of the Province of Pennsylvania* . . . *preceded by the Duke of York's Laws,* etc., 12. This is not to prejudice any masters " who have . . . Apprentices for Terme of Years, or other Servants for Term of years or Life." *Ibid.,* 12. Another clause directs that "No Servant, except such are duly so for life, shall be Assigned over to other Masters . . . for above the Space of one year, unless for good reasons offered ". *Ibid.,* 38.

[c] There is an evident distinction intended in the following: " A List of the Tydable psons James Sanderling and slave John Test and servant." One follows the other. MS. Rec. Court at Upland, Nov. 13, 1677. In 1686 the price of a negro, 30 pounds, named in a law-suit, is probably that of a slave. MS. Minute Book. Common Pleas and Quarter Sessions. Bucks Co., 1684-1730, pp. 56, 57. A will made in 1694 certainly disposed of the within mentioned negroes for life. "I do hereby give . . . powr . . . to my sd Exers . . . eithr to lett or hire out my five negroes . . . and pay my sd wife the one half of their wages Yearly during her life or Othrwise give her such Compensacon for her intrest therein as shee and my sd Exers shall agree upon and my will is that the other half of their sd wages

writing to his steward at Pennsbury, said that it would
be better to have blacks to work the place, since they
might be held for life.[6] In the same year by the terms of
a recorded deed a negro was sold to a new master " forever."[7] Three years later the Friends of Germantown
issued their celebrated protest against slavery,[8] while in
1693 George Keith denounced the practice of enslaving
men and holding them in perpetual bondage.[9] Meanwhile no law was made authorizing slavery in the colony, and no court seems to have been called upon to decide whether slavery was legal. It is not until 1700 that a
statute was passed bearing upon the subject. In that
year a law for the regulation of servants contains a section designed to prevent the embezzlement by servants
of their masters' goods. This section asserts that the
servant if white shall atone for such theft by additional

---

shall be equally Devided between my aforsd Children, and after my sd
wife decease my will also is That the sd negroes Or such of them and
their Offsprings as are then alive shall in kind or value be equally Devided
between my s^d Children " . . . Will of Thomas Lloyd. MS. Philadelphia
Wills, Book A, 267.

[6] Penn MSS., Domestic Letters, 17.

[7] " Know all men by these presents That I Patrick Robinson Countie
Clark of Philadelphia for and in Consideration of the Sum of fourtie
pounds Current Money of Pennsilvania . . . have bargained Sold and delivered . . . unto . . . Joseph Browne for himselfe, . . . heirs ex̄rs adm̄rs
and assigns One Negro man Named Jack, To have and to hold the Said
Negro man named Jack unto the said Joseph Browne for himself . . . for
ever. And I . . . the said Negro man unto him . . . shall and will warrant
and for ever defend by these presents." MS. Philadelphia Deed Book, E,
1, vol. V, 150, 151. This is similar to the regular legal formula afterward.
Cf. MS. Ancient Rec. Sussex Co., 1681-1709, Sept. 22, 1709.

[8] See below, p. 65.

[9] " And to buy Souls and Bodies of men for Money, to enslave them
and their Posterity to the end of the World, we judge is a great hinder-
ance to the spreading of the Gospel " . . . " neither should we keep them in
perpetual Bondage and Slavery against their Consent " . . . *An Exhortation and Caution To Friends Concerning buying or keeping of Negroes,*
reprinted in *Pa. Mag.,* XIII, 266, 268.

servitude at the end of his time sufficient to pay for double the value of the goods; but if black he shall be severely whipped in the most public place of the township.[10] It is probable that the law was so worded because it had come to be seen that there were few cases in which a negro could give satisfaction by additional time at the end of his term, since negroes were being held for life. If such be the case, this law may be said to contain the formal recognition of slavery in the colony.

The legal development of this slavery was rapid and brief. As it was not created by statutory enactment, so some of its most important incidents were never alluded to in the laws. The Assembly of Pennsylvania, unlike that of Virginia, never seems to have thought it necessary to define the status of the slave as property, the consequences of slave baptism, or the line of servile descent.[11] Some of these questions had been settled in other colonies before the founding of Pennsylvania, and there the results seem to have been accepted. Accordingly the steps in the development are neither obvious nor distinct. They rest not so much upon statute as upon court decisions interpreting usage, and in many cases the decisions do not come until the end of the slavery period. Notwithstanding all this there was a development, which may be said to fall into three periods. They were, first, the years from 1682 to 1700, when slavery was slowly diverging from servitude, which it still closely resembled; second, from 1700 to 1725-1726, when slavery was more sharply marked off from servi-

---

[10] " An Act for the better Regulation of Servants in this Province and Territories." *Stat. at L.*, II, 56.

[11] *Cf.* J. C. Ballagh, *A History of Slavery in Virginia*, chapter II.

tude; and third, the period from 1725-1726 to 1780, when nothing was added but some minor restrictions.

During the earliest years slavery in Pennsylvania differed from servitude in but little, save that servitude was for a term of years and slavery was for life. It may be questioned whether at first all men recognized even this difference. Many of Penn's first colonists were men who embarked upon their undertaking with high ideals of religion and right, and whose conception of what was right could not easily be reconciled with hopeless bondage.[12] The strength of this sentiment is seen in the well known provision of Penn's charter to the Free Society of Traders, 1682, that if they held blacks they should make them free at the end of fourteen years, the blacks then to become the Company's tenants.[13] It is the motive in Benjamin Furley's proposal to hold negroes not longer than eight years.[14] It is particularly evident in the protest made at Germantown in 1688.[15] It is seen in George Keith's declaration of principles in 1693.[16] And it gave impetus to the movement among the Friends, which, starting about 1696, led finally to the emancipation of all their negroes.

[12] *Cf.* letter of William Edmundson to Friends in Maryland, Virginia, and other parts of America, 1675. S. Janney, *History of the Religious Society of Friends, from Its Rise to the Year 1828*, III, 178.

[13] *The Articles Settlement and Offices of the Free Society of Traders in Pennsylvania*, etc., article XVIII. This quite closely resembles the ordinance issued by Governor Rising to the Swedes in 1654, that after a certain period negroes should be absolutely free. . . . "efter 6 åhr vare en slafvare alldeles fri." Sprinchorn, *Kolonien Nya Sveriges Historia*, 271.

[14] "Let no blacks be brought in directly. and if any come out of Virginia, Maryld. [or elsewhere *erased*] in families that have formerly bought them elsewhere Let them be declared (as in the west jersey constitutions) free at 8 years end." "B. F. Abridgmt. out of Holland and Germany." Penn MSS. Ford *vs.* Penn. etc., 1674-1716, p. 17.

[15] *Cf. Pa. Mag.*, IV, 28-30.

[16] *Ibid.*, XIII, 265-270.

Accordingly at first there may have been some negroes who were held as servants for a term of years, and who were discharged when they had served their time.[17] There is no certain proof that this was so,[18] and the probabilities are rather against it, but the conscientious scruples of some of the early settlers make it at least possible. In the growth of the colony, however, this feeling did not continue strong enough to be decisive. Economic adjustment, an influx of men of different standards, and motives of expediency, perhaps of necessity, made the legal recognition of an inferior status inevitable. Against this the upholders of the idea that negroes should be held only as servants, for a term of years, waged a losing fight. It is true they did not desist, and in the course of one hundred years their view won a complete triumph; but their success came in abolition, and in overthrowing a system established, long after they had utterly failed to prevent the swift growth and the statutory recognition of legal slavery for life and in perpetuity.

Aside from this one fundamental difference the incidents of each status were nearly the same. The negro held for life was subject to the same restrictions, tried in the same courts, and punished with the same punishments as the white servant. So far as either class was subject to special regulation at this time it was because of the laws for the management of servants, passed in 1683 and 1693, which concerned white servants equally with black slaves. These restrictions were as yet neither

---

[17] Negro servants are mentioned. See *Pa. Mag.*, VII, 106. *Cf.* below, p. 54. Little reliance can be placed upon the early use of this word.

[18] I have found no instance where a negro was indisputably a servant in the early period. The court records abound in notices of white servants.

numerous nor detailed, being largely directed against free people who abetted servants in wrong doing. Thus, servants were forbidden to traffic in their masters' goods; but the only penalty fell on the receiver, who had to make double restitution. They were restricted as to movement, and when travelling they must have a pass. If they ran away they were punished, the white servant by extra service, the black slave by whipping, but this different punishment for the slave was not enacted until 1700, the beginning of the next period. Whoever harbored them was liable to the master for damages.[19] The relations between master and servant were likewise simple. The servant was compelled to obey the master. If he resisted or struck the master, he was punished at the discretion of the court. On the other hand the servant was to be treated kindly.[20]

The period, then, prior to 1700 was characteristically a period of servitude. The laws spoke of servants white and black.[21] The regulations, the restrictions, the trials, the punishments, were identical. There was only the one difference: white servants were discharged with freedom dues at the end of a specified number of years; for negroes there was no discharge; they were servants for life, that is, slaves.

In the period following 1700 this difference gradually became apparent, and made necessary different treat-

---

[19] *Laws of the Province of Pennsylvania* . . . *1682-1700*, p. 153 (1683), 211, 213 (1693). For running away white servants had to give five days of extra service for each day of absence. *Ibid.*, 166 (1683), 213 (1693). Harboring cost the offender five shillings a day. *Ibid.*, 152 (1683), 212 (1693).

[20] *Ibid.*, 113 (1682); *ibid.*, 102 (Laws Agreed upon in England).

[21] *Ibid.*, 152. "No Servant white or black . . . shall at anie time after publication hereof be Attached or taken into Execution for his Master or Mistress debt" . . .

ment and distinct laws. This resulted from a recognition of the dissimilarity in character between property based on temporary service and that based on service for life. In the first place perpetual service gave rise to a new class of slaves. At first the only ones in Pennsylvania were such negroes as were imported and sold for life. But after a time children were born to them. These children were also slaves, because ownership of a negro held for life involved ownership of his offspring also, since, the negro being debarred by economic helplessness from rearing children, all of his substance belonging to his master, the master must assume the cost of rearing them, and might have the service of the children as recompense.[22] This was the source of the second and largest class of slaves. The child of a slave was not necessarily a slave if one of the parents was free. The line of servile descent lay through the mother.[23] Accordingly the child of a slave mother and a free father was a slave, of a free mother and a slave father a servant for a term of years only. The result

[22] The rearing of slave children was regarded as a burden by owners. A writer declared that in Pennsylvania " negroes just born are considered an incumbrance only, and if humanity did not forbid it, they would be instantly given away." *Pa. Packet,* Jan. 1, 1780. In 1732 the Philadelphia Court of Common Pleas ordered a man to take back a negress whom he had sold, and who proved to be pregnant. He was to refund the purchase money and the money spent " for Phisic and Attendance of the Said Negroe in her Miserable Condition." MS. Court Papers. 1732-1744. Phila. Co., June 9, 1732.

[23] The Roman doctrine of *partus sequitur ventrem.* This was never established by law in Pennsylvania, and during colonial times was never the subject of a court decision that has come down. That it was the usage, however, there is abundant proof. In 1727 Isaac Warner bequeathed " To Wife Ann . . . a negro woman named Sarah . . . To daughter Ann Warner (3) an unborn negro child of the above named Sarah." MS. Phila. Co. Will Files, no. 47, 1727. In 1786 the Supreme Court declared that it was the law of Pennsylvania, and had always been the custom. 1 Dallas 181.

of the application of this doctrine to the offspring of a negro and a white person was that mulattoes were divided into two classes. Some were servants for a term of years; the others formed a third class of slaves.

In the second place perpetual service gave to slave property more of the character of a thing, than was the case when the time of service was limited. The service of both servants and slaves was a thing, which might be bought, sold, transferred as a chattel, inherited and bequeathed by will; but in the case of a slave, the service being perpetual, the idea of the service as a thing tended to merge into the idea of the slave himself as a thing. The law did not attempt to carry this principle very far. It never, as in Virginia, declared the slave real estate. In Pennsylvania he was emphatically both person and thing, with the conception of personality somewhat predominating.[24] Yet there was felt to be a decided difference between the slave and the servant, and this, together with the desire to regulate the slave as a negro distinguished from a white man, was the cause of the distinctive laws of the second period.

[24] MS. Abstract of Phila. Co. Wills, Book A, 63, 71, (1693); Will of Samuel Richardson of Philadelphia in *Pa. Mag.*, XXXIII, 373 (1719). In 1682 the attorney-general in England answering an inquiry from Jamaica, declared " That where goods or merchandise are by Law forfeited to the King, the sale of them from one to another will not fix the property as against the King, but they may be seized wherever found whilst they remain in specie; And that Negros being admitted Merchandise will fall within the same Law ". MS. Board of Trade Journals, IV, 124. On several occasions during war negro slaves were captured from the enemy and brought to Pennsylvania, where they were sold as ordinary prize-goods—things. In 1745, however, when two French negro prisoners produced papers showing that they were free, they were held for exchange as prisoners of war—persons. MS. Provincial Papers, VII, Oct. 2, 1745. For the status of the negro slave as real estate in Virginia, *cf.* Ballagh, *Hist. of Slavery in Virginia*, ch. II. In 1786 the Supreme Court of Pennsylvania decided that " property in a Negroe may be obtained by a *bona fide* purchase, without deed." 1 Dallas 169.

The years from 1700 to 1725-1726 are marked by two great laws which almost by themselves make up the slave code of Pennsylvania. The first, passed in 1700 and passed again in 1705-1706, regulated the trial and punishments of slaves.[25] It marked the beginning of a new era in the regulation of negroes, in that, subjecting them to different courts and imposing upon them different penalties, it definitely marked them off as a class distinct from all others in the colony. In 1725-1726 further advance was made. Not only was the negro now subjected to special regulation because he was a slave, but whether slave or free he was now made subject to special restrictions because he was a negro. While some of these had to do with movement and behavior, the most important forbade all marriage or intercourse with white people.[26] These laws must be examined in detail.

From the very first was seen the inevitable difficulty involved in punishing the negro criminal as a person, and yet not injuring the master's property in the thing. The result of this was that masters were frequently led to conceal the crimes of their slaves, or to take the law into their own hands.[27] The solution was probably felt to be the removal of negroes from the ordinary courts. It is said, also, that Penn desired to protect the negro by clearly defining his crimes and apportioning his punishments. Accordingly he urged the law of 1700.[28]

[25] "An Act for the trial of Negroes." *Stat. at L.*, II, 77-79. Repealed in Council, 1705. *Ibid.*, II, 79; *Col. Rec.*, I, 612, 613. Passed again with slight changes in 1705-1706. *Stat. at L.*, II, 233-236.

[26] "An Act for the better regulating of Negroes in this Province." *Stat. at L.*, IV, 59-64. It became law by lapse of time. *Ibid.*, IV, 64.

[27] "An Act for the better regulating of Negroes in this Province", section 1. *Stat. at L.*, IV, 59.

[28] Cf. Enoch Lewis, " Life of William Penn " (1841), in *Friends' Library*, V, 315; J. R. Tyson, " Annual Discourse before the Historical Society of Pennsylvania " (1831), in *Hasard's Register*, VIII, 316.

Under this law negroes when accused were not to be tried in the regular courts of the colony. They were to be presented by the Courts of Quarter Sessions, but the cases were to be dealt with by special courts for the trial of negroes, composed of two commissioned justices of the peace and six substantial freeholders. On application these courts were to be constituted by executive authority when occasion demanded. Witnesses were to be allowed, but there was to be no trial by jury.[29] In such courts it was doubtless easier to regard the slave as property, and do full justice to the rights of the master.

Something was still wanting, however, for in case the slave criminal was condemned to death, the loss fell entirely on the master. From the earliest days of the colony owners had been praying for relief from this. In 1707 the masters of two slaves petitioned the governor to commute the death sentence to chastisement and transportation, and thus save them from pecuniary loss. The petition was granted. Such commutation was frequently sought, and in the special courts it could be more readily granted.[30] The real solution, however, was discovered in 1725-1726, when it was ordained that there-

[29] MS. Minutes Court of Quarter Sessions Bucks County, 1684-1730, p. 375 (1703); MS. "Bail, John Kendig for a Negro, 29. 9ᵇʳ 35," in Logan Papers, unbound; "An Act for the trial of Negroes," *Stat. at L.*, II, 77-79 (1700), 233-236 (1705-1706); *Col. Rec.*, III, 254; IV, 243; IX, 648, 680, 704, 705, 707; X, 73, 276. For the commission instituting one of these special courts (1762), see MS. Miscellaneous Papers, 1684-1847, Chester County, 149; also Diffenderffer, "Early Negro Legislation in the Province of Pennsylvania," in *Christian Culture*, Sept. 1, 1890. Mr. Diffenderffer cites a commission of Feb. 20, 1773, but is puzzled at finding no record of the trial of negroes in the records of the local Court of Quarter Sessions. It would of course not appear there. Special dockets were kept for the special courts. *Cf.* MS. Records of Special Courts for the Trial of Negroes, held at Chester, in Chester County. The law was not universally applied at first. In 1703 a negro was tried for fornication before the Court of Quarter Sessions. MS. Minutes Court of Quarter Sessions Bucks County, 1684-1730, p. 378.

[30] *Col. Rec.* I, 61; II, 405, 406.

28   THE NEGRO IN PENNSYLVANIA

after if any slave committed a capital crime, immediately upon conviction the justices should appraise such slave, and pay the value to the owner, out of a fund arising principally from the duty on negroes imported.[81]

These laws continued in force until 1780, and down to that time slaves were removed from the jurisdiction of the regular courts of the province; although after 1776 it was asserted that the clause about trial by jury in the new state constitution affected slaves as well as free men; and a slave was actually so tried in 1779.[82] Whether this view prevailed in all quarters it is impossible to say. In the next year the abolition act did away with the special courts entirely.[83]

[81] " An Act for the better regulating of Negroes," etc. *Stat. at L.*, IV, 59. For an instance of such valuation in the case of two slaves condemned for burglary, see MS. Provincial Papers, XXX, July 29, 1773. The governor, however, pardoned these negroes on condition that they be transported.

[82] " On the trials Larry the slave was convicted by a Jury of twelve Men and received the usual sentence of whipping, restitution and fine according to law. . . . This case is published as being the first instance of a slave's being tried in this state by a Grand and Petit Jury. Our constitution provides that these unhappy men shall have the same measure of Justice and the same mode of trial with others, their fellow creatures, when charged with crimes or offences." *Pa. Packet*, Feb. 16, 1779. Nevertheless a commission for a special court had been issued in August, 1777. *Cf.* " Petition of Mary Bryan," MS. Misc. Papers, Aug. 15, 1777.

[83] *Stat. at L.*, X, 72. What was the standing of negro slaves before the ordinary courts of Pennsylvania in the years between 1700 and 1780 it is difficult to say. They certainly could not be witnesses—not against white men, since this privilege was given to free negroes for the first time in 1780 (*Stat. at L.*, X, 70), and to slaves not until 1847 (*Laws of Assembly, 1847,* p. 208); while if they were witnesses against other negroes it would be before special courts. Doubtless negroes could sometimes seek redress in the ordinary courts, though naturally the number of such cases would be limited. There is, however, at least one instance of a white man being sued by a negro, who won his suit. " Francis Jnᵒson the Negro verbally complained agst Wᵐ Orion . . . and after pleading to on both sides the Court passed Judgment and ordered Wᵐ Orion to pay him the sd Francis Jnᵒson twenty shillings " . . . MS. Ancient Records of Sussex County, 1681 to 1709, 4th mo., 1687. Before 1700 negroes were tried before the ordinary courts, and there is at least one case where a negro witnessed against a white man. *Ibid.*, 8br 1687.

The law of 1700, which marked the differentiation of slaves from servants, marked also the beginning of discrimination. For negroes there were to be different punishments as well as a different mode of trial. Murder, buggery, burglary, or rape of a white woman, were to be punished by death; attempted rape by castration; robbing and stealing by whipping, the master to make good the theft.[34] This law was repeated in 1705-1706, except that the punishment for attempted rape was now made whipping, branding, imprisonment, and transportation, while these same penalties were to be imposed for theft over five pounds. Theft of an article worth less than five pounds entailed whipping up to thirty-nine lashes.[35] For white people at this time, whether servants or free, there was a different code.[36]

A far more important discrimination was made in 1725-1726 by the law which forbade mixture of the races. There had doubtless been some intercourse from the first. A white servant was indicted for this

[34] *Stat. at L.*, II, 77-79; *Col. Rec.*, I, 612, 613. Instances of negro crime are mentioned in MS. Records of Special Courts for the Trial of Negroes—Chester County. For a case of arson punished with death, *cf. Col. Rec.*, IV, 243. For two negroes condemned to death for burglary, *ibid.*, IX, 6, also 699. The punishment for the attempted rape of a white woman was the one point that caused the disapproval of the attorney-general in England, and, probably, led to the passage of the revised act in 1705-1706. *Cf.* MS. Board of Trade Papers, Prop., VIII, 40, Bb. For restitution by masters, which was frequently very burdensome, *cf.* MS. Misc. Papers, Oct. 9, 1780.

[35] *Stat. at L.*, II, 233-236. These punishments were continued until repealed in 1780, (*Stat. at L.*, X, 72), when the penalty for robbery and burglary became imprisonment. This bore entirely on the master, so that in 1790 Governor Mifflin asked that corporal punishment be substituted. *Hazard's Register*, II, 74. For theft whipping continued to be imposed, but guilty white people were punished in the same manner. MS. Petitions, Lancaster County, 1761-1825, May, 1784. MS. Misc. Papers, July, 1780.

[36] See below, p. 111.

offence in 1677; and a tract of land in Sussex County
bore the name of " Mulatto Hall." In 1698 the Chester
County Court laid down the principle that mingling of
the races was not to be allowed.⁷ The matter went beyond this, for in 1722 a woman was punished for abetting a clandestine marriage between a white woman and
a negro.²⁸ A few months thereafter the Assembly received a petition from inhabitants of the province,
inveighing against the wicked and scandalous practice
of negroes cohabiting with white people.²⁹ It appeared
to the Assembly that a law was needed, and they set
about framing one. Accordingly in the law of 1725-
1726 they provided stringent penalties. No negro was
to be joined in marriage with any white person upon
any pretense whatever. A white person violating this
was to forfeit thirty pounds, or be sold as a servant for
a period not exceeding seven years. A clergyman who
abetted such a marriage was to pay one hundred
pounds.⁴⁰

The law did not succeed in checking cohabitation,

⁷ " For that hee . . . contrary to the Lawes of the Governmt and
Contrary to his Masters Consent hath . . . got wth child a certaine molato
wooman Called Swart anna " . . . MS. Rec. Court at Upland, 19; Penn
MSS. Papers relating to the Three Lower Counties, 1629-1774, p. 193;
MS. Minutes Abington Monthly Meeting, 27 1st mo., 1693. " David
Lewis Constable of Haverfoord Returned A Negro man of his And A
white woman for haveing A Baster Childe . . . the negroe said she Intised
him and promised him to marry him: she being examined, Confest the
same: . . . the Court ordered that she shall Receive Twenty one laishes on
her beare Backe . . . and the Court ordered the negroe never more to meddle with any white woman more uppon paine of his life." MS. Min.
Chester Co. Courts, 1697-1710, p. 24.
²⁸ MS. Ancient Rec. of Phila., Nov. 4, 1722.
²⁹ Votes and Proceedings, II, 336.
⁴⁰ Stat. at L., IV, 62. Cf. Votes and Proceedings, II, 337, 345. For
marriage or cohabiting without the master's consent a servant had to atone
with extra service. Cf. Stat. at L., II, 22. This obviously would not
check a slave.

though of marriages of slaves with white people there is almost no record.[41] There exists no definite information as to the number of mulattoes in the colony during this period, but advertisements for runaway slaves indicate that there were very many of them. The slave register of 1780 for Chester County shows that they constituted twenty per cent. of the slave population in that locality.[42] It must be said that the stigma of illicit intercourse in Pennsylvania would not generally seem to rest upon the masters, but rather upon servants, outcasts, and the lowlier class of whites.[43]

Negro slaves were subject to another class of restrictions which were made against them rather as slaves than as black men. These concerned freedom of movement and freedom of action. During the earlier years of the colony's history regulation of the movements of the slaves rested principally in the hands of the owners. The continual complaints about the tumultuous assembling of negroes, to be noticed presently, would seem to

[41] Apparently such a marriage had occurred in 1722. MS. Ancient Rec. Phila., Nov. 4, 1722, which mention " the Clandestine mariage of Mr Tuthil's Negro and Katherine Williams." The petitioner, who was imprisoned for abetting the marriage, concludes: " I have Discover'd who maried the foresd Negroe, and shall acquaint your hon^rs."

[42] *American Weekly Mercury*, Nov. 9, 1727; *Pa. Gazette*, Feb. 7, 1739-1740; and *passim*. Mittelberger mentions them in 1750. *Cf. Journey to Pennsylvania*, etc., 107; MS. Register of Slaves in Chester County, 1780.

[43] " A circumstance not easily believed, is, that the subjection of the negroes has not corrupted the morals of their masters " . . . Abbé Raynal, *British Settlements in North America* I, 163. Raynal's authority is very poor. The assertion in the text rests rather on negative evidence. *Cf. Votes and Proceedings*, 1766, p. 30, for an instance of a white woman prostitute to negroes. *Ibid.*, *1767-1776*, p. 666, for evidence as to mulatto bastards by pauper white women. Also MS. Misc. Papers, Mar. 12, 1783. For a case (1715) where the guilty white man was probably not a servant *cf.* MS. Court Papers, Phila. Co., 1697-1732. Benjamin Franklin was openly accused of keeping negro paramours. *Cf. What is Sauce for a Goose is also Sauce for a Gander*, etc. (1764), 6; *A Humble Attempt at Scurrility*, etc. (1765), 40.

indicate that considerable leniency was exercised.⁴⁴ But frequently white people lured them away, and harbored and employed them.⁴⁵ The law of 1725-1726 was intended specially to stop this. No negro was to go farther than ten miles from home without written leave from his master, under penalty of ten lashes on his bare back. Nor was he to be away from his master's house, except by special leave, after nine o'clock at night, nor to be found in tippling-houses, under like penalty. For preventing these things counter-restrictions were imposed upon white people. They were forbidden to employ such negroes, or knowingly to harbor or shelter them, except in very unseasonable weather, under penalty of thirty shillings for every twenty-four hours. Finally it was provided that negroes were not to meet together in companies of more than four. This last seems to have remained a dead letter.⁴⁶

That this legislation failed to produce the desired effect is shown by the experience of Philadelphia in dealing with negro disorder. Such disorder was complained of as early as 1693, when, on presentment of the grand jury, it was directed that the constables or any other person should arrest such negroes as they might find gadding abroad on first days of the week, without written permission from the master, and take them to jail, where, after imprisonment, they should be given thirty-nine lashes well laid on, to be paid for by the master. This seems to have been enforced but laxly, for in 1702

⁴⁴ See below.
⁴⁵ Cf. Col. Rec., I, 117.
⁴⁶ Stat. at L., IV, 59-64, (sections IX-XIII). Tippling-houses seem to have given a good deal of trouble. In 1703 the grand jury presented several persons " for selling Rum to negros and others " . . . MS. Ancient Rec. of Phila., Nov. 3, 1703. Cf. also presentment of the grand jury, Jan. 2, 1744. Pa. Mag., XXII, 498.

the grand jury presented the matter again, and their
recommendation was repeated with warmth in the year
following.⁴⁷ A few years later they urged measures to
suppress the unruly negroes of the city.⁴⁸ In 1732 the
council was forced to recommend an ordinance to bring
this about, and such an ordinance was drawn up and
considered. Next year the Monthly Meeting of Friends
petitioned, and the matter was taken up again, but nothing came of it, so that the council was compelled to observe that further legislation was assuredly needed.⁴⁹
In 1741 the grand jury presented the matter strongly,⁵⁰
and an explicit order was at last given that constables
should disperse meetings of negroes within half an hour
after sunset.⁵¹ The nuisance, probably, was still not

⁴⁷ *Col. Rec.*, I, 380-381. " The great abuse and Ill consiquence of the
great multitudes of negroes who commonly meete togeither in a Riott and
tumultious manner on the first days of the weeke." MS. Ancient Rec. of
Phila., 28 7th mo., 1702; *ibid.*, Nov. 3, 1703.
⁴⁸ " The Grand Inquest . . . do present that whereas there has been Divers
Rioters . . . and the peace of our Lord the King Disturbers, by Divers In-
fants, bond Servants, and Negros, within this City after it is Duskish . . .
that Care may be taken to Suppress the unruly Negroes of this City accompanying to gether on the first Day of the weeke, and that they may
not be Suffered to walk the Streets in Companys after it is Darke without
their Masters Leave " . . . MS. Ancient Rec. of Phila., Apr. 4, 1717.
⁴⁹ *Minutes of the Common Council of the City of Philadelphia, 1704-1776*,
314, 315, 316, 326, 342, 376; *Col. Rec.*, IV, 224, (1737).
⁵⁰ " The Grand Inquest now met humly Represent to This honourable
Court the great Disorders Commited On the first Dayes of the week By
Servants, apprentice boys and Numbers of Negros it has been with
great Concearn Observed that the Whites in their Tumultious Resorts
in the markets and other placies most Darringly Swear Curse Lye Abuse
and often fight Striving to Excell in all Leudness and Obsenity which
must produce a generall Corruption of Such youth If not Timely Remi-
dieed and from the Concearn of Negroes Not only the above Mischeiffs
but other Dangers may issue " . . . MS. Court Papers, 1732-1744, Phila.
Co., 1741.
⁵¹ " Many disorderly persons meet every evg. about the Court house
of this city, and great numbers of Negroes and others sit there with
milk pails, and other things, late at night, and many disorders are there
committed against the peace and good government of this city." *Minutes Common Council of Phila.*, 405.

abated, for in 1761 the mayor caused to be published in the papers previous legislation on the subject.⁵² Nothing further seems to have been done.

The continued failure to suppress these meetings in defiance of a law of the province, must be attributed either to the intrinsic difficulty of enforcing such a law, or to the fact that the meetings were objectionable because of their rude and boisterous character, rather than because of any positive misdemeanor. More probably still this is but one of the many pieces of evidence which show how leniently the negro was treated in Pennsylvania.

The third period, from 1726 to 1780, is distinguished more because of the lack of important legislation about the negro than through any marked character of its own. The outlines of the colony's slave code had now been drawn, and no further constructive work was done. There is, however, one class of laws which may be assigned to this period, since the majority of them fall chronologically within its limits, though they are scarcely more characteristic of it than they are of either of the two periods preceding. All of these laws imposed restrictions upon the actions of negro slaves in matters in which white people were restricted also, but the restrictions were embodied in special sections of the laws, because of the negro's inability to pay a fine: the law imposing corporal punishment upon the slave, whenever it exacted payment in money or imprisonment from others.

Thus, an act forbidding the use of fireworks without the governor's permission, states that the slave instead

of being imprisoned shall be publicly whipped. Another provides that if a slave set fire to any woodlands
or marshes he shall be whipped not exceeding twenty-
one lashes. As far back as 1700 whipping had been
made the punishment of a slave who carried weapons
without his master's permission. In 1750-1751 participation in a horse-race or shooting-match entailed first
fifteen lashes, and then twenty-one, together with six
days' imprisonment for the first offense, and ten days'
imprisonment thereafter. In 1760 hunting on Indians'
lands or on other people's lands, shooting in the city, or
hunting on Sunday, were forbidden under penalty of
whipping up to thirty-one lashes. In 1750-1751 the
penalty for offending against the night watch in Philadelphia was made twenty-one lashes and imprisonment
in the work-house for three days at hard labor; for the
second offence, thirty-one lashes and six days. Sometimes it was provided that a slave might be punished as
a free man, if his master would stand for him. Thus a
slave offending against the regulations for wagoners
was to be whipped, or fined, if his master would pay the
fine.[83]

So far the slave was under the regulation of the state.
He was also subject to the regulation of his owner, who,

[83] " An Act for preventing Accidents that may happen by Fire," sect.
IV, *Stat. at L.*, III, 254 (1721); " An Act to prevent the Damages, which
may happen, by firing of Woods," etc., sect. III, *ibid.*, IV, 282 (1735);
" An Act for the trial of Negroes," sect. V, *ibid.*, II, 79 (1700); " An
Act for the more effectual preventing Accidents which may happen by
Fire, and for suppressing Idleness, Drunkenness, and other Debauch-
eries," sect. III, *ibid.*, V, 109, 110 (1750-1751); " An Act to prevent the
Hunting of Deer," etc., sect. VII, *ibid.*, VI, 49 (1760); " An Act for the
better regulating the nightly Watch within the city of Philadelphia," etc.,
sect. XXII, *ibid.*, V, 126 (1750-1751); repeated in 1756, 1763, 1766, 1771,
ibid., V, 241; VI, 309; VII, 7; VIII, 115; " An Act for regulating
Wagoners, Carters, Draymen, and Porters," etc., sect. VII, *ibid.*, VI, 68
(1761); repeated in 1763 and 1770, *ibid.* VI, 250; VII, 359, 360.

in matters concerning himself and not directly covered
by laws, could enforce obedience by corporal punishment. This was sometimes administered at the public
whipping-post, the master sending an order for a certain number of lashes.[54] But the slave was not given
over absolutely into the master's power. If he had to
obey the laws of the state, he could also expect the protection of the state.[55] The master could not starve him,
nor overwork him, nor torture him. Against these
things he could appeal to the public authorities. Moreover public opinion was powerfully against them. If
a master killed his slave the law dealt with him as
though his victim were a white man.[56] It is not probable,
to be sure, that the sentence was often carried out, but
such cases did not often arise.[57]

Such was the legal status of the slave in Pennsylvania.
Before 1700 it was ill defined, but probably much like
that of the servant, having only the distinctive incident
of perpetual service, and the developing incident of the
transmission of servile condition to offspring. Gradu-

[54] Cf. the story of Hodge's Cato, told in Watson, Annals of Philadelphia and Pennsylvania in the Olden Time, etc., II, 263.

[55] Cf. Achenwall, who got his information from Franklin, Anmerkungen,
25: " Diese Mohrensclaven geniessen als Unterthanen des Staats . . . den
Schutz der Gesetze, so gut als freye Einwohner. Wenn ein Colonist,
auch selbst der Eigenthumsherr, einen Schwarzen umbringt, so wird er
gleichfalls zum Tode verurtheilt. Wenn der Herr seinem Sclaven zu
harte Arbeit auflegt, oder ihn sonst übel behandelt, so kan er ihn beym
Richter verklagen." Also Kalm, Travels, I, 390.

[56] " Yesterday at a Supream Court held in this City, sentence of Death
was passed upon William Bullock, who was . . . Convicted of the Murder of
his Negro Slave." American Weekly Mercury, Apr. 29, 1742.

[57] Kalm (1748) said that there was no record of such a sentence being
carried out; but he adds that a case having arisen, even the magistrates
secretly advised the guilty person to leave the country, " as otherwise they
could not avoid taking him prisoner, and then he would be condemned
to die according to the laws of the country, without any hopes of saving
him". Travels, I, 391, 392. For a case cf. Pa. Gazette, Feb. 24, 1741-1742.

ally it became altogether different. To the slave now appertained a number of incidents of lower status. He was tried in separate courts, subject to special judges, and punished with different penalties. Admixture with white people was sternly prohibited. He was subject to restrictions upon movement, conduct, and action. He could be corrected with corporal punishment. The slave legislation of Pennsylvania involved discriminations based both upon inferior status, and what was regarded as inferior race. Nevertheless it will be shown that in most respects the punishments and restrictions imposed upon negro slaves were either similar to those imposed upon white servants, or involved discriminations based upon the inability of the slave to pay a fine, and upon the fact that mere imprisonment punished the master alone. Moreover, what harshness there was must be ascribed partly to the spirit of the times, which made harsher laws for both white men and black men. The slave code almost never comprehended any cruel or unusual punishments. As a legal as well as a social system slavery in Pennsylvania was mild.

CHAPTER III.

Social and Economic Aspects of Slavery.

The mildness of slavery in Pennsylvania impressed every observer. Acrelius said that negroes were treated better there than anywhere else in America. Peter Kalm said that compared with the condition of white servants their condition possessed equal advantages except that they were obliged to serve their whole lifetime without wages. Hector St. John Crèvecœur declared that they enjoyed as much liberty as their masters, that they were in effect part of their masters' families, and that, living thus, they considered themselves happier than many of the lower class of whites.[1] There is good reason for believing these statements, since a careful study of the sources shows that generally masters used their negroes kindly and with moderation.[2]

Living in a land of plenty the slaves were well fed and comfortably clothed. They had as good food as the white servants, says one traveller, and another says as good as their masters.[3] In 1759 the yearly cost of the food of a slave was reckoned at about twenty per cent. of his value. Likewise they were well clad, their

[1] Acrelius, *Description of New Sweden*, 169 (1759); Kalm, *Travels*, I, 394 (1748); Hector St. John Crèvecœur, *Letters from an American Farmer*, 222 (just before the Revolution).

[2] When one of Christopher Marshall's white servants "struck and kickt" his negro woman, he "could scarcely refrain from kicking him out of the House &c &c &c." MS. Remembrancer, E, July 22, 1779.

[3] Kalm, I, 394; St. John Crèvecœur, 221. Benjamin Lay contradicts this, but allowance must always be made for the extremeness of his assertions. *Cf.* his *All Slave-Keepers Apostates* (1737), 93.

[4] Acrelius, 169.

clothes being furnished by the masters. That clothes were a considerable item of expense is shown by the old household accounts and diaries. Acrelius computed the yearly cost at five per cent. of a slave's value.[5] In the newspaper advertisements for runaways occur particularly full descriptions of their dress.[6] Almost always they have a coat or jacket, shoes, and stockings.[7] It is true that when they ran away they generally took the best they had, if not all they had; but making due allowance it seems certain that they were well clad, as an advertiser declared.[8]

As to shelter, since the climate and economy of Pennsylvania never gave rise to a plantation life, rows of

[5] St. John Crèvecœur, 221; Kalm, I, 394; Acrelius, 169. Personal papers contain numerous notices. " To 1 pr Shoes for the negro . . . 6 " (sh.). MS. William Penn's Account Book, 1690-1693, p. 2 (1690). A " Bill rendered by Christian Grafford to James Steel " is as follows: " Making old Holland Jeakit and breeches fit for your Negero   0.3.0   Making 2 new Jeakits and 2 pair breeches of stripped Linen for both your Negeromans 0.14.0   And also for Little Negero boy 0.4.0 Making 2 pair Leather Breeches, 1 for James Sanders and another for your Negroeman Zeason 0.13.0." *Pa. Mag.*, XXXIII, 121 (1740). The bill rendered for the shoes of Thomas Penn's negroes in 1764-1765 amounted to £7 7 sh. 3d., the price per pair averaging about 7 sh. 6d. Penn-Physick MSS., IV, 223. Also *ibid.*, IV, 265, 267. *Cf.* Penn Papers, accounts (unbound), Aug. 19, 1741; Christopher Marshall's Remembrancer, E, June 1, 1779.

[6] Thus Cato had on " two jackets, the uppermost a dark blue half thick, lined with red flannel, the other a light blue homespun flannel, without lining, ozenbrigs shirt, old leather breeches, yarn stockings, old shoes, and an old beaver hat " . . . *Pa. Gazette*, May 5, 1748. A negro from Chester County wore " a lightish coloured cloath coat, with metal buttons, and lined with striped linsey, a lightish linsey jacket with sleeves, and red waistcoat, tow shirt, old lightish cloth breeches, and linen drawers, blue stockings, and old shoes." *Ibid.*, Jan. 3, 1782. Judith wore " a green jacket, a blue petticoat, old shoes, and grey stockings, and generally wears silver bobbs in her ears." *Ibid.*, Feb. 16, 1747-1748.

[7] *Amer. Weekly Mercury*, Jan. 31, 1721; Jan. 31, 1731; *Pa. Gazette*, Oct. 22, 1747; May 5, 1748; Apr. 16, 1761; Jan. 3, 1782; *Pa. Journal*, Feb. 5, 1750-1751; *Pa. Mag.*, XVIII, 385.

[8] *Pa. Gazette*, May 3, 1775. Supported by advertisements *passim*.

negro cabins and quarters for the hands never became a
distinctive feature. Slaves occupied such lodgings as
were assigned to white servants, generally in the house
of the master. This was doubtless not the case where
a large number was held. They can hardly have been
so accommodated by Jonathan Dickinson of Philadelphia, who had thirty-two.[9]

In the matter of service their lot was a fortunate one.
There seems to be no doubt that they were treated much
more kindly than the negroes in the West Indies, and
that they were far happier than the slaves in the lower
South. It is said that they were not obliged to labor
more than white people, and, although this may hardly
have been so, and although, indeed, there is occasional
evidence that they were worked hard, yet for the most
part it is clear that they were not overworked.[10] The
advertisements of negroes for sale show, as might be
expected, that most of the slaves were either house-
servants or farm-hands.[11] Nevertheless the others were

[9] MS. Dickinson Papers, unclassified. A farm with a stone house for
negroes is mentioned in *Pa. Gas.*, June 26, 1746. " Part of these slaves
lived in their master's family, the others had separate cabins on the
farm where they reared families " . . . " Jacob Minshall Homestead " in
Reminiscence, Gleanings and Thoughts, No. I, 12.

[10] Kalm, *Travels*, I, 394. For treatment of negroes in the West Indies,
cf. Sandiford, *The Mystery of Iniquity*, 99 (1730); Benezet, *A Short
Account of that Part of Africa Inhabited by the Negroes* (1762), 55, 56,
note; Benezet, *A Caution and Warning to Great Britain and Her Colonies in a Short Representation of the Calamitous State of the Enslaved
Negroes* (1766), 5-9; Benezet, *Some Historical Account of Guinea* (1771),
chap. VIII. For treatment in the South, cf. Whitefield, *Three Letters*
(1740), 13, 71; Chastellux, *Voyage en Amérique* (1786), 130. For treatment in Pennsylvania cf. Kalm, *Travels*, I, 394; St. John Crèvecœur,
Letters, 221. Acrelius says that the negroes at the iron-furnaces were
allowed to stop work for " four months in summer, when the heat is
most oppressive." *Description*, 168.

[11] *Mercury, Gazette*, and *Pa. Packet, passim*. Most of the taverns seem
to have had negro servants. Cf. MS. Assessment Book, Chester Co.,
1769, p. 146; of Bucks Co., 1779, p. 84.

engaged in a surprisingly large number of different occupations. Among them were bakers, blacksmiths, bricklayers, brush-makers, carpenters, coopers, curriers, distillers, hammermen, refiners, sail-makers, sailors, shoemakers, tailors, and tanners.[12] The negroes employed at the iron-furnaces received special mention.[13] The women cooked, sewed, did house-work, and at times were employed as nurses.[14] When the service of negroes was needed they were often hired from their masters, but as a rule they were bought.[15] They were frequently trusted and treated almost like members of the family.[16]

[12] *Mercury*, Mar. 3, 1723-1724; Dec. 15, 1724; July 4, 1728; Aug. 24, 1732; *Gazette*, Feb. 7, 1740; Dec. 3, 1741; May 20, 1742; Nov. 1, 1744; July 9, Dec. 3, 1761; *Packet*, July 5, 1733.

[13] " The laborers are generally composed partly of negroes (slaves) partly of servants from Germany or Ireland " . . . Acrelius, *Description*, 168. *Cf.* Gabriel Thomas, *An Historical and Geographical Account of the Province and Country of Pensilvania* (1698), etc., 28.

[14] *Mercury*, Jan. 16, 1727-1728; July 25, 1728; Nov. 7, 1728. *Gazette*, July 17, 1740; Mar. 31, 1743. " A compleat washerwoman " is advertised in the *Gazette*, Oct. 1, 1761; also " an extraordinary washer of clothes," *Gazette*, Apr. 12, 1775; Penn-Physick, MSS IV, 203 (1740).

[15] *Gazette*, May 19, 1743; July 11, 1745; Nov. 5, 1761; May 15, 1776; Dec. 15, 1779. *Cf.* notices in William Penn's Cash Book (MS.), 3, 6, 9, 15, 18; John Wilson's Cash Book (MS.), Feb. 23, 1776; MS. Phila. Account Book, 38 (1694); MS. Logan Papers, II, 259 (1707); Richard Hayes's Ledger (MS.), 88 (1716).

[16] *Cf.* the numerous allusions to his negro woman made by Christopher Marshall in his Remembrancer. An entry in John Wilson's Cash Book (MS.), Apr. 27, 1770, says: " paid his " (Joseph Pemberton's) " Negro woman Market mony . . . 7/6." The following advertisement is illustrative, although perhaps it reveals the advertiser's art as much as the excellence and reliability of the negress. " A likely young Negroe Wench, who can cook and wash well, and do all Sorts of House-work; and can from Experience, be recommended both for her Honesty and Sobriety, having often been trusted with the Keys of untold Money, and Liquors of various Sorts, none of which she will taste. She is no Idler, Company-keeper or Gadder abroad. She has also a fine, hearty young Child, not quite a Year old, which is the only Reason for selling her, because her Mistress is very sickly, and can't bear the Trouble of it." *Pa. Gazette*, Apr. 2, 1761.

When the day's work was over the negroes of Pennsylvania seem to have had time of their own which they were not too tired to enjoy. Some no doubt found recreation in their masters' homes, gossipping, singing, and playing on rude instruments.[17] Many sought each other's company and congregated together after nightfall. In Philadelphia, at any rate, during the whole colonial period, crowds of negroes infesting the streets after dark behaved with such rough and boisterous merriment that they were a nuisance to the whole community.[18] At times negroes were given days of their own. They were allowed to go from one place to another, and were often permitted to visit members of their families in other households.[19] Moreover, holidays were not grudged them. It is said that in Philadelphia at the time of fairs, the blacks to the number of a thousand of both sexes used to go to " Potter's Field," and there amuse themselves, dancing, singing, and rejoicing, in native barbaric fashion.[20]

If, now, from material comfort we turn to the matter of the moral and intellectual well-being of the slaves, we find that considering the time, surprising efforts were made to help them. In Pennsylvania there seems

[17] " Thou Knowest Negro Peters Ingenuity In making for himself and playing on a fiddle wth out any assistance as the thing in them is Innocent and diverting and may keep them from worse Employmt I have to Encourage in my Service promist him one from Engld therefore buy and bring a good Strong well made Violin wth 2 or 3 Sets of spare Gut for the Suitable Strings get somebody of skill to Chuse and by it " . . . MS. Isaac Norris, Letter Book, 1719, p. 185.

[18] See above, pp. 32-34.

[19] " Our Negro woman got leave to visit her children in Bucks County." Christopher Marshall's Remembrancer, D, Jan. 7, 1776. " This afternoon came home our Negro woman Dinah." Ibid., D, Jan. 15, 1776.

[20] Watson, Annals, I, 406. Cf. letter of William Hamilton of Lancaster: " Yesterday (being Negroes Holiday) I took a ride into Maryland." Pa. Mag., XXIX, 257.

never to have been opposition to improving them. Not
much was done, it is true, and perhaps most of the negroes were not reached by the efforts made. It must
be remembered, however, what violent hostility mere
efforts aroused in some other places.[21]

There is the statement of a careful observer that
masters desired by all means to hinder their negroes
from being instructed in the doctrines of Christianity,
and to let them live on in pagan darkness. This he ascribes to a fear that negroes would grow too proud on
seeing themselves upon a religious level with their
masters.[22] Some weight must be attached to this account, but it is probable that the writer was roughly ap-
plying to Pennsylvania what he had learned in other
places, for against his assertion much specific evidence
can be arrayed.

The attention of the Friends was directed to this subject very early. The counsel of George Fox was explicit. Owners were to give their slaves religious instruction and teach them the Gospel.[23] In 1693 the
Keithian Quakers when advising that masters should
hold their negroes only for a term of years, enjoined
that during such time they should give these negroes
a Christian education.[24] In 1700 Penn appears to have

[21] For the treatment of William Edmundson when he tried to convert
negroes in the West Indies, *cf.* his *Journal*, 85; Gough, *A History of the
People Called Quakers*, III, 61. *Cf.* MS. Board of Trade Journals, III,
191 (1680).

[22] Kalm, *Travels*, I, 397. "It's obvious, that the future Welfare of
those poor Slaves . . . is generally too much disregarded by those who
keep them." *An Epistle of Caution and Advice, Concerning the Buying
and Keeping of Slaves* (1754), 5. This, however, is neglect rather than
opposition.

[23] Fox's *Epistles*, in *Friend's Library*, I, 79 (1679).

[24] "An Exhortation and Caution to Friends Concerning buying or
keeping of Negroes," in *Pa. Mag.*, XIII, 267.

been able to get a Monthly Meeting established for them, but of the meeting no record has come down.[25] As to what was the actual practice of Friends in this matter their early records give meagre information. It seems certain that negroes were not allowed to participate in their meetings, though sometimes they were taken to the meeting-houses.[26] It is probable that in great part the religious work of the Friends among slaves was confined to godly advice and reading.[27] As to the amount and quality of such advice, the well known character of the Friends leaves no doubt.

The Moravians, who were most zealous in converting negroes, did not reach a great number in Pennsylvania, because few were held by them; nevertheless they labored successfully, and received negroes amongst them on terms of religious equality.[28] This also the Lutherans did to some extent, negroes being baptized among them.[29] It is in the case of the Episcopalians, however, that the most definite knowledge remains. The records of Christ Church show that the negroes who were baptized made no inconsiderable proportion of the total number baptized in the congregation. For a period of more than seventy years such baptisms are recorded, and are sometimes numerous.[30] At this church,

[25] Proud, *History of Pennsylvania*, 423; Gordon, *History of Pennsylvania*, 114.

[26] "Several" (negroes) "are brought to Meetings." MS. Minutes Radnor Monthly Meetings, 1763-1772, p. 79 (1764). "Most of those possessed of them . . . often bring them to our Meetings." *Ibid.*, 175 (1767).

[27] *Cf.* MS. Yearly Meeting Advices, 1682-1777, "Negroes or Slaves."

[28] Cranz, *The Ancient and Modern History of the Brethren . . . Unitas Fratrum*, 600, 601; Ogden, *An Excursion into Bethlehem and Nazareth in Pennsylvania*, 89, 90; 1 *Pa. Arch.*, III, 75; *Pa. Mag.*, XXIX, 363.

[29] *Cf.* Bean, *History of Montgomery County*, 302.

[30] MS. Records of Christ Church, Phila., I, 19, 43, 44, 46, 49, 132, 168, 271, 273, 274, 276, 277, 280, 281, 282, 283, 288, 293, 306, 312, 314, 333,

also, there was a minister who had special charge of the religious instruction of negroes.[81] It is possible that something may have been accomplished by missionaries and itinerant exhorters. This was certainly so when Whitefield visited Pennsylvania in 1740. Both he and his friend Seward noted with peculiar satisfaction the results which they had attained.[82] Work of some value was also done by wandering negro exhorters, who, appearing at irregular intervals, assembled little groups and preached in fields and orchards.[83]

Something was also accomplished for negroes in the maintenance of family life. In 1700 Penn, anxious to improve their moral condition, sent to the Assembly a bill for the regulation of their marriages, but much to his grief this was defeated.[84] In the absence of such

---

337, 341, 342, 344, 352, 353, 359, 371, 379, 383, 388, 392, 397, 399, 416, 440, 441. Baptisms were very frequent in the years 1752 and 1753. Very many of the slaves admitted were adults, whereas in the case of free negroes at the same period most of the baptisms were of children.

[81] William Macclanechan, writing to the Archbishop of Canterbury in 1760, says: " On my Journey to New-England, I arrived at the oppulent City of Philadelphia, where I paid my Compliments to the Rev'd Dr. Jenney, Minister of Christ's Church in that City, and to the Rev'd Mr. Sturgeon, *Catechist to the Negroes.*" H. W. Smith, *Life and Correspondence of the Rev. William Smith*, I, 238.

[82] " Many negroes came, . . . some enquiring, have I a soul? " Gillies and Seymour, *Memoirs of the Life and Character of . . . Rev. George Whitefield* (3d ed.), 55. " I believe near Fifty Negroes came to give me Thanks, under God, for what has been done to their Souls . . . Some of them have been effectually wrought upon, and in an uncommon Manner." *A Continuation of the Reverend Mr. Whitefield's Journal*, 65, 66. " Visited a Negroe and prayed with her, and found her Heart touched by Divine Grace. Praised be the Lord, methinks one Negroe brought to Jesus Christ is peculiarly sweet to my Soul." W. Seward, *Journal of a Voyage from Savannah to Philadelphia*, etc., Apr. 18, 1740.

[83] " This afternoon a Negro man from Cecil County maryland preached in orchard opposite to ours. there was Sundry people, they said he spoke well for near an hour." MS. Ch. Marshall's Remembrancer, E, July 13, 1779.

[84] " Then (the pror and Gov.) proposed to them the necessitie of a law . . . about the marriages of negroes." *Col. Rec.*, I, 598, 606, 610; *Votes*

46   THE NEGRO IN PENNSYLVANIA

legislation they came under the law which forbade
servants to marry during their servitude without the
master's consent.[35] Doubtless in this matter there was
much of the laxity which is inseparable from slavery,
but it is said that many owners allowed their slaves to
marry in accordance with inclination, except that a
master would try to have his slaves marry among themselves.[36] The marriage ceremony was often performed
just as in the case of white people, the records of Christ
Church containing many instances.[37] The children of
these unions were taught submission to their parents,
who were indulged, it is said, in educating, cherishing,

and Proceedings, I, 120, 121; Bettle, "Notices of Negro Slavery as
connected with Pennsylvania," in Mem. Hist. Soc. Pa., VI, 368; Clarkson, Life of Penn, II, 80-82. Clarkson attributes the defeat to the lessen-
ing of Quaker influence, the lower tone of the later immigrants, and
temporary hostility to the executive. More probably the bill failed because stable marriage relations have always been found incompatible
with the ready movement and transfer of slave property; and because at
this early period the slaveholders recognized this fact, and were not
yet disposed to allow their slaves to marry.

[35] Stat. at L., II, 22.   Cf. Commonwealth v. Clements (1814), 6
Binney 210.

[36] St. John Crèvecœur, Letters, 221; Kalm, Travels, I, 391. Kalm adds
that it was considered an advantage to have negro women, since otherwise the offspring belonged to another master.

[37] MS. Rec. Christ Church, 4239, 4317, 4361, 4370, 4371, 4373, 4376,
4379, 4381, 4404, 4405; MS. Rec. First Reformed Church, 4158, 4315;
MS. Rec. St. Michael's and Zion, 109. Among the Friends there are
very few records of such marriages. Cf. however, MS. Journal of Joshua
Brown, 5 2d mo., 1774: . . . "I rode to Philadelphia . . . and Lodged that
Night at William Browns and 5th day of the month I Spent in town and
Was at a Negro Wedding in the Eving Where Several per Mett and had
a Setting with them and they took Each other and the Love of God Seemd
to be Extended to them " . . . A negro marriage according to Friends'
ceremony is recorded in MS. Deed Book O, 234, West Chester. Cf.
Mittelberger, Journey, 106, "The blacks are likewise married in the
English fashion." There must have been much laxity, however, for only
a part of which the negroes were to blame. "They are suffered, with
impunity, to cohabit together, without being married, and to part, when
solemnly engaged to one another as man and wife " . . . Benezet, Some
Historical Account of Guinea, 134.

and chastising them.[37a] Stable family life among the slaves was made possible by the conditions of slavery in Pennsylvania, there being no active interchange of negroes. When they were bought or sold families were kept together as much as possible.[38]

In one matter connected with religious observances race prejudice was shown: negroes were not as a rule buried in the cemeteries of white people.[39] In some of the Friends' records and elsewhere there is definite prohibition.[40] They were often buried in their masters' orchards, or on the edge of woodlands. The Philadelphia negroes were buried in a particular place outside the city.[41]

Under the kindly treatment accorded them the negroes of colonial Pennsylvania for the most part behaved fairly well. It is true that there is evidence that crime among them assumed grave proportions at times, while the records of the special courts and items in the newspapers show that there occurred murder, poisoning, arson, burglary, and rape.[42] In addition there was fre-

[37] a St. John Crèvecœur, *Letters*, 222.

[38] " Accot of Negroes Dr. . . . for my Negroe Cuffee and his Wife Rose and their Daughter Jenny bot of Wm Banloft . . . 76/3/10." MS. James Logan's Account Book, 90 (1714). " Wanted, Four or Five Negro Men . . . if they have families, wives, or children, all will be purchased together." *Pa. Packet*, Aug. 22, 1778. *Cf.* also *Mercury*, June 4, 1724; June 21, 1739; *Independent Gazeteer*, July 14, 1792. *Cf.* however, Benezet, *Some Historical Account of Guinea*, 136; Crawford, *Observations upon Negro Slavery* (1784), 23, 24; *Pa. Packet*, Jan. 1, 1780.

[39] This was not always the case. The MS. Rec. of Sandy Bank Cemetery, Delaware Co., contains the names of two negroes.

[40] MS. Minutes Middletown Monthly Meeting, 2d Book A, 171, 558, 559; *Pa. Mag.*, VIII, 419; Isaac Comly, " Sketches of the History of Byberry," *in Mem. Hist. Soc. Pa.*, II, 194. There were exceptions, however. *Cf.* MS. Bk. of Rec. Merion Meeting Grave Yard.

[41] Bean, *Hist. Montgomery Co.*, 302; Martin, *Hist of Chester*, 80; Kalm, *Travels*, I, 44; *Pa. Gazette*, Nov. 15, 1775.

[42] *Stat. at L.*, IV, 59; *Col. Rec.*, II, 18; 1 *Pa. Arch.* XI, 667; *Mercury*, Apr. 12, 1739; *Phila. Staatsbote*, Jan. 16, 1764; *Pa. Gazette*, Nov. 12,

quent complaint about tumultuous assembling and boisterous conduct, and there was undoubtedly much pilfering.[43]   Moreover the patience of many indulgent masters was tried by the shiftless behavior and insolent
bearing of their slaves.[44]   Yet the graver crimes stand
out in isolation rather than in mass; and it is too much
to expect an entire absence of the lesser ones. The white
people do not seem to have regarded their negroes as
dangerous.[45] Almost never were there efforts for severe
repression, and a slave insurrection seems hardly to
have been thought of.[46]   There are no statistics whatever on which to base an estimate, but judging from the
relative frequency of notices it seems probable that crime
among the negroes of Pennsylvania during the slavery
period—no doubt because they were under better control—was less than at any period thereafter.

But there was a misdemeanor of another kind: negro

1761.   For an instance of a slave killing his master, cf. MS. Supreme
Court Papers, XXI, 3546. This was very rare. Pa. Mag., XIII, 449.
According to Judge Bradford's statement arson was "the crime of slaves
and children." Journal of Senate of Pa., 1792-1793, p. 52; Col. Rec., IV,
243, 244, 259; XII, 377; MS. Miscellaneous Papers, Feb. 25, 1780. Cf.
especially MS. Records of Special Courts for the Trial of Negroes; Col.
Rec., IX, 648; MS. Streper Papers, 55.

[43] In 1737 the Council spoke of the "insolent Behaviour of the Negroes
in and about the city, which has of late been so much taken notice of " . . .
Col. Rec., IV, 244; Votes and Proceedings, IV, 171. As to pilfering
Franklin remarked that almost every slave was by nature a thief. Works
(ed. Sparks), II, 315.

[44] The following has not lost all significance. "I was much Disturbed
after I came our girl Poll driving her same stroke of Impudence as when
she was in Philadᵃ and her mistress so hood-winked by her as not to see
it which gave me much uneasiness and which I am determined not to put
up with " . . . Ch. Marshall, Remembrancer, D, Aug. 4, 1777. Cf. also
Remarks on the Quaker Unmasked (1764).

[45] As shown by the very careless enforcement of the special regulations.

[46] Except immediately following the negro "insurrection" in New
York in 1712. Cf. Stat. at L., II, 433; 1 Pa. Arch., IV, 792; 2 Pa. Arch.,
XV, 368.

slaves frequently ran away. Fugitives are mentioned from the first,[47] and there is hardly a copy of any of the old papers but has an advertisement for some negro at large.[48] These notices sometimes advise that the slave has stolen from his master; often that he has a pass, and is pretending to be a free negro; and occasionally that a free negro is suspected of harboring him.[49]

The law against harboring was severe and was strictly enforced. Anyone might take up a suspicious negro; while whoever returned a runaway to his master was by law entitled to receive five shillings and expenses. It was always the duty of the local authorities to apprehend suspects. When this occurred the procedure was to lodge the negro in jail, and advertise for the master, who might come, and after proving title and paying costs, take him away. Otherwise the negro was sold

[47] " A negro man and a White Woman servant being taken up . . . and brought before John Simcocke Justice in Commission for runaways Who upon Examination finding they had noe lawful Passe Comitted them to Prison " . . . MS. Court Rec. Penna. and Chester Co., 1681-88, p. 75; MS. New Castle Ct. Rec., Liber A, 158 (1677); MS. Minutes Ct. Quarter Sess. Bucks Co., 1684-1730, p. 138 (1690); MS. Minutes Chester Co. Courts, 1681-1697, p. 222 (1694-1695). For the continual going away of Christopher Marshall's " Girl Poll," see his Remembrancer, vol. D.

[48] The following is not only typical, but is very interesting on its own account, since Abraham Lincoln was a descendent of the family mentioned. " RUN away on the 13th of *September* last from *Abraham Lincoln* of *Springfield* in the County of Chester, a Negro Man named Jack, about 30 Years of Age, low Stature, speaks little or no *English*, has a Scar by the Corner of one Eye, in the Form of a V, his Teeth notched, and the Top of one on his Fore Teeth broke; He had on when he went away an old Hat, a grey Jacket partly like a Sailor's Jacket. Whoever secures the said Negro, and brings him to his Master, or to *Mordecai* Lincoln . . . shall have *Twenty Shillings* Reward and reasonable Charges." Pa. *Gazette*, Oct. 15, 1730.

[49] *Mercury*, Apr. 18, 1723; July 11, 1723; *Gazette*, May 3, 1744; Feb. 22, 1775; July 28, 1779; Jan. 17, 1782; *Packet*, Oct. 13, 1778; Aug. 3, 1779. One negro indentured himself to a currier. *Gazette*, Aug. 30, 1775. Such negroes the community was warned not to employ. *Packet*, Feb. 27, 1779.

for a short time to satisfy jail fees, advertised again, and finally either set at liberty or disposed of as pleased the local court.[50]

This fleeing from service on the part of negro slaves, while varying somewhat in frequency, was fairly constant during the whole slavery period, increasing as the number of slaves grew larger. During the British occupation of Philadelphia, however, it assumed such enormous proportions that the number of negroes held there was permanently lowered.[51] Notwithstanding, then, the kindly treatment they received, slaves in Pennsylvania ran away. Nevertheless it is significant that during the same period white servants ran away more than twice as often.[52]

Many traits of daily life and marks of personal appearance which no historian has described, are preserved in the advertisements of the daily papers. Almost every negro seems to have had the smallpox. To have done with this and the measles was justly considered an enhancement in value. Some of the negroes kidnapped from Africa still bore traces of their savage ancestry. Not a few spoke several languages. Gener-

---

[50] The penalty was thirty shillings for every day. *Stat. at L.*, IV, 64 (1725-1726). There was need for regulation from the first. *Cf. Col. Rec.*, I, 117. An advertisement from Reading in *Gazette*, July 31, 1776, explains the procedure when suspects were held in jail. Such advertisements recur frequently. *Cf. Mercury*, Aug. 13, 1730 (third notice); *Gazette*, Dec. 27, 1774; *Packet*, Mar. 23, 1779.

[51] For negroes carried off or who ran away at this time *cf.* MS. Miscellaneous Papers, Sept. 1, 1778; Nov. 19, 1778; Aug. 20, 1779; and others. Numbers of strange negroes were reported to be wandering around in Northumberland County. *Ibid.*, Aug. 29, 1780. In 1732 the Six Nations had been asked not to harbor runaway negroes, since they were "the Support and Livelihood of their Masters, and gett them their Bread." 4 *Pa. Arch.*, II, 657, 658.

[52] So I judge from statistics which I have compiled from the advertisements in the newspapers.

ally they were fond of gay dress. Some carried fiddles
when they ran away. One had made considerable
money by playing. Many little hints as to character appear. Thus Mona is full of flattery. Cuff Dix is fond
of liquor. James chews abundance of tobacco. Stephen
has a "sower countenance"; Harry, "meek countenance"; Rachel, "remarkable austere countenance";
Dick is "much bandy legged"; Violet, "pretty, lusty,
and fat." A likely negro wench is sold because of her
breeding fast. One negro says that he has been a
preacher among the Indians. Two others fought a duel
with pistols. A hundred years has involved no great
change in character.[53]

Finally, on the basis of information drawn from rare
and miscellaneous sources it becomes apparent that in
slavery times there was more kindliness and intimacy
between the races than existed afterwards. In those
days many slaves were treated as if part of the master's
family : when sick they were nursed and cared for ; when
too old to work they were provided for ; and some were
remembered in the master's will.[54]   Negroes did run

---

[53] *Mercury*, Apr. 18, 1723; *Packet*, July 16, 1778; *Gazette*, June 12,
1740; Feb. 4, 1775; Jan. 3, 1776; July 2, 1781; *Gazette*, Nov. 17, 1748;
Feb. 21, 1775. "'Old Dabbo' an African Negro . . . call'd here for some
victuals . . . He had three gashes on each cheek made by his mother when
he was a child . . . His conversation is scarcely intelligible"; MS. Diary
of Joel Swayne, 1823-1833, Mar. 27, 1828. *Mercury*, Aug. 6, 1730;
Packet, Aug. 26, 1779; *Gazette*, July 31, 1739-1740; *Mercury*, June 24,
1725; *Packet*, June 22, 1789; *Packet*, Dec. 31, 1778; *Gazette*, Sept. 10,
1741; July 21, 1779; Sept. 11, 1746; Oct. 16, 1776; July 30, 1747; May
14, 1747; Oct. 22, 1747; Aug. 30, 1775; Mar. 22, 1747-1748; July 24,
1776; Apr. 23, 1761; July 5, 1775; *Packet*, Jan. 26, 1779.
[54] "My Dear Companion . . . has really her hands full, Cow to milk,
breakfast to get, her Negro woman to bath, give medicine, Cap up with
flannels, as She is allways Sure to be poorly when the weather is cold,
Snowy and Slabby. its then She gives her Mistriss a deal of fatigue and
trouble in attending on her." Ch. Marshall, Remembrancer, E, Mar. 25,
1779. "To Israel Taylor p order of the Com[s] for Cureing negro Jack

away, and numbers of them desired to be free, but when manumission came not a few of them preferred to stay with their former owners. It was the opinion of an advocate of emancipation that they were better off as slaves than they could possibly be as freemen.[55]

Such was slavery in Pennsylvania. If on the one hand there was the chance of families being sold apart; if there was seen the cargo, the slave-drove, the auction sale; it must be remembered that such things are inseparable from the institution of slavery, and that on the other hand they were rare, and not to be weighed against the positive comfort and well-being of which there is such abundant proof. If ever it be possible not to condemn modern slavery, it might seem that slavery as it existed in Pennsylvania in the eighteenth century was a good, probably for the masters, certainly for the

---

legg . . . 4/10   To Roger Parke for Cureing negro sam . . . /9/9." MS. William Penn's Account Book, 1690-1693, p. 8.   A bill for £10 10 sh. 4d. was rendered to Thomas Penn for nursing and burying his negro Sam.   Some of the items are very humorous.   MS. Penn Papers, Accounts (unbound), Feb. 19, 1741.   The bill for Thomas Penn's negroes, Hagar, Diana, and Susy, for the years 1773 and 1774, amounted to £5 5 sh. Penn-Physick MSS., IV, 253.   An item in a bill rendered to Mrs. Margaretta Frame is: " To bleeding her Negro man Sussex . . . /2/6." MS. Penn Papers, Accounts (unbound), June 5, 1742.   St. John Crèvecœur, *Letters,* 221.   Masters were compelled by law to support their old slaves who would otherwise have become charges on the community.   *Cf. Stat. at L.,* X, 70; *Laws of Pa., 1803,* p. 103; *1835-1836,* pp. 546, 547.   In very many cases, however, old negroes were maintained comfortably until death in the families where they had served.   *Cf.* MS. Phila. Wills, X, 94 (1794).   There are numerous instances of negroes receiving property by their master's wills.   *Cf.* West Chester Will Files, no. 3759 (1785).   For the darker side *cf.* Lay, *All Slave-Keepers Apostates,* 93.

⁵⁵ " Many of those whom the good Quakers have emancipated have received the great benefit with tears in their eyes, and have never quitted, though free, their former masters and benefactors."   St. John Crèvecœur, *Letters, 222; Pa. Mag.,* XVIII, 372, 373; Buck, MS. *History of Bucks Co.,* marginal note of author in his scrapbook.   For the superiority of slavery *cf.* J. Harriot, *Struggles through Life,* etc., II, 409.   Also Watson, *Annals,* II, 265.

slaves.[56] The fact is that it existed in such mitigated form that it was impossible for it to be perpetuated. Whenever men can treat their slaves as men in Pennsylvania treated them, they are living in a moral atmosphere inconsistent with the holding of slaves. Nothing can then preserve slavery but paramount economic needs. In Pennsylvania, since such needs were not paramount, slavery was doomed.

[56] It has been suggested that it was milder than the system under which redemptioners were held, and that hence " Quaker scruples against slavery were either misplaced or insincere." C. A. Herrick, " Indentured Labor in Pennsylvania," (MS. thesis, University of Pa.), 89. An examination of the Quaker records would have shown that the last part of this statement is not true. See below, chaps. IV, V.

CHAPTER IV.

The Breaking up of Slavery—Manumission.

In Pennsylvania the disintegration of slavery began as soon as slavery was established, for there were free negroes in the colony at the beginning of the eighteenth century.[1] Manumission may have taken place earlier than this, for in 1682 an owner made definite promise of freedom to his negro.[2] The first indisputable case now known, however, occurred in 1701, when a certain Lydia Wade living in Chester County freed her slaves by testament.[3] In the same year William Penn on his return to England liberated his blacks likewise.[4] Judging from the casual and unexpected references to free ne-

[1] It is of course possible that some of these negroes had been servants, and that their period of service was over.

[2] " Where As William Clark did buy . . . An negor man Called and knowen by the name of black Will for and during his natrill Life; never the Less the said William Clark doe for the Incourigment of the sd neagor servant hereby promise Covenant and Agree; that if the said Black Will doe well and Truely sarve the said William Clark . . . five years . . . then the said Black Will shall be Clear and free of and from Any further or Longer Sarvicetime or Slavery . . . as wittnes my hand this Thirteenth day of . . . June Anno; Din; 168$\frac{2}{2}$." MS. Ancient Rec. of Sussex Co., 1681-1709, p. 116.

[3] " My will is that my negroes John and Jane his wife shall be set free one month after my decease." Ashmead, *History of Delaware County*, 203.

[4] " I give to . . . my blacks their freedom as is under my hand already " . . . MS. Will of William Penn, Newcastle on Delaware, 30th 8br, 1701. This will, which was left with James Logan, was not carried out. Penn's last will contains no mention of his negroes. He frequently mentions them elsewhere. *Cf.* MS. Letters and Papers of William Penn (Dreer), 29 (1689), 35 (1690); *Pa. Mag.*, XXXIII, 316 (1690); MS. Logan Papers. II, 98 (1703). *Cf.* also Penn. MSS., Official Correspondence, 97.

groes which come to light from time to time, it seems
probable that other masters also bestowed freedom. At
any rate the status of the free negro had come to be recognized about this time as one to be protected by law, for
when in 1703 Antonio Garcia, a Spanish mulatto, was
brought to Philadelphia as a slave, he appealed to the
provincial Council, and presently was set at liberty.[5] In
1717 the records of Christ Church mention Jane, a free
negress, who was baptized there with her daughter.[6]

This freeing of negroes at so early a time in the history of the colony is sufficiently remarkable. It might be
expected that manumission would have been rare; and,
indeed, the records are very few at first. Nevertheless
a law passed in 1725-1726 would indicate that the practice was by no means unusual.[7]

It is not possible to say what was the immediate cause
of the passing of that part of the act which refers to
manumission. It may have been the growth of a class
of black freemen, or it may have been the desire to check
manumission;[8] but it was probably neither of these
things so much as it was the practice of masters who set
free their infirm slaves when the labor of those slaves
was no longer remunerative.[9] This practice together
with the usual shiftlessness of most of the freedmen
makes the resulting legislation intelligible enough. It

[5] *Col. Rec.,* II, 120.

[6] Jane " a free negro woman " . . . MS. Rec. Christ Church, 46.

[7] " Whereas 'tis found by experience that free negroes are an idle,
slothful people and often prove burdensome to the neighborhood and afford ill examples to other negroes " . . . " An Act for the better regulating
of Negroes in this Province." *Stat. at L.,* IV, 61.

[8] " Our Ancestors . . . for a long time deemed it policy to obstruct the
emancipation of Slaves and affected to consider a free Negro as a useless
if not a dangerous being " . . . Letter of W. Rawle (1787), in MS. Rec.
Pa. Soc. Abol. Slavery.

[9] *Votes and Proceedings,* II, 336, 337.

provided that thereafter if any master purposed to set his negro free, he should obligate himself at the county court to secure the locality in which the negro might reside from any expense occasioned by the sickness of the negro or by his inability to support himself. If a negro received liberty by will, recognizance should be entered into by the executor immediately. Without this no negro was to be deemed free. The security was fixed at thirty pounds.[10]

Whatever may have been the full purpose of this statute, there can be no question that it did check manumission to a certain extent. A standing obligation of thirty pounds, which might at any moment become an unpleasant reality, when added to the other sacrifices which freeing a slave entailed, was probably sufficient to discourage many who possessed mildly good intentions. Several times it was protested that the amount was so excessive as to check the beneficence of owners;[11] and on one occasion it was computed that the thirty pounds required did not really suffice to support such negroes as became charges, but that a different method and a smaller sum would have secured better results.[12] The

[10] " An Act for the better regulating of Negroes in this Province." Stat. at L., IV, 61 (1725-1726).

[11] " This is however very expensive for they are obliged to make a provision for the Negro thus set at liberty, to afford him subsistence when he is grown old, that he may not be driven by necessity to wicked actions, or that he may be at anybody's charge, for these free Negroes become very lazy and indolent afterwards." Kalm, Travels, I, 394 (1748).

[12] Cf. Votes and Proceedings, 1767-1776, p. 30. The author of Brief Considerations on Slavery, and the Expediency of Its Abolition (1773) argued that the public derived benefit from the labor of adult free negroes, and that the public should pay the surety required. By an elaborate calculation he endeavored to prove that a sum of about five shillings deposited at interest by the community each year of the negro's life after he was twenty-one, would amply suffice for all requirements. Pp. 8-14 of the second part, entitled " An Account Stated on the Manumission

burden to owners was no doubt felt very grievously during the latter half of the eighteenth century, when manumission was going on so actively, and it is known that the Assembly was asked to give relief.[13] Nevertheless nothing was done until 1780 when the abolition act swept from the statute-books all previous legislation about the negro, slave as well as free.[14]

In spite of the obstacles created by the statute of 1725-1726, the freeing of negroes continued. In 1731 John Baldwin of Chester ordered in his will that his negress be freed one year after his decease. Two years later Ralph Sandiford is said to have given liberty to all of his slaves. In 1742 Judge Langhorne in Bucks County devised freedom to all of his negroes, between thirty and forty in number. In 1744 by the will of John Knowles of Oxford, negro James was to be made free on condition that he gave security to the executors to pay the thirty pounds if required. Somewhat before this time John Harris, the founder of Harrisburg, set free the faithful negro Hercules, who had saved his life from the Indians. In 1746 Samuel Blunson manumitted his slaves at Columbia. During this period negroes were occasionally sent to the Moravians, who gave them religious training, baptized them, and after a time set them at liberty. During the following years the records of some of the churches refer again and again to free negroes who were married in them, bap-

---

of Slaves." He says " As the laws stand at present in several of our northern governments, the act of manumission is clogged with difficulties that almost amount to a prohibition." *Ibid.*, 11.

[13] *Votes and Proceedings, 1767-1776,* p. 696.

[14] *Stat. at L.,* X, 72.

tized in them, or who brought their children to them to be baptized.[15] At an early date there was a sufficient number of free black people in Pennsylvania to attract the attention of philanthropists; and it is known that Whitefield as early as 1744 took up a tract of land partly with the intention of making a settlement of free negroes.[16] Up to this time, however, manumission probably went on in a desultory manner, hampered by the large security required, and practised only by the most ardent believers in human liberty. The middle of the eighteenth century marked a great turning-point.

The southeastern part of Pennsylvania, in which most of the negroes were located, was peopled largely by Quakers, who in many localities were the principal slave-owners, and who at different periods during the eighteenth century probably held from a half to a third of all the slaves in the colony. But they were never able to reconcile this practice entirely with their religious belief and from the very beginning it encountered strong opposition. As this opposition is really part of the history of abolition in Pennsylvania it will be treated at length in the following chapter. Here it is sufficient to say that from 1688 a long warfare was carried on, for the most part by zealous reformers who gradually won adherents, until about 1750 the Friends' meetings declared against slavery, and the members who were not slave-owners undertook to persuade those who still owned negroes to give them up.

[15] Martin, *History of Chester*, 480; Watson, *Annals*, II, 265; *Pa. Mag.*, VII, 82; Davis, *History of Bucks County*, 798; MS. in Miscellaneous Collection, Box 10, Negroes; Morgan, *Annals of Harrisburg*, 11; Smedley, *History of the Underground Railroad in Chester*, etc., 27; *Pa. Mag.*, XII, 188; XXIX, 363, 365; MS. Rec. Christ Church, 46, 352, 356, 379, 400, 403, 404, 440, 441, 455, 475, 4126, 4330, 4356; MS. Rec. First Reformed Church, 4126, 4248; MS. Rec. St. Michael's and Zion, 97.
[16] *Cf.* Conyngham's " Historical Notes," in *Mem. Hist. Soc. Pa.*, I, 338.

The feeling among some of the Friends was extraordinary at this time. They went from one slaveholder to another expostulating, persuading, entreating. It was then that the saintly John Woolman did his work; but he was only the most distinguished among many others. It is hardly possible to read over the records of any Friends' meeting for the next thirty years without finding numerous references to work of this character; and in more than one journal of the period mention is made of the obstacles encountered and the expedients employed.[17]

The results of their efforts were far-reaching. Many Friends who would have scrupled to buy more slaves, and who were convinced that slave-holding was an evil, yet retained such slaves as they had, through motives of expediency, and also because they believed that negroes held in mild bondage were better off than when free. Against this temporizing policy the reformers fought hard, and aided by the decision of the Yearly Meeting that slaveholders should no longer participate in the affairs of the Society, carried forward their work with such success that within one more generation slavery among the Friends in Pennsylvania had passed away.

During the period, then, from 1750 to 1780 manumission among the Friends became very frequent. Many slaves were set free outright, their masters assuming the liability required by law. Others were manumitted on condition that they would not become chargeable.[18] Some owners gave promise of freedom at the end of a certain number of years, considering the service during those years an equivalent for the financial obligation

[17] See below, p. 74.
[18] MS. Miscellaneous Papers, 1684-1847, Chester Co., 101 (1764).

which at the end they would have to assume.[19]   Often the negro was given his liberty on condition that at a future time he would pay to the master his purchase price.[20]   In 1751 a writer said that numerous negroes had gained conditional freedom, and were wandering around the country in search of employment so as to pay their owners.   The magistrates of Philadelphia complained of this as a nuisance.[21]

Just how many slaves gained their freedom during this period it is impossible to say.   The church records mention them again and again ; and they become, what they had not been before, the occasion of frequent notice and serious speculation.[22]   Other people began now to follow the Friends' example,[23] and the belief in abstract principles of freedom aroused by the Revolutionary struggle gave further impetus to the movement.[24]   In every quarter, now, manumissions were constantly be-

[19] They were generally held longer than apprentices or white servants—until twenty-eight or thirty years of age, but many of the Friends protested against this. MS. Diary of Richard Barnard, 24 5 mo., 1782; MS. Minutes Exeter Monthly Meeting, Book B, 354 (1779).

[20] " I do hereby Certify that Benjamin Mifflin hath given me Directions to sell his Negro man Cuff to himself for the Sum of Sixty Pounds if he can raise the Money having Repeatedly refused from Others seventy Five Pounds and upwards for him." MS. (1769) in Misc. Coll., Box 10, Negroes.

[21] Pa. Gazette, Mar. 5, 1751.

[22] Cf. Benezet, Some Historical Account of Guinea, 134, 135, where he laments the difficulties under which free negroes labor. Also same author, A Mite Cast into the Treasury, 13-17, where he argues that negro servants should not be held longer than white apprentices.

[23] " Die mährischen Brüder folgten diesem rühmlichen Beispiel; so auch Christen von den übrigen Bekenntnissen." Ebeling, in Erdbeschreibung, etc., IV, 220.

[24] Cf. preamble to the act of 1780. Stat. at L., X, 67, 68. A negro twenty-one years old was manumitted because " all mankind have an Equal Natural and Just right to Liberty." MS. Extracts Rec. Goshen Monthly Meeting, 415 (G. Cope).

ing made.[25] Any estimate as to how many negroes, servants and free, there were in Pennsylvania by 1780 must
be largely a conjecture, but it is perhaps safe to say that
there were between four and five thousand.[26]

The act of 1780, which put an end to the further
growth of slavery in Pennsylvania, marked the beginning of the final work of the liberators. Coming at a time
when so many people had given freedom to their slaves,
and passing with so little opposition in the Assembly as
to show that the majority of Pennsylvania's people no
longer had sympathy with slavery, it was the signal to
the abolitionists to urge the manumission of such negroes as the law had left in bondage. The task was
made easier by the fact that not only was the value of the
slave property now much diminished, but a man no
longer needed to enter into surety when he set his slaves
free. Doubtless many whose religious scruples had been
balanced by material considerations, now saw the way
smooth before them, or arranged to make the sacrifice cost them little or nothing at all. During this period
manumission took on a commercial aspect which formerly had not been so evident. This was brought about
in several ways.

Sometimes negroes had saved enough to purchase
their liberty.[27] Many, as before, received freedom upon

[25] MS. General Quarter Sessions of the Peace, Phila. Co., 1773-1780.
Franklin, Letter to Dean Woodward, Apr. 10, 1773, in *Works* (ed.
Sparks), VIII, 42.

[26] In 1751 the number of negroes in Pennsylvania, including Delaware,
was thought to be 11,000. *Cf.* above, p. 12. The negroes in Pennsylvania alone by 1780 probably did not exceed the same number. Of these
6,000 were said to be slaves. *Cf.* above, *ibid.* In some places by this
time manumission was nearly complete. *Cf.* W. J. Buck, in *Coll. Hist.
Soc. Pa.*, I, 201.

[27] MSS. Misc. Coll., Box 10, Negroes.

binding themselves to pay for it at the expiration of a certain time.[28]   In this they often received assistance from well-disposed people, in particular from the Friends, who had by no means stopped the good work when their own slaves were set free.[29] At times the entire purchase money was paid by some philanthropist.[30] Frequently one member of a negro family bought freedom for another, the husband often paying for his wife, the father for his children.[31] Furthermore it had now become common to bind out negroes for a term of years, and many owners who desired their slaves to be free, found partial compensation in selling them for a limited period, on express condition that all servitude should be terminated strictly in accordance with the contract.   By

[28] MS. Rec. Pa. Soc. Abol. Sl., I, 19, 27, 29, 43, 67, and *passim*.

[29] A MS. dated Phila., 1769, contains a list of persons who had promised to contribute towards purchasing a negro's freedom.   Among the memoranda are: " John Head agrees to give him Twenty Shillings and not to be Repaid . . . John Benezet twenty Shillings . . . Christopher Marshall /7/6 . . . If he can raise with my Donation enough to free him I agree to give him three pounds and not otherwise I promise Saml Emlen jur . . . Joseph Pemberton by his Desire [Five *erased*] pounds £3." MS. Misc. Coll., Box 10, Negroes.   •

[30] Misc. MSS. 1744-1859. Northern, Interior and Western Counties, 191 (1782).

[31] In 1779 a negro of Bucks County to secure the freedom of his wife gave his note to be paid by 1783.   In 1782, having paid part, he was allowed to take his wife until the next payment.   In 1785 she was free. MS. Rec. Pa. Soc. Abol. Sl., I, 27-43.   In 1787 negro Samson had purchased his wife and children for ninety-nine pounds. *Ibid.*, I, 67. James Oronogue, who had been hired by his master to the keeper of a tavern, gained by his obliging behavior sixty pounds from the customers within four years' time, and at his master's death was allowed to purchase his freedom for one hundred pounds.   He paid besides fifty pounds for his wife. *Ibid.*, I, 69. When Cuff Douglas had been a slave for thirty-seven years his master promised him freedom after four years more.   On the master agreeing to take thirty pounds in lieu of this service, Douglas hired himself out, and was free at the end of sixteen months.   He then began business as a tailor, and presently was able to buy his wife and children for ninety pounds, besides one son for whom he paid forty-five pounds. *Ibid.*, I, 72. Also *ibid.*, I, 79, 91.

furthering such transactions the benevolent tried to help negroes to gain freedom.[82] Occasionally the slave liberated was bound for a term of years to serve the former master.[83] Even at this period, however, negroes continued to be manumitted from motives of pure benevolence. Some received liberty by the master's testament, and others were held only until assurance was given the master that he would not become liable under the poor law.[84]

As the result of the earnest efforts that were made slavery in Pennsylvania dwindled steadily. In the course of a long time it would doubtless have passed away as the result of continued individual manumission. As a matter of fact, it had become almost extinct within two generations after 1750. This was brought about by work that affected not individuals, but whole classes, and finally all the people of the state; which was designed to strike at the root of slavery and destroy it altogether. This was abolition.

[82] "Wanted to purchase, a good Negro Wench . . . If to be sold on terms of freedom by far the most agreeable." *Pa. Packet*, Aug. 22, 1778. In 1791 Caspar Wistar bought a slave for sixty pounds "to extricate him from that degraded Situation " . . . , his purpose being to keep the negro for a term of years only. MS. Misc. Coll., Box 10, Negroes. Numerous other examples among the same MSS.

[83] "I, John Lettour from motives of benevolence and humanity . . . do . . . set free . . . my Negro Girl Agathe Aged about Seventeen Years. On condition . . . that she . . . bind herself by Indenture to serve me . . . Six years " . . . . MS. *ibid. Cf.* MS. Abstract Rec. Abington Monthly Meeting, 372 (1765).

[84] "I Manumit . . . my Negro Girl Abb when she shall Arrive to the Age of Eighteen Years . . . (on Condition that the Committee for the Abolition of slavery shall make entry according to Law . . . so as to secure me from any Costs or Trouble on me or my Estate on said Negro after the age of Eighteen Years). . . Hannah Evans." MS. Misc. Coll., Box 10, Negroes. *Cf. Stat. at L.,* X, 70. At times this might become an unpleasant reality. *Cf.* MS. State of a Case respecting a Negro (Ridgway Branch).

CHAPTER V.

The Destruction of Slavery—Abolition.

The events which led to the extinction of slavery in Pennsylvania fall naturally into four periods. They are, first, the years from 1682 to about 1740, during which the Germans discountenanced slave-holding, and the Friends ceased importing negroes; second, the period of the Quaker abolitionists, from about 1710 to 1780, by which time slavery among the Quakers had come to an end; third, from 1780 to 1788, the years of legislative action; and finally, the period from 1788 to the time when slavery in Pennsylvania became extinct through the gradual working of the act for abolition.

Opposition to slaveholding arose among the Friends. Slavery had not yet been recognized in statute law when they began to protest against it. This protest, faint in the beginning and taken up only by a few idealists, was never stopped afterwards, but, growing continually in strength, was, as the events of after years showed, from the first fraught with foreboding of doom to the institution. Opposition on the part of the Friends had begun before Pennsylvania was founded. In 1671 Fox, travelling in the West Indies, advised his brethren in Barbadoes to deal mildly with their negroes, and after certain years of servitude to make them free. Four years later William Edmundson in one of his letters asked how it was possible for men to reconcile Christ's command, to do as they would be done by, with the prac-

64

tice of holding slaves without hope or expectation of freedom.[1] Nevertheless in the first years after the settlement of Pennsylvania Friends were the principal slaveholders. This led to differences of opinion, but at the start economic considerations prevailed.

The reform really began in 1688, a year memorable for the first formal protest against slavery in North America.[2] Germantown had been settled by German refugees who in religious belief were Friends. These men, simple-minded and honest, having had no previous acquaintance with slavery, were amazed to find it existing in Penn's colony. At their monthly meeting, the eighteenth of the second month, 1688, Pastorius and other leaders drew up an eloquent and touching memorial. In words of surpassing nobleness and simplicity they stated the reasons why they were against slavery and the traffic in men's bodies. Would the masters wish so to be dealt with? Was it possible for this to be in accord with Christianity? In Pennsylvania there was freedom of conscience; there ought likewise to be freedom of the body. What report would it cause in Europe that in this new land the Quakers handled men as there men treated their cattle? If it were possible that Christian men might do these things they desired to be so informed.[3]

---

[1] Edmundson's *Journal*, 61. Janney, *History of the Friends*, III, 178.

[2] Pennypacker, " The Settlement of Germantown," in *Pa. Mag.*, IV, 28; McMaster, " The Abolition of Slavery in the United States," in *Chatauquan*, XV, 24, 25 (Apr., 1892). For the protest against slavery and the slave-trade (*De instauranda Æthiopum Salute*, Madrid, 1647) of the Jesuit, Alfonso Sandoval, *cf.* Saco, *Historia de la Esclavitud de la Raza Africana en el Nuevo Mundo*, 253-256.

[3] Pennypacker, *place cited;* Learned, *Life of Francis Daniel Pastorius,* 261, 262. Facsimile of protest in Ridgway Branch of the Library Company of Philadelphia.

This protest they sent to the Monthly Meeting at Richard Worrel's. There it was considered, and found too weighty to be dealt with, and so it was sent on to the Quarterly Meeting at Philadelphia, and from thence to the Yearly Meeting at Burlington, which finally decided not to give a positive judgment in the case.[4] For the present nothing came of it; but the idea did not die. It probably lingered in the minds of many men; for within a few years a sentiment had been aroused which became widespread and powerful.

In 1693 George Keith, leader of a dissenting faction of Quakers, laid down as one of his doctrines that negroes were men, and that slavery was contrary to the religion of Christ; also that masters should set their negroes at liberty after some reasonable time.[5] At a meeting of Friends held in Philadelphia in 1693 the prevailing opinion was that none should buy except to set free. Three years later at the Friends' Yearly Meeting it was resolved to discourage the further bringing in of slaves.[6] In 1712 when the Yearly Meeting at Philadelphia desiring counsel applied to the Yearly Meeting at London, it received answer that the multiplying of negroes might be of dangerous consequence.[7] In the next and the following years the Meetings strongly advised Friends not to import and not to buy slaves.[8] From 1730 to 1737 reports showed that the importation of

[4] The Monthly Meeting declared " we think it not expedient for us to meddle with it here." Pennypacker, *place cited*, 30, 31.

[5] Watson, *Annals*, II, 262. " An Exhortation and Caution To Friends Concerning buying or keeping of Negroes," in *Pa. Mag.*, XIII, 265-270. This is said to have been the first printed protest against slavery in America. *Cf.* Hildeburn, *A Century of Printing*, etc., I, 28, 29; Gabriel Thomas, *Account*, 53; Bettle, *Notes*, 367.

[6] Clarkson, *Life of Penn*, II, 78, 79.

[7] *Cf.* Bettle, 372.

[8] *Ibid.*, 373.

negroes by Friends was being largely discontinued. By
1745 it had virtually ceased.[9]

It is generally believed that Pennsylvania's restrictive
legislation, that long series of acts passed for the purpose of keeping out negroes by means of prohibitive
duties, was largely due to Quaker influence. This is
probably true, but it is not easy to prove. The proceedings of the colonial Assembly have been reported so
briefly that they do not give the needed information.
When, however, the strong feeling of the Friends is
understood in connection with the fact that they con-
trolled the early legislatures, it is not hard to believe that
the high duties were imposed because they wished the
traffic at an end. Their feeling about the slave-trade
and their desire to stop it are revealed again and again
in the meeting minutes.[10] The most drastic law was
certainly due to them.[11]

[9] *Ibid.*, 377.
[10] " Whereas several Papers have been read relating to the keeping and
bringing in of Negroes . . . it is the advice of this Meeting, that Friends
be careful not to encourage the bringing in of any more Negroes " . . .
MS. " Negroes or Slaves," Yearly Meeting Advices, 1682-1777 (1696).
" This meeting is also dissatisfied with Friends buying and incouriging
the bringing in of Negroes " . . . MS. Chester Quarterly Meeting Minutes,
6 6th mo., 1711. " There having a conscern Come upon severall friends
belonging to this meeting Conscerning the Importation of Negros . . . after
some time spent in the Consideration thereof it is the Unanimous sence
of this meeting that friends should not be concerned hereafter in the
Importation thereof nor buy any " . . . MS. Chester Monthly Meeting
Minutes, 27 4th mo., 1715. MS. Chester Quarterly Meeting Minutes,
1 6th mo., 1715. " This meeting have been for some time under a
Conscern by reason of the great Quantity of Negros fetched and imported into this Country." *Ibid.*, 11 6th mo., 1729. MS. Yearly Meeting
Minutes, 19-23 7th mo., 1730. As soon as Friends had been brought to
cease the importation of negroes, attack was made upon the practice of
Friends buying negroes imported by others. *Cf.* MS. Chester Q. M. M.,
11 6th mo., 1729; 9 9th mo., 1730. The MS. Chester M. M. M. mention
100 books on the slave-trade for circulation.
[11] " We also kindly received your advice about negro slaves, and we are
one with you, that the multiplying of them, may be of a dangerous con-

But the small number of negroes in Pennsylvania as compared with the neighboring northern colonies was above all due to the early and continuous aversion to slavery manifested by the Germans. The first German settlers opposed the institution for religious reasons.[12] This opposition is perhaps to be ascribed to them as Quakers rather than as men of a particular race. But as successive swarms poured into the country it was found, it may be from religious scruples, more probably because of peculiar economic characteristics and because of feelings of sturdy industry and self-reliance, that they almost never bought negroes nor even hired them.[13] As the German element in Pennsylvania was

sequence, and therefore a Law was made in Pennsylvania laying Twenty pounds Duty upon every one imported there, which Law the Queen was pleas'd to disanull, we would heartily wish that a way might be found to stop the bringing in more here, or at least that Friends may be less concerned in buying or selling, of any that may be brought in, and hope for your assistance with the Government if any farther Law should be made discouraging the importation. We know not of any Friend amongst us that has any hand or concern in bringing any out of their own Country." MS. Yearly M. M., 22 7th mo., 1714. This was written in reply to the London Yearly Meeting, and alludes to the act passed in 1712. See above, p. 3.

[12] See above, p. 65. *Cf.* also P. C. Plockhoy's principle laid down in his *Kort en Klaer Ontwerp* (Amsterdam, 1662): " No lordship or servile slavery shall burden our Company." Quoted in Pennypacker, *Settlement of Germantown*, 204, 292.

[13] " The Germans seldom hire men to work upon their farms." Rush, *An Account of the Manners of the German Inhabitants of Pennsylvania* (1789), 24. " They never, as a general thing, had colored servants or slaves." *Ibid.*, 24 (note by Rupp). " Slaves in Pennsylvania never were as numerous in proportion to the white population as in New York and New Jersey. To our German population this is certainly attributable— Wherever they or their numerous descendants located they preferred *their own* labor to that of negro slaves." Buck, MS. *History of Bucks County*, 69. " Of all the nations who have settled in America, the Germans have availed themselves the least of the unjust and demoralizing aid of slavery." W. Grimshaw, *History of the United States*, 79. The truth of these statements is revealed in the tax-lists of the different counties. Thus, in Berks County there were 2692 German tax-payers (61%) and 1724 (39%) not Germans. Of these 44 Germans held 62 slaves,

very considerable, amounting at times to one-third of
the population, such a course, though lacking in dra-
matic quality, and though it has been unheralded by
the historians, was nevertheless of immense and decisive importance.[14]

During this period, then, much had been accomplished. Not only had the Germans turned their backs
upon slave-holding, but the Friends, brought to perceive
the iniquity of the practice, had ceased importing slaves,
and for the most part had ceased buying them. It was
another generation before the conservative element
could be brought to advance beyond this position. It
was not so easy to make them give up the slaves they
already had.

The succeeding period was characterized by an inevitable struggle which ensued between considerations
of economy and ethics. The attitude of many Friends
was that in refusing to buy any more slaves they were

and 57 of other nationalities held 92 slaves. 3 *Pa. Arch.*, XVIII, 303-
430. In York County, where there were 2051 German property-holders
(34%) and 3993 who were not Germans (66%), 27 Germans held 44
slaves as against 178 others who held 319 slaves. 3 *Pa. Arch.*, XXI,
165-324. (Both these estimates are for 1780.) In Lancaster County the
property-holders included approximately 3475 Germans (48%) and 3706
not Germans (52%). Here 31 Germans held 46 slaves, while 200 not
Germans held 402 slaves. 3 *Pa. Arch.*, XVII, 489-685 (1779). The
records of the German churches rarely mention slaves.

[14] The small number of negroes in Pennsylvania was often.noticed.
Burnaby, *Travels through the Middle Settlements*, 63, said "there are few
negroes or slaves " . . . (1759), Anburey, *Travels through the Interior
Parts of America*, II ,280-281, said, " The Pennsylvanians . . . are more
industrious of themselves, having but few blacks among them." (1778).
Cf. Proud, *History*, II, 274. Estimates as to the number of Germans in
Pennsylvania vary from 3/5 (1747, *cf.* Rupp's note in Rush, *Account*, 1)
to 1/3 (1789, *ibid.*, 54). For many estimates *cf.* Diffenderffer, *German
Immigration into Pennsylvania*, pt. II, *The Redemptioners*, 99-108. Some
few Germans had intended to hold slaves from the first. *Cf.* the articles
of agreement between the members of the Frankfort Company (1686):
. . . " alle . . . leibeigenen Menschen . . . sollen unter Allen Interes-
senten pro rato der Ackerzahl gemein seyn." MS. in possession of S. W.
Pennypacker, Philadelphia.

fulfilling all reasonable obligations. Sometimes there was a desire to hush up the whole matter and get it out of mind. Isaac Norris tells of a meeting that was large and comfortable, where the business would have gone very well but for the warm pushing by some Friends of Chester in the matter of negroes. But he adds that affairs were so managed that the unpleasant subject was dropped.[15] What would have been the result of this disposition cannot now be known; but it proved impossible to smooth matters away. There had already begun an age of reformers, forerunners by a hundred years of Garrison and his associates, men who were content with nothing less than entire abolition.

The first of the abolitionists was William Southeby of Maryland, who went to Pennsylvania. For years the subject of slavery weighed heavily upon his mind. As early as 1696 he urged the Meeting to take action. His petition to the Provincial Assembly in 1712 asking that all slaves be set free was one of the most memorable incidents in the early struggle against slavery. But the Assembly resolved that his project was neither just nor convenient; and his ideas were so far in advance of the times that not only did he a little later lose favor among the Friends, but long after it was the judgment that his ill-regulated zeal had brought only sorrow.[16]

[15] Watson, (MS.) Annals, 530. The same spirit is apparent much later. "There generally appeared an uneasiness in their minds respecting them, tho all are not so fully convinced of the Iniquity of the practice as to get over the difficulty which they apprehend would attend their giving them their liberty " . . . MS. Abstract Rec. Gwynedd Monthly Meeting, 278 (1770). "Perhaps thou wilt say, ' I do not buy any negroes: I only use those left me by my father.' But is it enough to satisfy your own conscience? " Benezet, Notes on the Slave Trade, 8.

[16] Votes and Proceedings, II, 110; The Friend, XXVIII, 293, and following; A. C. Thomas, " The Attitude of the Society of Friends toward Slavery in the Seventeenth and Eighteenth Centuries, Particularly in Relation to Its Own Members," in Amer. Soc. Church History, VIII, 273, 274.

The next in point of time was Ralph Sandiford (1693-1733), a Friend of Philadelphia. His hostility to slavery was aroused by the sufferings of negroes whom he had seen in the West Indies; and his feeling was so strong that on one occasion he refused to accept a gift from a slaveholder. In 1729 he published his *Mystery of Iniquity,* an impassioned protest against slavery. Although threatened with severe penalties if he circulated this work, he distributed it wherever he felt that it would be of use.[17] Such enmity did he arouse that he was forced to leave the city.[18]

His work was carried forward by Benjamin Lay (1677-1759), an Englishman who came from Barbadoes to Philadelphia in 1731. He too aroused much hostility by his violence of expression and eccentric efforts to create pity for the slaves. He gave his whole life to the cause, but owing to his too radical methods he was much less influential than he might have been.[19]

A man of far greater power was John Woolman (1720-1772), perhaps the greatest liberator that the Friends ever produced. Woolman gave up his position as accountant rather than write bills for the sale of negroes. He was very religious, and most of his life he spent as a minister travelling from one colony to another trying to persuade men of the wickedness of

[17] " Ralph Sandiford C^r for Cash receiv'd of Benj^a Lay for 50 of his Books which he intends to give away . . . 10 " (sh.) MS. Benjamin Franklin's Account Book, Feb. 28, 1732-1733.

[18] Sandiford, *Mystery of Iniquity,* 43; Vaux, *Memoirs of the Lives of Benjamin Lay and Ralph Sandiford; The Friend,* L, 170; Thomas, *Attitude,* 274; Franklin, *Works* (ed. Sparks), X, 403.

[19] *Cf. American Weekly Mercury,* Nov. 2, 1738, for notice in which the Friends' Meeting denounces his *All Slave-Keepers . . . Apostates* (1737). *Cf.* anecdotes related by Vaux; Bettle, *Notices,* 375, 376; *The Friend,* L, 170; Thomas, *Attitude,* 274.

slavery. In 1754 he published the first part of his book, *Some Considerations on the Keeping of Negroes,* of which the second part appeared in 1762. He was stricken with smallpox while on a visit to England, and died there.[20]

The last was Anthony Benezet (1713-1784), a French Huguenot who joined the Society of Friends. He came to Philadelphia as early as 1731, but it was about 1750 that his attention was drawn to the negroes. From that time to the end of his life he was their zealous advocate. By his writings upon Africa, slavery, and the slave-trade, he attracted the attention and enlisted the support of many. He was untiring in his efforts. Frequently he talked with the negroes and strove to improve them; he endeavored to create a favorable impression of them; he was influential in securing the passage of the abolition act; and at his death he bequeathed the bulk of his property to the cause which he had served so well in his life.[21]

That these Quaker reformers, particularly men like Woolman and Benezet, exerted an enormous influence against slavery in Pennsylvania, there can be no doubt.[22] Their influence is attested by numerous contemporary allusions, but it is proved far better by the change in sentiment which was gradually brought about. Southeby, Sandiford, and Lay were before their time and were

[20] Bettle, *Notices,* 378-382; Thomas, *Attitude,* 245, 275-279; Tyler, *Literary History of the American Revolution,* II, 339-347; *The Friend,* LIII, 190; Woolman, *Journal.*

[21] Vaux, *Memoirs of Benezet; The Friend,* LXXI, 369; Thomas, 274, 275; Bettle, 382-387; Benezet's own writings.

[22] Thomas, 273. There must have been a great many other reformers of considerable influence, but of less fame, about whose work little has come down. *Cf.* "Thos. Nicholson on Keeping Negroes" (1767). MS. in Misc. Coll., Box 10, Negroes.

treated as fanatics. Woolman and Benezet who came afterward were able to reap the harvest which had been sown.

The movement which had been urged with violent rapidity from without was all the while proceeding slowly and quietly within. For many years the Friends considered slavery, and almost every year the Meetings made reports upon the subject. These reports showed that the number of Quakers who bought slaves was constantly decreasing.[23] In 1743 an annual query was instituted.[24] In 1754 the Yearly Meeting circulated a printed letter strongly condemning slavery.[25] The second decisive step followed when it was made a rule that Friends who persisted in buying slaves should be disowned. The measure was effective and this part of the work was soon accomplished.[26] Finally in 1758 the third step was taken when it was unanimously agreed that Friends should be advised to manumit their slaves, and that those who persisted in holding them should not

[23] *Cf.* MS. Chester Q. M. M., 14 6th mo., 1738; 8 6th mo., 1743.
[24] Needles, *Memoir,* 13.
[25] Bettle, 377.
[26] The MS. Chester Q. M. M., 8 8th mo., 1763, say . . . " we are not quite clear of dealing in Negro's, but care is taken mostly to discourage it . . ." Three years later they add . . . " clear of importing or purchasing Negro's." *Ibid.,* 11 8th mo., 1766. *Cf.* also *ibid.,* 10 8th mo., 1767; MS. Chester M. M. Miscellaneous Papers, 28 1st mo., 1765; MS. Darby M. M. M., II, 11, 12, 16, 19, (1764), 24, 27, 31, 33, 35, 38, 40, 42, 45, 46, (1764-1765). These references concern the case of Enoch Eliot, who, having purchased two negroes, was repeatedly urged to set them free, and finally did so. MS. Abstract Rec. Abington M. M., 28 7th mo., 1760; 25 8th mo., 1760. " One of the fr^ds app^d to visit Jonathan Jones reports they all had an oppertunity With him s^d Jonathan, and that he gave them exspectation of not making any more purchases of that kind, as also he is sorry for the purchace he did make " . . . *Ibid.,* 24 11th mo., 1760; also *ibid.,* 24 11th mo., 1760; 20 9th mo., 1762; 29 10th mo., 1764.

be allowed to participate in the affairs of the Society.[27] John Woolman and others were appointed on committees to visit slaveholders and persuade them.[28]

The work of these visiting committees is as remarkable as any in the history of slavery. Self-sacrificing people who had freed their own slaves now abandoned their interests and set out to persuade others to give negroes the freedom thought to be due them. In southeastern Pennsylvania are old diaries almost untouched for a century and a half which bear witness of characters odd and heroic; which contain the story of men and women sincere, brave, and unfaltering, who united quiet mysticism with the zeal of a crusader. The committees undertook to persuade a whole population to give up its slaves. There is no doubt that the task was a difficult one. Again and again the writers speak of obstacles overcome. They tell of owners who would not be convinced, who acknowledged that slavery was wrong, and promised that they would buy no more slaves, but who affirmed that they would keep such as they had. The diaries speak of repeated visits, of the

[27] MS. Yearly M. M., 23-29 9th mo., 1758, where Friends are earnestly entreated to " sett them at Liberty, making a Christian Provision for them according to their Ages etc " . . . *Cf.* report about George Ragan: . . . " as to his Buying and selling a Negro, he saith he Cannot see the Evil thereof, and therefore cannot make any satisfaction, and as he has been much Laboured with by this m[s] to bring him to a sight of his Error, This m[s] therefore agreeable to a minute of our Yearly M[s] can do no Less than so far Testify ag[st] him . . . as not to Receive his Collections, neither is he to sit in our m[gs] for Discipline until he can see his Error " . . . MS. Abst. Abington M. M., 288 (1761). *Cf.* Michener, *Retrospect of Early Quakerism,* 346, 347; *A Brief Statement of the rise and Progress of the Testimony of the Religious Society of Friends, against Slavery and the Slave Trade,* 21-24; Sharpless, *A History of Quaker Government in Pennsylvania,* II, 229; Needles, 13. For the fervid feeling at this time *cf. Journal of John Churchman* (1756), in *Friends' Library,* VI, 236.

[28] Bettle, 378; Sharpless, II, 229. *Cf.* also *Journal of Daniel Stanton,* in *Friends' Library,* XII, 167.

arguments employed, of slow ånd gradual yielding, and
of final triumph. If ever Christian work was carried
on in the spirit of Christ, it was when John Woolman,
Isaac Jackson, James Moon, and their fellow missionaries put an end to slavery among the Quakers of Pennsylvania.[29]

The penalties denounced by the Meeting were imposed with firmness. In 1761 the Chester Quarterly
Meeting dealt with a member for having bought and
sold a slave.[30] Through this and the following years
there are many records in the Monthly Meetings of
manumissions, voluntary and persuaded; record being
made in each case to ensure the negro his freedom.[31]
In 1774 the Philadelphia Meeting resolved that Friends
who held slaves beyond the age at which white apprentices were discharged, should be treated as disorderly persons.[32] The work of abolition was practically
completed in 1776 when the resolution passed that
members who persisted in holding slaves were to be

[29] MS. Abst. Abington M. M., 328, 336, 347, 351, 358, 368, 372, 398;
MS. Min. Sadsbury M. M., 1737-8—1783, pp. 270, 290; MS. Min. Radnor
M. M., 1772-1782, pp. 63, 66, 71, 102, 103, 107, etc.; MS. Min. Women's Q.
M., Bucks Co., 26 8th mo., 1779; 30 8th mo., 1781; MS. Darby M. M. M.,
II, 87, 91, 93, (1769), 178 (1774), 180, 181, 184, 186, 190 (1775), 309,
312 (1780); MS. Women's Min. Darby M. M., 2 2d mo., 1775; 30 3rd
mo., 1775; 3 8th mo., 1780; 31 8th mo., 1780; MS. Extracts Buckingham
M. M., 128, 130, 136 (1767-1768); MS. Diary of Richard Barnard, 24
9th mo., 1774; 7 6th mo., 1780; MS. Journal of Joshua Brown, 11th mo.,
1775; above all the MS. Diary of James Moon, *passim*. *Cf.* Sharpless,
Quakerism and Politics, 159-178; Whittier's introduction to John Woolman's *Journal*.

[30] Futhey and Cope, *History of Chester Co.*, 423.

[31] *Cf.* Abst. Rec. Gwynedd M. M., 201, 204, 213, 218, 240, 270, 271,
273, 278, 280, 307, 311, 312, 316, 321, 322, 323, 336, 348, 374, 471; MS.
Papers Middletown M. M., 1759-1786, pp. 386, 388, 389, 390; Franklin,
Works, (ed. Sparks), VIII, 42.

[32] *Brief Statement*, 49.

disowned.[33] If this is understood in connection with the fact that in the Meetings questions were rarely decided except by almost unanimous vote, it is clear that so far as the Friends were concerned slavery was nearly extinct. This was almost absolutely accomplished by 1780.[34]

The wholesale private abolition of slavery by the Friends of Pennsylvania is one of those occurrences over which the historian may well linger. It was not delayed until slavery had become unprofitable,[35] nor was it forced through any violent hostility. It was a result attained merely by calm, steady persuasion, and a disposition to obey the dictates of conscience unflinchingly. As such it is among the grandest examples of the triumph of principle and ideal righteousness over self-interest.[36] It may well be doubted whether any body of

[33] MS. Yearly M. M., 27 9th mo., 1776; *Brief Statement,* 24-27; Needles, 13; Thomas, 245; Sharpless, *History of Quaker Government in Pennsylvania,* II, 138, 139.

[34] *Brief Statement,* 31-35; Needles, 13; Sharpless, II, 226. For some years the Meetings continued to make regular reports on this subject. " 7th No Slaves among us and such of their Offspring as are under our Care are generally pretty well provided for." MS. Rec. Warrington Q. M., 25 8th mo., 1788.

[35] In the absence of a plantation system slavery in Pennsylvania never was profitable in the same sense as in Virginia or South Carolina, and where white labor could be obtained slavery could not compete. *Cf.* Franklin, *Works,* II, 314, 315 (1751). But as it was almost impossible to obtain sufficient white labor, or at least to retain it, slavery as it existed in Pennsylvania was profitable throughout the colonial period. For the strong desire to import, see above, chap. I. For the high prices paid in the first quarter of the nineteenth century for the right to hold negroes to the age of 28, see below, p. 94.

[36] This is my judgment after a careful investigation of the Friends' records. Adam Smith, who had not seen these records, but who wrote just when the work was being completed, thought differently. *Wealth of Nations* (ed. Rogers), I, 391.

men and women other than the Friends were capable of
such conduct at this time.[87]

So far the checking of slavery in Pennsylvania had
been the result of two great factors; that the Germans
would not hold slaves, and that the Friends gradually
gave them up. Another factor now made it possible to
bring about the end of the institution altogether. There
began the period of the long contest of the Revolution,
when Pennsylvania was stirred to its depths by the
struggle for independence.

Almost at the beginning of the war, in 1776, the Assembly received from citizens of Philadelphia two petitions that manumission be rendered easier. These petitions accomplished nothing,[38] but the feeling which had
been gathering strength for so many years went forward unchecked, and by 1778 there existed a powerful
sentiment in favor of legislative abolition. Therefore
in February, 1779, the draft of a bill was prepared and
recommended by the Council; but for a while no progress was made. ₋₁ce the Assembly, though it approved
the princip ₋elieved that such a measure should orig-
inate in itself.[39] Toward the end of the year the matter
was taken up in earnest, and a bill was soon drafted.
Public sentiment was thoroughly aroused now. Petitions for and against the bill came to the Assembly, and
letters were published in the newspapers. The friends
of the measure were untiring in their efforts. Anthony
Benezet is said to have visited every member of the As-

[87] Other sects followed the example of the Friends, cf. Ebeling, IV,
220, but their work was mostly significant in connection with the legislative work of the Assembly. For the effects of the work of the Friends
cf. Bowden, History of the Friends, II, 221.

[38] Votes and Proceedings, 1767-1776, p. 696.

[39] 1 Pa. Arch., VII, 79; Journal of House of Rep., 1776-1781, p. 311.

sembly. On March 1, 1780, the bill was enacted into a law, thirty-four yeas and twenty-one nays.[40]

The " Act for the gradual Abolition of Slavery " provided that thereafter no child born in Pennsylvania should be a slave; but that such children, if negroes or mulattoes born of a slave mother, should be servants until they were twenty-eight years of age; that all present slaves should be registered by their masters before November 1, 1780; and that such as were not then registered should be free.[41] It abolished the old discrimina-

[40] *Col. Rec.*, XII, 99; *Pa. Packet*, Sept. 16, 1779; *Journals of House, 1776-1781*, pp. 392, 394, 399, 412, 424, 435; *Packet*, Mar. 13, 1779; Dec. 25, 1779; Jan. 1, 1780; *Gazette*, Dec. 29, 1779; Vaux, *Memoirs of Benezet*, 92. The distribution of the vote seems to have had no political, no religious, and probably no economic significance. The measure was popular in and out of the Assembly. *Packet*, Dec. 25, 1779; *Jour. of House, 1776-1781*, p. 435. An earlier bill had been published in the *Packet*, Mar. 4, 1779. It is very interesting. The bill as finally drafted became the first act for the abolition of slavery in the United States. Accordingly its authors had to do much original and constructive work. In the course of the work their ideas underwent some change, and the transition is easily seen in comparing the first bill of 1779 with the act as passed in 1780. In some respects the first is more liberal than the second; in other respects less so. Thus at first it was intended to make the children of slaves servants until twenty-one only. (*Packet*, Mar. 4, 1779). "A Citizen" discussing this objected that the master would receive inadequate compensation for rearing negro children, and urged that the age limit be made twenty-eight or even thirty. (*Packet*, Mar. 13, 1779), and so pay for the unproductive years, which was but just. The law made the age twenty-eight. On the other hand it was at first proposed to continue the prohibition of intermarriage and the permission to bind out idle free negroes. (*Packet*, Mar. 4, 1779). Both these provisions were omitted from the law.

[41] *Stat. at L.*, X, 67-73; 2 Sergeant and Rawle, ˙305-309. Many of the Friends thought that negroes ought not to be held after they were twenty-one. *Cf.* MS. Rec. Pa. Soc. Abol. Sl., I, 23. Very many masters lost their negroes through failing to register them, through ignorance of the provision requiring registry, or through carelessness in complying with it. *Cf.* Rush, *Considerations upon the Present Test-Law*, (2nd ed.), 7 (note); *Journals of House, 1776-1781*, p. 537, and following; 4 *Pa. Arch.*, III, 822. *Cf.* Christopher Marshall's Remembrancer, F, Oct. 10, 1780: . . . " gott our Negro Recorded." *Cf. York Herald*, Apr. 26, 1797. The limit was extended to Jan. 1, 1783, in favor of the citizens of Wash-

tions, for it provided that negroes whether slave or free should be tried and punished in the same manner as white people, except that a slave was not to be admitted to witness against a freeman.[42] The earlier special legislation was repealed.[43]

The act of 1780, which was principally the work of George Bryan,[44] was the final, decisive step in the destruction of slavery in Pennsylvania. The buying and selling of human beings as chattels had become repugnant to the best thought of the state, and it had partly passed away. The practice still survived, however, in many quarters, and strengthened as it was by considerations of economy and convenience, it would probably have gone on for many years. Against this the abolition law struck a mortal blow. From the day of March 1, 1780, the little remnant of slavery slowly withered and passed away. In the course of a generation, except for some scattered cases, it had vanished altogether.

Pennsylvania was the first state to pass an abolition law.[45] In after years this became a matter of great

---

ington and Westmoreland counties, previously under the jurisdiction of Virginia. *Stat. at L.*, X, 463. Runaways from other states were of course not made free by this provision. *Cf.* sect. VIII of act.

[42] The repeal of this section was proposed the next year, but failed by three votes. *Cf. Journals of House, 1776-1781*, p. 605. It was finally repealed in 1847.

[43] Sect. X of act.

[44] For the view that it was drafted by William Lewis, *cf. Pa. Mag.*, XIV, 14; Robert E. Randall, *Speech on the Laws of the State relative to Fugitive Slaves*, 6; Horace Binney, *Leaders of the Old Bar of Philadelphia*, 25. There can be little doubt, however, that full credit should be given to Bryan. "He framed and executed the ' act ' " . . . Obituary notice in the *Gazette*, Feb. 2, 1791. *Cf.* inscription on his tomb-stone, copy in Inscriptions in the Burying Ground of the Second Presbyterian Church Phila. (MS. H. S. P.); *Mem. Hist. Soc. Pa.*, I, 408-410; Konkle, *Life and Times of Thomas Smith*, 105.

[45] Vermont had forbidden slavery by her constitution of 1777. Poore, II, 1859.

pride. Her legislators and statesmen frequently boasted of it. Not only was the priority a glory in itself, but the manner in which Pennsylvania conceived the law, and the success with which she carried it out, furnished the states that lay near her a splendid example and a strong incentive which not a few of them followed shortly thereafter.[46]

Yet this law was open to some objections, and for different reasons received much criticism. First, it was loosely and obscurely drawn in some of its sections, and these gave rise to litigation.[47] In the second place, it was largely ineffectual to prevent certain abuses which had been foreseen when it was discussed, and which assumed alarming proportions in a few years. Some Pennsylvanians openly kept up the slave-trade outside of Pennsylvania, and masters within the state sold their slaves into neighboring states, whither they sent also their young negroes, who there remained slaves instead of acquiring freedom at twenty-eight.[48] They even sent away for short periods their female slaves when pregnant, so that the children might not be born on the free soil of Pennsylvania. Besides this

[46] Its significance in this respect is remarked by Bowden, *History of the Friends*, II, 220. Connecticut and Rhode Island provided for abolition in 1784, New York in 1799, New Jersey in 1804. The same was accomplished in Massachusetts in 1780, and in New Hampshire in 1792, by construction of the constitution. Among many instances where Pennsylvania pointed to her great act with pride, *cf. Acts of Assembly, 1819-20*, p. 199; 4 *Pa. Arch.*, VI, 242, 290. Albert Gallatin, writing to Charles Brown, Mar. 1, 1838, says: "It is indeed a great subject of pride . . . that as one of the United States she was the first to abolish slavery " . . . *Writings* (ed. Adams), II, 523, 524.

[47] 1 Dallas 469; 14 Sergeant and Rawle 443-446; 1 *Pa. Arch.*, VIII, 720.

[48] *Pa. Mag.*, XV, 372, 373. The selling-price elsewhere was greater since it included the price of the posterity.

the kidnapping of free negroes went on unchecked.[49] These practices did not escape unprotested. The Friends were indefatigable in their efforts to stop them, and the government was not disposed to allow the work of 1780 to be undone.[50] So in 1788 was passed an act to explain and enforce the previous one. It provided that the births of the children of slaves were to be registered; that husband and wife were not to be separated more than ten miles without their consent; that pregnant females should not be sent out of the state pending their delivery; and it forbade the slave-trade under penalty of one thousand pounds. Heavy punishments were provided for such chicanery as had previously been employed.[51]

This legislation was enforced by the courts in constructions which favored freedom wherever possible. Exact justice was dealt out, but if the master had neglected in the smallest degree to comply with the precise conditions specified in the laws, whether through carelessness, mistake, or unavoidable circumstance, the authorities generally showed themselves glad to declare the slave free.[52] The Friends and abolitionists were particularly active in hunting up pretexts and instituting

[49] Brissot de Warville, *Mémoire sur les Noirs de l'Amérique Septentrionale*, 19.

[50] *Minutes of Assembly, 1787-1788*, pp. 104, 134, 135, 137, 159, 164, 177, 197; *Packet*, Mar. 13, 1788; *Diary of Jacob Hiltzheimer*, 144.

[51] *Laws of Pennsylvania* (Carey and Bioren), III, 268-272. Despite this many negroes continued to be sold out of the state, and in 1795 the Pa. Soc. Abol. Sl. was asking for a more stringent law. *Cf.* MS. Rec. of Soc., IV, 191. Also MS. Supreme Court Papers, nos. 3, 4, (1795). As late as 1796 the author of the *Reise von Hamburg nach Philadelphia* says: " Häufig kommen, in Philadelphia vorzüglich . . . grosze Transporte von Sclaven von Africa vorüber," p. 24.

[52] 1 Dallas 491, 492; 2 Dallas 224-228; 3 Sergeant and Rawle 396-402; 2 Yeates 234, 449; 3 *id*. 259-261; 4 *id*. 115, 116; 6 Binney 206-211; MS. Sup. Ct. Papers, I, 1; MS. Rec. Pa. Soc. Abol. Sl., I, 197.

law-suits for the purpose of setting at liberty the negroes of people who believed they were obeying the
laws, but who had neglected to comply with some technical point.[53]

While these devotees of freedom were harassing the
enemy they were engaged in operations much more
drastic. The laws for abolition, respecting as they did
the sacredness of right in property, had not abrogated
existing titles to slaves.[54] This the abolitionists denounced as theft, and resolved to get justice by cutting
out slavery root and branch.[55]

First they attacked it in the courts. The declaration
of rights in the constitution of 1790 declared that all
men were born equally free and independent, and had an
inherent right to enjoy and defend life and liberty.[56] In
1792 a committee of the House refused the petition of
some slaveholders on the ground that slavery was not
only unlawful in itself, but also repugnant to the constitution.[57] This point was seized upon by the abolitionists, who resolved to test it before the law. Accordingly they arranged the famous case of Negro Flora *v.*
Joseph Graisberry, and brought it up to the Supreme
Court of the state in 1795. It was not settled there,
but went up to what was at that time the ultimate judicial authority in Pennsylvania, the High Court of Errors and Appeals. Some seven years after the question
had first been brought to law this august tribunal de-

---

[53] 2 Rawle, 204-206; 1 Penrose and Watts 93. *Cf. Min. of Assembly,
1785-1786*, pp. 168, 169.

[54] 14 Sergeant and Rawle 442; Brissot, *Mémoire, 20.*

[55] Brissot, *Mémoire,* 21. *Cf.* the severe censure in *Why Colored People
in Philadelphia Are Excluded from the Street Cars* (1866), 23.

[56] Art. IX, sect. 1.

[57] *Journal of the House, 1792-1793,* pp. 39, 55.

cided after lengthy and able argument that negro slavery did legally exist before the adoption of the constitution of 1790, and that it had not been abolished thereby.[58]

Failing to destroy slavery in the courts the abolitionists strove to demolish it by legal enactment. For this purpose they began a campaign that lasted for two generations. In 1793 the Friends petitioned the Senate for the complete abolition of slavery, and in 1799 they sent a memorial showing their deep concern at the keeping of slaves. In the following year citizens of Philadelphia prayed for abolition, and a few days later the free blacks of the city petitioned that their brethren in bondage be set free, suggesting that a tax be laid upon themselves to help compensate the masters dispossessed. The demand for freedom was supported in other quarters of the state, and undoubtedly a strong feeling was aroused. The Pennsylvania Society for the Abolition of Slavery began the practice, which it kept up for so many years, of regularly memorializing the legislature. Later on some of the leading men of the state took up the cause, and once the governor in his message referred to the galling yoke of slavery and its stain upon the commonwealth.[59]

[58] MS. Docket Supreme Court of Pennsylvania, XXVII, 379. The suit was on a writ " de homine replegiando." *Cf.* Stroud, *Sketch of the Laws Relating to Slavery in the Several States of the United States of America* (2d ed.), 227 (note); MS. Docket of the High Court of Errors and Appeals, 1780-1808, p. 126; *Pa. Gazette,* Feb. 3, 1802; Report of Pa. Soc. Abol. Sl. in *Minutes Sixth Convention Abol. Soc., Phila., 1800,* p. 7. It was the different decision of an exactly similar question that abolished slavery in Massachusetts. *Cf.* Littleton *v.* Tuttle, 4 Massachusetts 128.

[59] *Journal of Senate, 1792-1793,* pp. 150, 151; *1798-1799,* p. 149; *J. of H., 1799-1800,* pp. 76, 123, 153, 160, 172, 190; *J. of S., 1799-1800,* p. 223; *J. of S., 1800-1801,* pp. 134, 135; *J. of H., 1802-1803,* p. 218; *J. of H., 1811-1812,* pp. 24, 216; 4 *Pa. Arch.,* IV, 757, for Governor Snyder's message.

It is probable, however, that the majority of the people in the state believed that enough had been done, and desired to see the little remaining slavery quietly extinguished by the operation of such laws as were effecting the extinction. Be this as it may, it is certain that although many bills were proposed to effect total and immediate abolition, some of which had good prospects of success, yet each one was gradually pared of its most radical provisions, and in the end was always found to lack the support requisite to make it a law.

In 1797 the House had a resolution offered and a bill prepared for abolition. This measure dragged along through the next two sessions, but in 1800 so much encouragement came from the city and counties that the work was carried on in earnest. The course of this bill illustrates the progress of others. At first the proposed enfranchisement was to be immediate and for all; then it was modified to affect only negroes over twenty-eight. In this form it passed the House by a handsome majority, but in the Senate it was postponed to the next session. When finally its time came the committee having it in charge reported that as slavery was not in accordance with the constitution of 1790, a law to do away with slavery was not needed. The measure was still mentioned as unfinished business about the time that the High Court decided that slavery was in accordance with the constitution after all.[60]

The abolitionists did not lose heart. They tried again in 1803, and again the following year. In 1811 a little

[60] J. of H., 1796-1797, pp. 283, 308, 354, 355; J. of H., 1797-1798, pp. 75, 269; J. of H., 1798-1799, pp. 20, 354; J. of H., 1799-1800, pp. 23, 76, 93, 123, 153, 160, 162, 172, 176, 190, 236, 303, 304, 306, 309, 310, 313, 314, 330, 358, 376; J. of S., 1799-1800, pp. 144, 223, 235. The bill passed the House 54 to 15. J. of S., 1800-1801, p. 175; J. of S., 1801-1802, p. 24.

was done in the House, and in 1821 the matter was discussed in the Senate. In this latter year a bill was prepared and debated, but nothing passed except the motion to postpone indefinitely. Indeed the movement had now spent its force, and was thereafter confined to futile petitions that showed more earnestness of purpose than expectation of success.[61]

This is easily explicable when it is understood how rapidly slavery had declined. The number of slaves in Pennsylvania had never been large. By the first Federal census they were put at less than four thousand; but within a decade they had diminished by more than half, and ten years later there were only a few hundred scattered throughout the state.[62] The majority of these slaves during the later years were living in the western counties that bordered on Maryland and Virginia, where slavery had begun latest and lingered longest.[63]

[61] *J. of H.*, *1802-1803*, pp. 361, 362; *1804-1805*, p. 61; *Pa. Gazette*, Feb. 1, 1804; *J. of H.*, *1811-1812*, pp. 58, 67, 216; *J. of S.*, *1820-1821*, p. 33; *Phila. Gazette*, Mar. 6, 1821; *J. of S.*, *1820-1821*, pp. 105, 308, 469, 531, 532, 535, 536. For the provisions of such a bill—the abolition of slavery and of servitude until twenty-eight—compensation of owners—permission for negroes to remain slaves if they so desired—*cf. House Report* no. 399 (1826); *J. of H.*, *1825-1826*, pp. 370, 375, 396, 497, 498. Also *J. of S.*, *1841*, vol. I, 249, 294.

[62] The numbers were 1790, 3737; 1800, 1706; 1810, 795; 1820, 211; 1830, 67; 1840, 64 (?). The U. S. Census Reports do not mention any after 1840, but it is said that James Clark of Donegal Township, Lancaster County, held a slave in 1860. *Cf.* W. J. McKnight, *Pioneer Outline History of Northwestern Pennsylvania*, 311. It is necessary to remark that the U. S. Census reported 386 as the number of slaves in 1830. As this was in increase of 175 over the number reported in 1820, it aroused consternation in Pennsylvania and amazement elsewhere, so that a committee of the Senate was immediately appointed to investigate. Their account showed that there had been no increase but a substantial diminution in numbers; and that the U. S. officers had been grossly careless, if not positively ignorant in their work. *J. of S.*, *1832-1833*, vol. I, 141, 148, 482-487; *Hazard's Register*, IV, 380; IX, 270-272, 395; XI, 158, 159; *African Repository and Colonial Journal*, VII, 315.

[63] *Cf. J. of S.*, *1821-1822*, pp. 214, 215.

In Philadelphia and the older counties it had almost
entirely disappeared. So rapid was the decline that as
early as 1805 the Pennsylvania Abolition Society reported that in the future it would devote itself less to
seeking the liberation of negroes than to striving to improve those already free. This could only mean that
they were finding very few to liberate.[64]

That the decreasing agitation for the entire abolition
of slavery in Pennsylvania was due to the decline of
slavery and not to any decrease in hostility to it, is shown
by the character of other legislation demanded, and the
readiness with which stringent laws were passed. The
act of 1780 permitted the resident of another state to
bring his slave into Pennsylvania and keep him there
for six months.[65] A very strong feeling developed
against this. In 1795 it was necessary for the Supreme
Court to declare that such a right was valid. It was
afterwards decided, however, that if the master continued to take his slave in and out of Pennsylvania for
short periods, the slave should be free. Again and
again the legislature was asked to withdraw the privilege. It is needless to recount the petitions that never
ceased to come, and at times poured in like a flood. At
last the pressure of popular feeling could no longer be
held back, and after the legislation of 1847 following
the memorable case of Prigg *v.* Pennsylvania, when a
slave was brought by his master within the bounds of
Pennsylvania, that moment by state law he was free.[66]

[64] *Minutes Tenth American Convention Abol. Sl., Phila., 1805,* p. 13.
[65] *Stat. at L.,* X, 71.
[66] Respublica *v.* Richards, 2 Dallas 224-228; Commonwealth *v.* Smyth, 1
Browne 113, 114; *Laws of Assembly, 1847,* p. 208. This law was affirmed
by the courts in 1849. Kauffman *v.* Oliver 10 *Pa. State Rep.* (Barr),
517-518. It was at times contested by the citizens of other states, as in

Long before this time the passage through the state of slaves bound with chains had awakened the pity of those who saw it.[67] In 1816 it was decided that in certain cases if a runaway slave gave birth to a child in Pennsylvania the child was free.[68] Later the legislature forbade state officers to give any assistance in returning fugitives; and at last lacked but little of giving fugitives trial by jury.

If it be asked whether at this time Pennsylvania was not rather decrying slavery among her neighbors than destroying it within her own gates, since beyond denial she still had slavery there, it must be answered that first, her slavery as regards magnitude was a veritable mote, and secondly, since after 1830, for example, there was not one slave in Pennsylvania under fifty years old, it was far more to the advantage of the negroes to remain in servitude where the law guaranteed them protection and good treatment, than to be set free, when their color and their declining years would have rendered their well-being doubtful. It is probable that such slavery as existed there in the last years was based rather on the kindness of the master and the devotion of the slave, than on the power of the one and the suffering of the other. It was a peaceful passing away.

the famous episode of J. H. Wheeler's slaves in 1855. *Cf. Narrative of Facts in the Case of Passmore Williamson.* In this case the Federal District Court held that Pa. had no jurisdiction over the right of transit. In 1860 a negress was brought from Va. to Pa. She was at once told that she was free; but when her master returned she went back with him. *Phila. Inquirer,* Aug. 29, 1860.

[67] *J. of H., 1821-1822,* pp. 628, 637, 950; *J. of S., 1821-1822,* pp. 325, 330, 331. For a vivid description cf. Parrish, *Remarks on the Slavery of the Black People* (1806), 21.

[68] If the mother had absconded before she became pregnant. Commonwealth *v.* Holloway (1816), 2 Sergeant and Rawle 305. *Cf. Niles's Weekly Register,* X, 400.

And so in connection with slavery Pennsylvania is seen to have been fortunate. Seeing at an early time the pernicious consequences of such an institution she was able, such were the circumstances of her economic environment, and such was the character of her people, to check it so effectually that it never assumed threatening bulk. Almost as quick to perceive the evil of it, she acted, and while others moralized and lamented, she set her slaves free. Moreover as if to atone for the sin of slave-keeping she granted her freedmen such privileges that it seemed to her ardent idealists that the future could not but promise well.

Whether this liberality came to be a matter of regret in after years, and whether because of circumstances sure to come, but as yet unforeseen, it was possible for the experience of Pennsylvania with her free black population to be as happy as that with her slaves, it will be the purpose of later chapters to enquire.

CHAPTER VI.

INTERMEDIATE STATUS—SERVITUDE AND APPRENTICESHIP.

IN Pennsylvania the rise of the negro from slavery to complete freedom was a process long, gradual, and slow. The change from the lower to the higher status was not resisted so long that it came at last in sudden and entire transformation. There was no instantaneous creation of a great body of freedmen, but the negro was liberated by voluntary acts and by gradual abolition, so that his enfranchisement was normal and accomplished by degrees. There was no upheaval, no new era, no universal emancipation, no sudden abolition. The process was strictly an evolution throughout.

In the course of this slow rise from complete servitude to complete freedom the negro occupied successively two distinct intermediate positions; he was generally a servant before he became a free man; sometimes he was an apprentice. It is true that in numerous instances negro slaves were made negro free men, and received their freedom under such circumstances, and accompanied with such assistance, as to make it possible for them to enjoy complete liberty. In most cases, however, this was not so. For reasons social and economic the ascent was slow and laborious, and the negro was compelled to halt for long periods on his way up. As a race movement it was rather a rise from slavery into limited servitude, from servitude to apprenticeship, and from apprenticeship to entire and continuous freedom.

It is by no means true that even a large minority of the slaves in Pennsylvania became first servants and then apprentices before becoming free. It was very rare that in the case of any particular individual there was more than one intermediate stage in the progress. But since probably the majority of the slaves were for a number of years servants before they became free, and as the children of free negroes were in almost every case either servants or apprentices before they became free, so it may be said that the negroes of Pennsylvania, beginning, many of them, about 1680 as slaves, passed during a period of about six generations through one or more of these stages, until about 1840 nearly all of them had become entirely free. It is proposed to investigate the circumstances that attended this evolution.

In Pennsylvania there was from the first an unfree class whose members were not slaves, but who were subject to ownership and were not free. The owner's title was in theory vested only in the possession of the service; but as a matter of fact he owned the body of the person held to service as fully as if that person were a slave. He could buy, sell or transfer the servant, and in these transactions as well as in his treatment of the servant his power was limited only by such restrictions as the law specifically imposed.

There is a certain symmetry about the development of the status of non-freedom. Modern research has shown that in Virginia, for example, negroes were at first legally servants, and then gradually became slaves.[1] In the early part of the nineteenth century a Southern writer predicted that the reverse would next

[1] Ballagh, *White Servitude in the Colony of Virginia*, ch. 1.

take place, and that from being first slaves and then servants negroes would at last become free.² The entire process if unarrested and given time would thus have been from freedom to servitude, from servitude to slavery, from slavery back to servitude, and from servitude to entire freedom. In Pennsylvania the later stages in this process, from slavery to freedom, found full development, but it is not clear that the first existed. In this colony negro servitude for a limited time does not seem to have preceded negro slavery as a general legal system, although even in the earliest years it is quite possible that some negroes may have been servants. From 1682 to 1700, while negro slavery closely resembled white servitude in most of its incidents, it was yet fundamentally different in that white servants were held temporarily while negroes were held for life. Accordingly the general laws concerning servitude seem to have been made primarily for indentured servants and redemptioners. When later there arose a class of negro servants they came not only under these laws, but also under special laws affecting them alone.³

After 1700 negro servants begin to appear. The act of 1725-1726 for the regulation of negroes recognized four classes of such servants. They were, first, those negroes who were unable or unwilling to support themselves. Such were to be bound out by the justices of

² St. George Tucker. *Cf.* Ballagh, *Slavery in Virginia,* 134, 135.
³ Prior to the special legislation of 1700 negro slaves were regulated by the laws for servants, but the regulation was rough and ill defined, since the status of slavery had not yet been adjusted to the legal system of the colony. See above, pp. 21-23. Certain evidence seems to indicate that there may have been negro servants before 1700, but I have found no positive instance of one. *Cf.* above, p. 22.

the peace for periods of a year at a time. Secondly,
all children of free negroes without exception were
to be bound out by the same justices until twenty-
four years of age, if male, until twenty-one, if female.
Thirdly, such negroes as were sold for crime, the
servitude being either a satisfaction of court expenses
or jail fees, or in graver cases a punishment for the
crime itself, as in the case of fornication with a white
person, when the penalty for the first offense was seven
years. Fourthly, all mulatto children who were not
slaves for life, were to be bound out until they were
thirty-one years of age.[4]

The number of blacks who were servants prior to
1780 must therefore have been considerable. It is
hardly probable, indeed, that the class was greatly
swelled by free negroes who were sold because they
were not self-supporting, or even by the accession of
many negroes sold for crime; but on the other hand it
grew continually with the growth in numbers of the
free negroes themselves, since all of their children became servants temporarily, while it was largely increased by the mulattoes not slaves, of whom Pennsylvania always had many.[5]

The most notable enlargement of the class of negro
servants was made by the abolition act of 1780, one of
the provisions of which was that all of the future children of registered slaves should become servants until

[4] *Stat. at L.*, IV, 62, 63. The children of poor white people were
bound out until twenty-one and eighteen respectively. *Cf.* "An Act
for the Relief of the Poor" (1770-1771). *Stat. at L.*, VIII, 79. Sometimes free negroes held for jail fees bound themselves to serve a master
who purchased their release. *Cf.* MS. Miscellaneous Papers, Feb. 4, 5,
1782.

[5] See above, p. 31.

they were twenty-eight.[6]   Within twenty years after
1780 there were probably in Pennsylvania more negro
servants than slaves.

The number was further augmented by negroes who
were brought from other places.   In a state where
labor was in demand, but where slavery was being abolished, servitude for a number of years became a valuable commodity.   Hence, after 1780, there arose a considerable traffic in young negroes of Delaware, Maryland, and Virginia, of fourteen years or older, who
were taken by their masters to Pennsylvania and there
manumitted.   In return for this the negroes indentured
themselves as servants until they were twenty-eight
years of age.   The indentures could then be assigned to
residents of the state.[7]   This assignment for such a
long period was thought by some to be an infringement
of the spirit of the act of 1780, and was soon assailed
as a violation of liberty.   When the matter was brought
before the courts, however, it was pleaded that the
servitude was after all for a limited period, in the case
of men who otherwise would not have been brought
from places where they would have remained slaves all
their days, while in Pennsylvania they had the certainty
of freedom before them.   Therefore the spirit of liberty was really being served, although the law was

---

[6] See above p. 78.

[7] *Stat. at L.*, X, 68, 69; Respublica *v.* the Gaoler of Philadelphia
County (1794), 1 Yeates 368, 369; MS. Rec. Pa. Soc. Abol. Sl., VII, 15.
A good illustration is a power of attorney from Adam King of Georgetown to Captain John Hand on the way to Philadelphia. " You are
hereby authorized . . . to dispose of the above named Negros to the best
advantage, vizt Frederick to serve till he arrives at the age of Twenty
eight Years say ten years to serve . . . Harriet till she is twenty-one years
old say five years, or if the Laws of the State will Admit of it a Longer
time say till She is Twenty five, ten years " . . . MS. in Misc. Coll., Box
10, Negroes.

apparently infringed. This reasoning prevailed, and the practice was thereafter recognized as legal.[8]

It was with this sanction that slaveholders from the South and from the West Indies brought their negroes to Pennsylvania and held them there until they were twenty-eight years old.[9] They continued to do this for some time, while the traffic in servants from the neighboring states lasted until at least 1845.[10] So great was the demand for these servants, that, although they were sold only for a limited period, the young negroes brought more than half as much as they would have brought had they been sold as slaves in the states from which they came.[11] The traffic entailed some abuses, however. In 1821 it had become necessary to enact a law declaring that whoever brought in a negro servant more than twenty-eight years old should be answerable

[8] Yeates 368, 369. The privilege was strictly construed. Cf. The Commonwealth v. Hambright (1818), 4 Sergeant and Rawle 217-221.

[9] Cf. de la Rochefoucault Liancourt, Travels through the United States of North America . . . in the Years 1795, 1796, and 1797, II, 355.

[10] A negro girl from Kentucky, aged nine, was entered for nineteen years in Washington County in 1845. Her servitude would thus have expired in 1864. Cf. Crumrine, Histofy of Washington County, 261.

[11] Cf. Porcupine's Gazette, May 15, 1799; Phila. Gazette, May 18, 1809; Aurora, Jan. 15, 1814. John Clark of Lancaster County bought three negro boys in Delaware in 1814. For one boy of fourteen he paid three hundred dollars; for two boys, nineteen and eleven respectively, three hundred and sixty dollars. Clark MSS. Cf. also 3 Penrose and Watt 237, 238; J. of S., 1832-1833, vol. I, 486. The report in the latter says " about half the usual price of a slave is paid for this limited assignment." The average value of a negro in the South was supposed to be about three hundred dollars in 1822. The price rose from two hundred dollars about 1800 to six hundred dollars in 1830. Cf. Hart, Slavery and Abolition, 128. The reasons why Southern owners could be brought to sell their negroes in the North for less than they could obtain in the South, are not always clear, for the negroes sold do not seem to have been of an inferior class. In some cases the owners may have been those who desired enfranchisement 'for their slaves, and were glad to receive some compensation.

to the overseers of the poor. In 1836 this law was made more stringent.[12]

Such were the sources of negro servants. Their legal status was distinct from that of any other class in Pennsylvania. In some respects it closely resembled that of white servants, in others that of negro slaves. From the latter it differed because it was limited in time, from the former because it was circumscribed by additional laws. The members of this class at different times were subject to three sets of laws; those which concerned them as servants, and which regulated all servants, white or black; those which concerned them as negro servants; and those which concerned them as negroes, and regulated all negroes, slaves, servants, and free.

The laws about servitude in general were intended both to safeguard the servant in his helpless condition and to secure the rights of the master. Thus in 1682 there was ordained a registry for servants, to preserve the exact terms of each one's servitude.[13] In the following year their whole position, its duties and its obligations, was defined; while in 1693 the entire matter was again dealt with at length.[14] In 1700 masters were forbidden to sell their servants out of the province, or to assign them without proper legal scrutiny, while the gifts due at the expiration of servitude were carefully

---

[12] " An Act to Prevent the Increase of Pauperism in This Commonwealth," *Acts of Assembly, 1821*, p. 254; " An Act Relating to the Support and Employment of the Poor," *Laws of Assembly, 1835-1836*, p. 546.

[13] *Laws of the Province of Pennsylvania . . . 1682-1700*, pp. 101, 119; *Col. Rec.*, I, 40; *Hazard's Register*, X, 280. The courts would assist a servant retained by his master over time. *Cf.* MS. Rec. of the Court at Upland, p. 96 (1678); MS. Court Rec. of Penna. and Chester Co., 1681-1688, p. 46 (1686); MS. Court Papers, 1732-1744, Phila. Co., Nov. 8, 1732.

[14] *Laws of the Province of Pennsylvania . . . 1682-1700*, pp. 152, 153 (1683); 212, 213 (1693).

and clearly defined.[15]   On the other hand runaways were
to make satisfaction by extra time of servitude, a reward
was established for anyone who returned a runaway,
and harboring of such an one was strictly forbidden.[16]
Another act of the same year forbade servants to marry
without the master's consent, the penalty being service
for an additional year.[17]   In 1705 extra service was likewise made the penalty for having a bastard child.[18]   In
1729-1730 the marriages of servants were further regulated.[19]   And finally in 1771 all previous legislation on
the subject was supplemented and more clearly defined.[20]
During this whole period servants were protected from
the cruelty of the master, and if badly treated they
might, on application to the courts, be set free.[21]

As a servant the negro was during the period of his
indenture practically the property of his master.   He
could be bought and sold like a slave, except that the
authorities were supposed to scrutinize such transfers
carefully lest the conditions of service be violated.[22]   The

[15] " An Act for the better Regulation of Servants in This Province
and Territories," *Stat. at L.*, II, 54, 55.   *Cf.* MS. Phila. Court Rec.,
1685-1686, 4 9th mo., 1685; MS. Ancient Records of Phila., 1 12th mo.,
1703-1704; MS. Court Papers, 1732-1744, Phila. Co., 1741; MS. John
Wilson's Cash Book, Oct. 30, 1775.
[16] *Stat. at L.*, II, 55, 56.   *Cf.* MS. Court Rec. Penna. and Chester Co.,
1681-1688, p. 37 (1685); MS. Phila. Court Rec., 1685-1686, 6 3d mo.,
1686.   The number of servants who ran away was enormous.   Almost
every copy of the old newspapers has several advertisements for them.
[17] " An Act for the Preventing of Clandestine Marriages," *Stat. at L.*,
II, 22.   Repeated in 1705.   *Ibid.*, II, 161.
[18] Not less than one nor more than two years.   " An Act against
Adultery and Fornication," *Stat. at L.*, II, 182.   *Cf.* MS. Phila. Court
Rec., 1685-1686, Feb. 3, 1685.
[19] *Stat. at L.*, IV, 153.
[20] *Stat. at L.*, VIII, 29-31.
[21] *Cf.* MS. Docket Court Quarter Sessions, Chester Co., 1723-1733.
Also MS. Court Rec. Penna. and Chester Co., 1681-1688, p. 23 (1684).
[22] By the act of 1729-1730 it was provided that all sales or assignments
in Philadelphia should be made before the mayor.   Failure to do this entailed a penalty of ten pounds.   The mayor was to keep a register of
servants, a record of their indentures, and a record of the time of their

master could compel the servant to work, and could insist on his obedience. In return he must support the servant, giving him sufficient food, clothing, and shelter. In the period after 1780 when all forms of servitude in Pennsylvania were becoming milder or disappearing the master frequently contracted to give a certain amount of schooling or instruction.[23] At the expiration of his time the servant was to receive certain gifts. The early legislation had specified clothing and sundry farming tools,[24] but the law enjoining the latter was repealed in 1771,[25] and thereafter the freedom dues were as a rule two suits of clothes.[26]

assignment. *Stat. at L.*, IV, 170, 171. At times traffic in servants became flourishing. *Cf. Pa. Gazette*, July 3, 1776; *Pa. Packet*, Aug. 18, 1788; *Porcupine's Gazette*, Jan. 1, 1799; *Harrisburg Courant*, May 28, 1800; (Lancaster) *Constitutional Democrat*, Aug. 26, 1806; *Phila. Gazette*, Jan. 15, 1807; *General Advertiser*, July 23, 1807; *Dauphin Guardian* Feb. 2, 1808; (Lancaster) *Times*, Mar. 28, 1809; *Democratic Press*, May 2, 1815; (Harrisburg) *Chronicle*, Mar. 8, 1819. The advertisements are very frequent in the period 1800-1812. Some persons made a business of facilitating exchanges. Baker's General Intelligence and Exchange Office advertised: " For Sale, a black girl, 18 years old and 10 to serve, do. 14 and 4, do. 20 and 8; do. 10 and 8. A Black Boy 19 and 2; do. 15 and 6; do. 13 and 8. do. 11 and 10." *Phila. Gazette*, Feb. 9, 1815.

[23] A negro indentured in 1792 was to be " taught to read well in the Bible." In 1808 a negress indentured for twelve years was to have eighteen months of half-day schooling, and was to be taught to read and write. MS. Misc. Coll., Box 10, Negroes.

[24] In 1683 the gifts at freedom were to be " One new Sute of apparell, ten bushels of Wheat or fourteen bushels of Indian-corn, one Ax, two howes one broad and another narrow." *Laws of the Province of Pennsylvania . . . 1682-1700*, p. 153. In 1700 . . . " two complete suits of apparel, whereof one shall be new; . . . one new ax, one grubbing hoe and one weeding hoe " . . . *Stat. at L.*, II, 55.

[25] *Stat. at L.*, VIII, 31.

[26] " 2 suits one new " . . . " Usual freedom dues " . . . " Necessaries befitting his Station." MSS. in Misc. Coll., Box 10, Negroes. In 1771 summary power was given to the justices of the Courts of Quarter Sessions to compel the payment of dues, many masters having failed to do this, and the servants being unable to prosecute for legal redress. *Stat. at L.*, VIII, 30.

For his part the servant owed his master service, and must obey his commands. Without permission he could not leave the master's premises, nor absent himself without leave. If he ran away he atoned with extra service. In 1700 this penalty had been fixed at five days for every day of absence. In 1771 the same penalty was reaffirmed.[27] When servants ran away anyone might take them up, and on returning them to the master claim a reward fixed by law.[28] This the master was obliged to pay whether he wanted the servant back or not, though in the latter case he frequently sought to evade payment by advertising for the servant and offering to pay some ridiculously low reward, such as six cents, or even at times not more than a cent.[29] Many servants, particularly the white redemptioners, ran away, but they seem generally to have been well treated. There is rarely any complaint about severity or overwork. The negro servants were given such employment as was usually given to slaves.[30]

Negro servants were subject to these laws as long as the laws regulated servitude in Pennsylvania. These laws they obeyed in common with all other servants. If they were forbidden to go around at will, or to marry

[27] Stat. at L., II, 13, 55; VIII, 31.
[28] Ten shillings if the negro was taken up within ten miles of the master's abode, twenty shillings if farther away. Stat. at L., II, 55.
[29] Cf. Porcupine's Gazette, July 9, 1799; Phila. Gazette, Nov. 25, 1808; General Advertiser, Apr. 9, 1808; Aurora, Jan. 3, 1818; Harrisburg Argus, July 26, 1828; Union Times, June 13, 1834.
[30] For runaway servants see Pennsylvania newspapers, passim. At times this fleeing from service was a great source of trouble to the owner. In 1732 James Forcues petitioned for extra time from his mulatto servant, Ben, showing in an itemized statement that the mulatto had lost more than four hundred days and cost him more than five pounds in fines and charges. MS. Court Papers, Phila. Co., 1697-1732 (1724-1732). Occupations are given in the advertisements of servants for sale. Newspapers, passim.

without the master's consent, if they were obliged to
obey the master, to do such work as he gave them, and
to serve their terms out, white servants were restricted
in exactly the same way. There were other incidents,
however, which made the status of white and black
servants very different.

First, there were discriminations concerning a servant
because he was a negro servant. These had to do entirely with length of service. They fall into two periods; from 1725-1726 to 1780, and from 1780 to the time
when black servitude in Pennsylvania disappeared. The
period of servitude for white servants in the colony was
as a rule four years.[31] In the case of the negro it might
be four years if a free negro so contracted; but it might
be seven or less for crime, a period extending to the
twenty-fourth or the twenty-first year in the case of the
children of free parents, or to the thirty-first in the
case of mulattoes.[32] These discriminations were all
swept away by the act of 1780, which put free negroes
upon the footing of white people, and left the regulation of their children to themselves; nevertheless this
very act instituted a marked discrimination for a new
class of servants, when it declared that the future
children of slaves should be servants until twenty-eight
years of age. This practice of holding negroes for a
longer term than white persons, which lasted for a
longer time than had originally been contemplated,

---

[31] In 1683 the period had been made five years for a young person,
not to extend beyond his twenty-second year. *Laws of the Province of
Pennsylvania . . . 1682-1700*, p. 153. In 1693 this age limit for young persons
was made twenty-one years, but the term for older servants remained
five years. *Ibid.*, 237. In 1700 the time was made four years or more.
Stat. at L., II, 55.

[32] *Stat. at L.*, IV, 62, 63. *Cf. Pa. Gazette*, Oct. 23, 1776. MS. Slave
Register of 1780 for Chester County.

since it was allowed to apply to negroes brought into Pennsylvania from other states, bade fair to perpetuate itself and last longer still.   About 1800 there arose the practice of holding until twenty-eight not only the children of slaves, but also the children of such female servants, if these children were born during the servitude of their mothers.   For a while there was no interference with this, and some of the inferior courts even decided that it was legal.[83]   In 1824, however, it was declared that the practice was unlawful; and finally in 1826 in the case of Miller *v.* Dwilling the Supreme Court affirmed that because of birth no person could be held to servitude until twenty-eight but one whose mother was a slave at the time of his birth.[84]   After this time the number of negroes born in Pennsylvania, who could be held for a longer term than white servants, became relatively small.

In the second place negro servants were subject to regulations which affected them because they were negroes.   Thus by the laws of 1700 and 1705-1706 they were tried in special courts, punished with special penalties, and excluded from bearing witness against white people.[85]   To this extent their status was that of the slave.   These provisions were all repealed in 1780, but meanwhile the act of 1725-1726 had subjected them to additional discriminations.   Like a slave a negro servant, if taken up more than ten miles from his master's habitation without written consent from the master, was to be whipped with as many as ten lashes.[86]   He was

[83] Communication of the Pa. Soc. Abol. Sl. in *Minutes of Seventeenth Session of the Amer. Conv. Abol. Sl.,* 11.

[84] 14 Sergeant and Rawle 442-446; *Hazard's Register,* XI, 158.

[85] *Stat. at L.,* II, 77-79.

[86] *Ibid.,* IV, 63.   The person taking him up was to receive five shillings from the owner.

not to be allowed to ramble about seeking employment even though he had permission from the master, and though he had covenanted to pay him money.[37]   No negro was to be found tippling or drinking near any place where liquors were sold; nor was he to be away from his master's house after nine o'clock at night, unless he had license from the master.[38]   The penalty was whipping up to ten lashes.[39]   In 1780 these restrictions were entirely removed.

Thus the negro servant occupied an intermediate status, lower than that of the white servant, higher than that of the black slave.   He was the property of his master for a period, must obey the master, could not marry without the master's permission, and could be bought and sold by him like a slave.   On the other hand he had the law's protection, the master must treat him kindly, and at the end of his service must give him freedom dues.   To this extent his position was that of the white servant.   But it was different and lower in that the service was longer, and that before 1780 he was under special restrictions as to movement and conduct, and was even subject to the special trials and punishments of the slave.   Because the period of his service was limited, however, his status was always higher than that of the slave.

Toward the end of the slavery period some negroes had risen sufficiently high to be able to occupy an intermediate status of non-freedom higher than the preceding.   They began to be held in a servitude of a more

[37] *Ibid.*, IV, 63, 64.   A master so permitting was to be fined twenty shillings.   This law was not strictly enforced.   Negroes frequently hired themselves of their masters.

[38] *Ibid.*, IV, 63.

[39] *Ibid.*

limited and more dignified character than that of the common servant; a servitude, moreover, of which the incidents were the same for negroes as for the white persons included in it.[40] That is, they had been able to become apprentices.

Apprenticeship is a species of servitude in which the master gives instruction and the apprentice gives service. In some respects it is hardly to be distinguished from the lower forms of servitude, since the service of the apprentice is absolutely owned by the master for a term of years. It differs from the lower forms theoretically since while a servant works in return for money advanced to another person by the master, the apprentice serves in return for tuition in some art or mystery. It differs in fact because the character of the servant's work is not clearly defined, but the service of the apprentice is supposed to be limited to the mystery specified in his indenture.[41]

Apprenticeship, which was well known in both the law and custom of England and the colonies, grew up in Pennsylvania in connection with children, and even adults, whose support was not otherwise well provided for, and who lacked the facilities for learning some trade.[42] In 1705-1706 it was made lawful for the overseers of the poor with the consent of two or more justices of the peace to apprentice the children of parents

[40] Previous to 1780 negro apprentices like negro servants were subject to the discriminations which affected all negroes, but apprenticeship itself involved no discriminatory incidents.

[41] The law of Pennsylvania always considered apprenticeship a higher form of servitude than that of the indentured servant. *Cf.* Yeates 233; 3 Rawle 307.

[42] For early examples see MS. Ancient Rec. of Sussex Co., 1681-1709, p. 97 (1681); MS. Germantown Rec. of the Courts, 1691-1707, p. 5 (1692); MS. Min. Chester Co. Courts, 1697-1710, p. 28 (1698-1699).

who were living but unable to support them;[43] while in 1713 the Orphans Court was authorized to apprentice poor children whose parents were dead.[44] As yet there was no comprehensive legislation on the subject, however, and for many years the obligations of the status were not clearly defined in the colony's statute law.[45] It is probable that at this time the laws concerning servants were looked upon as roughly concerning apprentices also, but when the latter became numerous enough to be noticeable it was found that existing legislation did not regulate them sufficiently.[46] Therefore in 1762-1763 a law was passed carefully defining their duties and privileges.[47] This law, which was re-enacted with slight modifications in 1769-1770, became the basis upon which rested the regulation of apprentices throughout the succeeding period.[48]

The law of 1769-1770 provided that the apprentice should be bound by indenture.[49] This was to be done with the consent of the child together with that of the parent, guardian, or next friend, or that of the overseers of the poor with the assent of two justices of the peace.[50]

[43] *Stat. at L.*, II, 253.

[44] *Ibid.*, III, 19.

[45] *Cf. Votes and Proceedings*, IV, 283.

[46] *Cf. Stat. at L.*, VI, 246; VII, 360; *Votes and Proceedings*, IV, 283; 3 Rawle 304-311.

[47] " An Act for the Regulation of Apprentices within this Province," *Stat. at L.*, VI, 246-249.

[48] " An Act for the Regulation of Apprentices within this Province," *Stat. at L.*, VII, 360-363.

[49] For numerous examples in the case of negro apprentices, see MS. indentures in Misc. Coll., Box 10, Negroes.

[50] The infant had to consent and be a party to the contract. *Cf.* 1 Ashmead 123-126; *Stat. at L.*, VII, 360, 361; 6 Sergeant and Rawle 340-342; 2 *Pa. Law Journal Rep.* (510)-(511); 5 Wharton 128-131. The father's consent was required, *cf.* 8 Watts and Sergeant 339-340; but if the father was an unfit person, as for example a drunkard, the mother's assent was lawful; see 1 Ashmead 71-73; 2 Rawle 269-271; 1 Rawle 190-195. The master himself could not act as best friend; *cf.* 1 Sergeant and Rawle 336-337; 3 *id.* 158-167.

The binding was to be done for the purpose of learning some mystery, art, or occupation.[51] The courts guarded the wording of the indenture with great care.[52] By this covenant the apprentice was to be bound till the age of eighteen, if a girl, or twenty-one, if a boy.[53]

The master, who was a party to the contract, was obliged to fulfil his covenant as promised, that is, he must teach the mystery specified in the indenture,[54] and give the apprentice food, clothing, and shelter, unless otherwise specially contracted.[55] He was obliged to fulfil the contract in person, for he could not transfer the apprentice at will as he could a slave or a servant.[56] The indenture could only be assigned with the consent of the apprentice and that of his parent or guardian,[57] and the apprentice could not be taken out of the state.[58] In addition to giving support the master was expected to give other things, such as a certain amount of schooling and instruction, matters which, at first fixed by custom, came afterwards to be regarded as legally neces-

[51] *Stat. at L.*, VII, 360. This was construed very widely so as to include such general training as housewifery, and such a lowly occupation as that of a chimpey-sweep. *Cf.* 1 Browne 197-199; 2 Browne 275-276. For a negro " chimney sweeper " (1815), *cf.* 1 Sergeant and Rawle 330-333; also *ibid.*, 252, where, however, the court seemed reluctant to give a construction wide enough to include housewifery.

[52] 10 Sergeant and Rawle 416-417; 13 *id.* 186-189.

[53] *Stat. at L.*, VII, 361.

[54] 5 *Pa. State Rep.*, 269-272; 1 Wharton 112-115.

[55] *Cf.* Commonwealth *v.* Conrow (1845), 2 *Pa. State Rep.*, 402-403, where in lieu of the usual meat, drink, and washing, the contract called for a weekly wage. In this case Justice Gibson said that the law-makers of 1770 had evidently intended that the apprentice should be an inmate of the master's house, and that such was still the case in the country; but he noticed that a different custom had gradually arisen in the cities.

[56] See above, pp. 25, 96.

[57] *Cf.* 1 Sergeant and Rawle 248; 1 Ashmead 405.

[58] 6 Binney 203.

essary.[59] If the master failed to do what he had
covenanted to do, or if he treated the apprentice cruelly,
or caused him to do work injurious to his morals, then
on application the justice of the peace and the Court
of Quarter Sessions could coerce the master or set the
apprentice free.[60] At the expiration of his time the apprentice was to receive gifts of clothing or a sum of
money.[61]

The apprentice owed the master only such service
as was specified in the indenture, and the master could
compel him to perform no other.[62] During the period
of his service he could not leave the master's premises
without permission, nor without permission could he
marry.[63] If he was not obedient to lawful commands,
or if he failed to fulfil his share of the contract, he might
be committed to the workhouse on complaint of the
master by the Court of Quarter Sessions, or he might
be imprisoned at hard labor.[64] If he ran away he might
be arrested and committed to jail until he consented to

[59] *Cf.* Commonwealth *v.* Pennott (1849), 1 Brightly 189-190, where an
indenture not covenanting to give a reasonable amount of schooling was
held void. In 1792 a negro apprentice was to be taught " to read well
in the Bible." MS. in Misc. Coll., Box 10, Negroes. An indenture for a
negro apprentice in 1794 calls for " Six months Night and Six months
Day Schooling." *Ibid.* In 1812 an indenture covenants to send a negro
apprentice " Eighteen Months to School." *Ibid.*

[60] *Stat. at L.,* VII, 361; 1 Browne 24-29. *Cf.*, however, 2 Browne 205-
211.

[61] *Cf.* indentures in Misc. Coll., Box 10, Negroes.

[62] *Cf.* 4 *Pa. Law Journal Rep.* (440)-(443).

[63] *Cf.* 2 Yeates 321-323. In an indenture of 1812 a negro is to obey
the lawful commands of his master; do no damage to his master nor
permit others to do it; neither to waste nor lend his master's goods, and
not to buy or sell any goods without permission; not to absent himself
without leave, nor haunt taverns or places of amusement; not to commit
fornication, and not to marry. MS. in Misc. Coll., Box 10, Negroes.

[64] *Stat. at L.,* VII, 362. The master himself was permitted to employ
moderate correction. *Cf.* 1 Ashmead 267.

return home.[65] The penalty for harboring an apprentice
was twenty shillings for each day, to be paid to the
master.[66]

The laws of apprenticeship in Pennsylvania were
made primarily for white people, but after 1780 they
applied to a great many negroes also. There were some
negro apprentices before this,[67] and there are extant numerous indentures immediately following the abolition
act.[68] From 1790 on the number is large.[69] For some
years after the act of 1780 it is probable that many
negroes, who according to law should have been bound
as apprentices, were held and treated as servants; and
even as late as 1814 a plea was made before the Supreme Court that a black boy was not in fact an apprentice, but a servant; but this was decisively overruled
by the Court, and thereafter no more was heard of it.[70]
After the abolition act was passed the friends of the
negro took care to bind out negro children and see that
the terms of the indentures were strictly and justly construed.[71] Indeed the apprenticing of negroes now be-

[65] *Stat. at L.*, VII, 362. By a law of 1799 a runaway was liable for
damages when he became of age. *Acts of Ass., 1799*, p. 475. *Cf.* (Pittsburg) *Allegheny Democrat*, Nov. 21, 1826; *Mifflin Eagle*, Apr. 28, 1831.
[66] *Stat. at L.*, VII, 363.
[67] MS. Record of Indentures of Apprentices, Servants, Redemptioners,
etc., 81 (1771), 129 (1772), 662 (1773).
[68] MS. Misc. Papers, Dec. 14, 1783. MS. Rec. Pa. Soc. Abol. Sl., I,
91 (1787). MSS. in Misc. Coll., Box 10, Negroes.
[69] *Ibid.* and MS. Return of Directors of the Poor, Chester Co., 1802.
For an instance *cf.* Boucher, *History of Westmoreland Co.*, 325.
[70] *Cf.* MS. Rec. Pa. Soc. Abol. Sl., I, 89; Commonwealth *v.* Vanlear, 1
Sergeant and Rawle, 248-253; Respublica *v.* Catharine Keppele, 1 Yeates
233-237, where it is laid down that while formerly the children of free
negroes and mulattoes might be bound as servants, this was only under
the sanction of a special statute (the act of 1725-1726, repealed in 1780),
and that now no minor could be bound as a servant even by his parent.
Cf. Commonwealth *v.* Baird, 1 Ashmead 267: "In Pennsylvania, a parent cannot make his child a servant" . . .
[71] *Cf.* Moore and Jones's *Traveller's Directory* (1802), p. 9.

came so frequent that opportunities arose for abusing it. It began to be a regular practice for unscrupulous men, under pretext of relieving poor negroes of the burden of their children and of providing comfortable places for them, to induce these negroes to bind out their children for a term of years, often paying them a sum of money to further the transaction. Such a master would then assign his indenture for a valuable consideration, and it frequently proved impossible to trace the apprentice thereafter. For a time this evil defied all efforts made to check it; but it was directly contrary to the law of apprentices, and the zealous work of the Pennsylvania Abolition Society finally brought it to an end about 1817.[72]

Such were the steps from slavery to freedom. In 1700 probably most of the negroes in Pennsylvania were slaves. In 1830 slavery was almost extinct there. The long, slow transformation was now nearly complete. That the ascent had been very gradual, that the negro had mounted up from one elevation to another, there still remained undeniable evidence, for negro slaves, servants, and apprentices were to be found side by side with negro freemen. But the older in time the status was the fewer were the persons comprehended in it. There were now very few slaves; there were not many servants; there was a moderate number of apprentices; and there were a great many negroes who were entirely free. Each status had constantly changed in relative importance. From 1680 to 1700 life servitude had existed, while from 1700 to 1780 was the

---

[72] 1 Sergeant and Rawle 249-250; Report of Pa. Soc. Abol. Sl. in *Minutes Fourteenth American Convention Abol. Sl., Phila., 1816*, p. 8; Commonwealth *v.* Vanlear (1814), 1 Sergeant and Rawle 249-250; Commonwealth *v.* . . . Jones (1817), 3 Sergeant and Rawle 158-167.

characteristic period of slavery. In the first seventy years of this time nearly every negro was a slave, a few were free, while some were servants soon to become free. In the next thirty years, from 1750 to 1780, slavery still predominated, but no longer to the same extent, since manumission was making free negroes more numerous, while servitude was becoming wide-spread and important. The next period, from 1780 to about 1810, was the period characterized by servitude. There were still many slaves at first; but slavery was waning, sentiment was against it, and the abolition act had been passed. On the other hand this very act had created a new body of servants; under a construction of one of its parts many servants were being brought from other states; and many negroes were now becoming servants through partial manumission. In addition there arose a class of negro apprentices, who occupied a position above that of servants. Last of all were the free negroes, becoming more numerous than all the others combined. In the third period, from 1810 to about 1830, slavery almost disappeared; the servants were gradually becoming free; and apprenticing stopped because of the race prejudice which was developing. In Pennsylvania the negroes as a race had emerged into freedom.[73]

[73] Some remnants of both slavery and servitude lasted in Pennsylvania down to the Civil War.

CHAPTER VII.

THE LEGAL STATUS OF THE FREE NEGRO.

IT has been shown that the rise of the negro in Pennsylvania was gradual, and that he passed out of slavery up to freedom through servitude more or less limited. After he became free his progress continued to be of the same character. In some respects his freedom was still incomplete, for he was not so free as a free white man. In civil position this inequality lasted until 1780; in political status until 1870.

Up to 1780 the free negro in common with the negro servant was subject to some of the regulations made for negro slaves. This was so in the matter of trials and punishments. Before 1700 negroes when tried were brought before the same courts as white men.[1] In that year was passed a law to regulate the trial of negroes, which declared that they should no longer be tried in the usual courts, but in special courts only.[2] This law, renewed and amended in 1705-1706, was passed at a time when free negroes in Pennsylvania had not yet attracted the attention of the law-givers, but it remained

---

[1] For an instance cf. MS. Min. Court Quarter Sess., Bucks Co., 1684-1730, p. 93 (1688). In 1700 a negro killed a white man and was committed to prison. Shortly thereafter the act for the trial of negroes was passed and it became a question how the negro should be tried. There was considerable discussion, but finally it was decided that although he might properly be tried by the special court, yet it was safer not to do so. "Order'd, That there should be forthwith issued a Commission of Oyer and Terminer, to try them by Juries." *Col. Rec.*, II, 11, 12, 18.

[2] *Stat. at L.*, II, 77-79.

in force until 1780. During the period which inter-
vened there arose a class of free negroes constantly
increasing. They were not specifically included in the
law, nevertheless, while the law seemed to have in view
slaves and servants, it spoke of negroes, and free negroes were tried in the special courts.[3] Accordingly
during this time they were debarred from the right of
trial by jury.[4] The same laws provided punishments
for negroes convicted. When these punishments were
established they were undoubtedly intended for slaves,
but again the wording of the law included all negroes.[5]
During part of the time before 1780 some of these pen-

[3] *Stat. at L.*, II, 233-236. . . . " All such offences committed by any
negro or negroes within this government." *Ibid.*, II, 77, 78 (1700).
" It shall and may be lawful for two justices of the peace of this
province, who shall be particularly commissionated by the governor for
that service, within the respective counties thereof, and six of the most
substantial freeholders of the neighborhood, to hear, examine, try and
determine all such offences committed by any negro or negroes within
this province." *Ibid.*, II, 234 (1705-1706). *Cf.* order authorizing a
special court to be held: . . . " to Jno Hannum and J (?) Morton . . . Es-
quires two of our Justices of our peace within the County of Chester . . .
Know Ye that for the hearing trying and determining all and s[undry]
the Crimes and offences that have been committed or shall be hereafter
committed by any Negro or Negroes whet[her slave]s or free within the
said County of Chester . . . We have assigned you . . . to hold such special
Court or Courts " . . . MS. Misc. Papers, 1684-1847, Chester Co., 149
(1762).
[4] In the controversy of 1837-1838 concerning the negro's right to the
franchise this was often pointed out as one of the proofs that full rights
had never been extended to him in early times. Notwithstanding there is
room for some little doubt. The records of the courts both ordinary and
special are so scanty as to afford small clue to what the prevailing usage
was. There is at least one instance of a mulatto being brought before
the Court of Quarter Sessions at Philadelphia. *Cf.* MS. Rec. General
Quarter Sessions of the Peace, 1773-1780, June 6, 1774. After 1776 it
was believed that even slaves had the right to a jury trial; and it was
asserted that the constitution gave equal legal rights to free men whether
white or black. Neither before nor after 1776 was any test-case brought,
so that it is difficult to ascertain the truth. After 1780 by the abolition
of the special courts the discrimination was entirely removed.
[5] *Stat. at L.*, II, 79, 235.

alties were harsher than those imposed upon white
people guilty of the same crimes. Thus, the punishment
for murder, arson, burglary, buggery, or rape, was
death.⁶ In the case of white people these crimes with
the exception of murder were not capital before 1718.⁷
It is accordingly evident both from the manner in which
he was judged and the penalties to which he was subject that the free negro occupied a status inferior to that
of the white man.

In 1725-1726, when free negroes had become fairly
numerous, they were subjected to additional discriminations. First there were provisions against vagrancy.
Just as security was demanded when a negro was made
free on the ground that free negroes had been found
to be idle and slothful people, so it was provided that if
any free negro being able-bodied and fit to work should
fail to do so or become a vagrant, then any two magistrates having jurisdiction should bind out such negro
from year to year as they might think fit.⁸ This provision does not seem to have been enacted in a spirit hostile to the negro, but appears to have been directed
solely against such negroes as were unwilling or unable
to become self-supporting. In Pennsylvania after 1750

⁶ *Ibid.*
⁷ For burglary, imprisonment, branding and whipping, *Stat. at L.,*
II, 173, 174 (1705-1706). In 1718 the death penalty was provided for one
who entered a house with intent to commit felony or kill. *Ibid.,* III, 203,
204. For buggery, life imprisonment and whipping. *Ibid.,* II, 183, 184
(1705-1706). For rape, seven years imprisonment at hard labor, public
whipping and forfeiture; for the second offense, castration and branding.
Ibid., II, 7 (1700). In 1705-1706 castration was abolished for branding
with the letter R. *Ibid.,* II, 178. In 1718 the death penalty was provided for arson, buggery, sodomy, highway robbery, rape, and murder.
Ibid., III, 203, 204.
⁸ " An Act for the better Regulation of Negroes," *Stat. at L.,* IV, 61, 62.

the negro had so many friends that if he was willing to work he could generally succeed.

Secondly, there were parts of the act of 1725-1726 which had to do with the relations of free negroes to slaves. In these relations white people were restricted also, but in the case of the free negro the penalties were made heavier, because there was greater need to suppress the nuisance involved in the harboring of slaves by their friends who were free, or in the receiving on the part of free negroes of goods stolen by slaves; there being greater difficulty to prevent these things taking place between one negro and another, than between a negro and a white man. Accordingly, if a free negro harbored any slave without the master's consent, that negro was to forfeit five shillings for the first hour, and one shilling for each hour succeeding. For a similar offense a white man paid thirty shillings a day.[9] If a free negro traded with any slave unless the master gave consent, he was to make restitution and be whipped not exceeding twenty-one lashes.[10] This offense involved for a white person repayment of thrice the value of the goods.[11] It was further enacted that if the negro did not pay the fines incurred, then the justices might order satisfaction by servitude.[12]

Thirdly, the law strove to prevent intermixture of the races. Upon white people offending it imposed stringent penalties, but upon free negroes it bore much more heavily. Thus, if a free negro man or woman married a white person, that negro was to be sold by

[9] *Stat. at L.*, IV, 62, 64. For concealing servants the penalty was twenty shillings a day. *Ibid.*, II, 56.
[10] *Stat. at L.*, IV, 62.
[11] *Stat. at L.*, II, 56.
[12] *Stat. at L.*, IV, 62.

the justices of the Quarter Sessions as a slave for life. For a white person offending the penalty was seven years of servitude, or a fine of thirty pounds.[13] If the offense was fornication or adultery the free negro was to be sold as a servant for seven years. The white person thus guilty was to be punished by whipping, imprisonment, or branding with the letter A.[14] That these sections prevented intermarriage before 1780 there is little doubt; but that they failed to prevent illicit intercourse decisive proof is afforded by the large number of mulattoes.[15]

Finally, it seems probable that the laws forbidding negroes to frequent tippling-houses, or to carry arms, or to assemble in companies, applied to the free negro as well as the slave; but these laws were all enforced so loosely that it is probable that the application was more theoretical than real.

Thus, before 1780 a negro even if free was far from being as free as a white man. He had no political rights and could have none.[16] He could not marry a white person and hence could never aspire to social equality. In his family relations he was not permitted to have charge of the raising of his own children.[17] He had no access to the ordinary courts of the colony, but was subjected to special jurisdiction and trial without jury. In his dealings with fellow members of his own race who were not free, he was closely watched and strictly circumscribed. Even in his personal movements he was not altogether free, since when he travelled from one place

[13] *Stat. at L.,* IV, 63.
[14] *Stat. at L.,* II, 180, 181.
[15] See above, p. 31.
[16] See below, chap. X.
[17] See above, p. 92.

to another it was necessary for him to have a pass.[18] And finally, even this status of freedom, imperfect as it was, could be reached only with difficulty and retained only with effort. It was as easy to lose as it was hard to attain. The way up was obstructed by the law about manumission; other parts of the same law made reversion toward slavery easy. For laziness or small crimes the free negro might be made a servant; for graver offenses he might again become a slave. That his position was less hard than might appear was because the laws were not rigorously applied. There was as yet no bitterness between the races.

In 1780 the old laws relating to the negro were abolished; the restrictions placed upon him were removed, and after that time he stood upon a plane of legal equality with the white man, except that the state constitution did not give him the right of suffrage, and that acts of the Legislature denied him the right of becoming part of the state militia.[19] This latter was no serious hardship, while his right to vote had as yet been neither urged nor questioned. He was now tried in the same courts, punished with the penalties, and given the same civil rights as a white person.

In the period after 1780 the only laws made in Pennsylvania to affect the legal position of the negro were made in his favor. Because of his peculiar situation, his recent connection with slavery, and his present proximity to slavery in the South, it was found that the general legislation of the commonwealth did not sufficiently

---

[18] Cf. advertisement in Pa. Gazette, May 19, 1748: . . . "And as got a pass as a free Negroe." This was probably based on the old provision which required servants and strangers when travelling to be provided with a pass. Laws of the Province of Pennsylvania . . . 1682-1700, p. 211 (1693).

[19] See below, p. 182, note 47.

protect him. From kidnapping he could be guarded only by special laws.

In Pennsylvania the history of kidnapping falls into three periods: the years prior to 1820, when owing to inadequate penalties it was largely unchecked; from 1820 to 1847, during which time stringent laws were gradually bringing it to an end; and the period after 1847, when the growth of popular indignation made the crime too dangerous to carry on. During all this time the practice was abhorred, and efforts to suppress it were continually being made not only by the Friends and the abolitionists, but by the great majority of the people of the commonwealth. There was rarely any lack of sympathy for the negro victim even when he was otherwise an object of detestation.

The stealing of free negroes seems to have occurred from time to time in colonial days;[20] but after 1780, when so many of the negroes in Pennsylvania were free, the crime became much more frequent, and soon aroused strong feeling.[21] In 1789 President Mifflin mentioned a young negro lured away and sold into Louisiana.[22] Two years later, when governor, he spoke of several miscreants who had been indicted for the crime in Washington County.[23] In 1799 seventy-four

[20] *Cf.* "Petition of Negro Harry," MS. Misc. Papers, Aug. 18, 1777. *Cf.* letter to the clergyman in *Pa. Packet*, Jan. 1, 1780.

[21] The *Federal Gazette*, Sept. 7, 1789, speaking of some kidnappers who had been operating in Delaware says: "Such nefarious wretches deserve to be extirpated, as there is no creature on the face of the earth with whom they can with propriety be ranked." *Cf.* also memorial to the governor of the state: "The Memᵗˢ humbly apprehend that a Crime of deeper dye is not to be found in the Criminal Code of this State than that of taking a Freeman and carrying off with Intent to sell him and actually selling him as a Slave *in Gross.*" MS. Rec. Pa. Soc. Abol. Sl., III, 49 (1791).

[22] 1 *Pa. Arch.*, XI, 567.

[23] 4 *Pa. Arch.*, IV, 179-181; *J. of S., 1790-1791*, p. 274.

free negroes of Philadelphia protested against the Federal Fugitive Slave Law of 1793, declaring that it gave opportunities for kidnapping.[24] In 1801 a particularly daring attempt occurred at West Nottingham near the Maryland line,[25] while several negroes were actually carried away from Philadelphia about the same time.[26]

During the years following the attention of the public was drawn to this practice more and more. Kidnappers, supposedly from the South, hovered around the mouth of the Delaware.[27] Sometimes the negro was lured away by the basest treachery; at times he was decoyed by some traitor of his own color;[28] occasionally he was attacked with shocking brutality in the streets of Philadelphia itself.[29] The matter was taken up by the Abolition Society in its reports for various years. In 1812 its members petitioned the Legislature for a more stringent law; but in 1816 they were forced to complain that nothing had been done.[30] Very occasionally some of the worst offenders were tried and punished.[31]

[24] J. Parrish, *Remarks on the Slavery of the Black People*, 49-51.

[25] *Pa. Gazette*, Nov. 25, 1801.

[26] *Reflections on Slavery . . . by Humanitas*, 23-32.

[27] Sutcliff, *Travels in Some Parts of North America in the Years 1804, 1805, and 1806*, p. 257.

[28] One man courted and married mulatto women, and then sold them as slaves. Torrey, *Portraiture of Domestic Slavery in the United States*, 52, 56, 57. *Phila. Gazette*, Sept. 23, 1819, for the case of a negro decoy in Philadelphia. *Ibid.*, June 24, 1825, for riot caused by two negro decoys at York. One of them was dreadfully beaten by the mob of infuriated blacks. *Cf. Greensburg Gazette*, July 1, 1825. Also MS. Diary of Joel Swayne, Mar. 16, 1824.

[29] *Phila. Gazette*, July 25, 1818.

[30] MS. Rec. Pa. Soc. Abol. Sl., VI, 13, 17, 21; Report of Pa. Soc. Abol. Sl. in *Minutes Fourteenth Conv. Abol. Sl.*, Phila., 1816, pp. 6, 7; *J. of S.*, 1811-1812, p. 109.

[31] In 1818 a certain William Young of Philadelphia was sentenced to pay three hundred pounds and serve three years in prison. He had lured

The basis of the law against kidnapping was the act of 1788, which imposed imprisonment and a fine of one hundred pounds.[32] The futility of this punishment was soon recognized, and owing to repeated outrages the Legislature considered a new law on several occasions.[33] Nothing was done, however, until at last the urgent messages of Governor Findlay and the strength of public sentiment caused a bill to be passed in 1820.[34] This was entitled "An Act to Prevent Kidnapping". It rigidly defined the crime as the selling or stealing of a free negro or mulatto, or assisting in the same. It then provided as penalty a fine of not less than five hundred nor more than two thousand dollars, one-half of which was to go to the prosecutor, and imprisonment at hard labor for not less than seven nor more than twenty-one years. Under heavy penalties it forbade aldermen and justices of the peace to try cases of fugitive slaves, and it provided that when a fugitive was remanded under the United States law of 1793, the judge should file a description and report with the clerk of Quarter Sessions.[35]

The severity of these provisions, which no doubt did check the practice, would seem to have left nothing to

---

three negroes to Delaware. They were never heard of again. *Phila. Gazette,* Oct. 2, 1818. In 1819 a tin peddler was caught at Easton with two negro children. The enraged villagers cut off one of his ears. *Niles's Register,* XV, 384.

[32] Dallas, *Laws of Pennsylvania,* II, 589.

[33] *J. of H., 1803-1804,* pp. 376, 567, 592, 593; *J. of H., 1805-1806,* p. 142; *J. of H., 1806-1807,* pp. 26, 31, 264; *J. of S., 1811-1812,* pp. 109, 186, 214; *J. of S., 1817-1818,* pp. 363, 370, 371, 406, 410, 442, 443; 4 *Pa. Arch.,* V, 105, 159.

[34] *J. of H., 1818-1819,* pp. 238, 354; *J. of S., 1818-1819,* pp. 148, 158; *J. of H., 1819-1820,* pp. 232, 254, 402, 719; also 121, 175, 233, 302, 323, 381, 430, 983, 987, 1069, 1081, 1088.

[35] *Acts of Assembly, 1820,* pp. 104-106.

be desired; yet cases continued to be reported; and
various attempts were made to obtain a stricter law.[36]
Nevertheless the act of 1820 remained substantially
unmodified. In 1826, when Pennsylvania in compliance
with the wishes of Maryland undertook to facilitate the
capture of fugitive slaves,[37] the penalties upon kidnapping were renewed unchanged;[38] and so they remained
until 1847, when the suit of Prigg v. Pennsylvania made
new legislation necessary, and the punishment was
made somewhat heavier.[39]

After this time the sentiment of the state was
thoroughly aroused, and the law was rigorously enforced. Cases of kidnapping did occur still, but in
number they were relatively few.[40] In 1850 an attack
was made upon the constitutionality of Pennsylvania's
legislation on this subject, since, it was alleged, the
enactments interfered with the Federal laws concerning
fugitive slaves. This attack failed, and it was held

[36] *Phila. Gazette,* May 22, 1822; July 2, 1823; Feb. 8, May 3, 1828;
African Observer, 5th mo., 1827. In 1827 a certain Purnell at Philadel-
phia was fined four thousand dollars and sentenced to forty-two years
in the penitentiary (two offenses). *Niles's Reg.,* XXXII, 279. *Cf.* MS.
Rec. Pa. Soc. Abol. Sl., X, 91, 173, 175; Rep. Pa. Soc. Abol. Sl., in *Min.
Twentieth Sess. Con. Abol. Sl., Balto., 1827; Pa. Freeman,* Mar. 21,
May 9, 1844; *Adams Sentinel,* Aug. 11, 1845; *J. of S., 1822-1823,* p. 525;
J. of S., 1829-1830, p. 340; *J. of S., 1831-1832,* p. 111; *J. of S., 1842-1843,*
p. 307; *J. of H., 1843,* pp. 263, 286.

[37] See below, p. 233.

[38] *Acts of Assembly, 1825-1826,* pp. 150-155.

[39] The fine remained as before, but the imprisonment was made solitary
confinement at hard labor for from five to twelve years for the first offense,
and twenty-one years for the second. *Laws of Pa., 1847,* pp. 206-207.

[40] *Public Ledger,* Mar. 24, 1851; *Laws of Pa., 1852,* pp. 631, 632, 637;
(Harrisburg) *Whig State Journal,* Feb. 5, July 29, 1852; *Evening Bulletin,* Aug. 1, 1853; (Harrisburg) *Daily Patriot,* Dec. 16, 1859. On kidnapping in connection with the Fugitive Slave Law of 1850 see below, p.
242.

that even though slavery was a subject for national regulation, yet Pennsylvania in protecting her population of free negroes had full right to take necessary measures.[41] Within her bounds, then, the state by vigorous action had succeeded in bringing the nefarious practice almost to an end.

Such was the legal position of the free negro after 1780. In most matters equality had been given him. Henceforth the chief obstacles to his well-being were poverty, ignorance, and oppression. But lately a slave, and now in many instances starting at the very bottom of the industrial scale, he was as yet little fitted to endure competition with the white man, even when that competition was not hostile. Owing to what was in some respects a very dependent and helpless situation, he was particularly liable to that oppression which results even under just laws when one portion of the community takes advantage, because it can take advantage, of the other. Even without this disadvantage because of his lowly economic condition he would have found it very difficult to share in the better part of the civilization by which he was surrounded; but in addition there was soon to make its appearance an ominous prejudice, which had not been apparent during slavery days. This was destined to grow in increasing volume thenceforward, and because of it he was to find that without the assistance of zealous friends it would be impossible for him to enforce his legal rights or procure betterment for his children or himself. Yet

[41] Commonwealth *v.* Auld, (Court Quarter Sessions, Cumberland Co.), 4 *Pa. Law Journal Rep.* (431)-(436).

though his lot in the future might be a hard one, the most insuperable obstacles were now removed from his advancement. He was no longer legally an alien. At last he was living under the common laws of the state. For the first time in any real sense he was a member of the commonwealth.

CHAPTER VIII.

Economic and Social Progress.

It is probable that no body of free negroes ever began their economic rise with more assistance and better wishes than the negroes of Pennsylvania. During the colonial period there was nothing to embitter the relations of the races; the general attitude toward negroes was a kindly one; and assistance was readily given them. The great movement among the Quakers which resulted in the manumission of all their slaves had largely a religious character, so that the Friends felt bound to assist the new freedmen as a matter of course. Moreover in Pennsylvania the oldest, the ablest, and the most intelligent of all the abolition societies continually gave the negro wise and efficient aid. If the state could have dealt only with its native black people perhaps most of them would have obtained material well-being in a generation after becoming free.

In colonial days negroes were not only set free, but were frequently provided for. An excellent example is the provision made by Judge Langhorne in 1742. According to his will, which gave liberty to all of his slaves, the older ones were to stay on the premises; to six of the others he gave land to hold free or on lease, and in addition horses, cows, sheep, agricultural instruments, and household goods; while each of the younger negroes was to receive ten pounds when twenty-four

years of age.[1] The local histories contain many other
instances like this.

From the first the Friends recognized their obligation
to give assistance. In 1758 the Yearly Meeting declared that Christian provision should be made for
manumitted slaves, and such was generally made.[2]
Many of the Friends believed, moreover, that it was
not sufficient to set slaves free, or even to endow their
liberty with gifts; but that, since the negro had been
wronged by being kept in any slavery at all, it was the
duty of Christian masters to make payment now for the
service which had been wrongfully exacted.[3] In 1779
the Meeting recommended that freedmen be compen-
sated for their labor done while slaves.[4] This principle
was adopted during the next two years, committees
being appointed to visit the former masters and to give
the freed negroes help.[5]

The work of the Pennsylvania Society for the Abolition of Slavery must be described in another place.
Here it is sufficient to say that the abolitionists together
with the Friends made every effort to better the condition of former slaves. Schools were organized, religious instruction was furnished, and all sorts of en-
deavors were made to get the negroes started in life.
After 1797 the Society had regular committees to improve the morals and the education of negroes, to find

---

[1] Pa. Mag., VII, 79, 80, 82; Buck, History of Bucks Co., (author's
scrap-book), MS. note to chap. XII.
[2] Sharpless, A Quaker Experiment, 32; Futhey and Cope, History of
Chester Co., 423.
[3] Cf. story told by Woolman, Journal, in Friends' Library, IV, 375.
[4] An Address to Friends and Friendly People, etc. (1848), 21.
[5] Brief Statement of the Rise and Progress of the Testimony of the
Religious Society of Friends, 51.

them employment, and to apprentice their children where they could learn some useful trade.[6]

Under these favorable conditions the negro made excellent progress. The first freedmen remained largely in the service of their former masters.[7] Soon, however, they began hiring themselves to others, or working as day laborers.[8] It was not long before they began to venture into business for themselves.[9] In 1789 those who kept small shops were described as doing moderately well, though hindered by inability to borrow money.[10] The travellers who came to Philadelphia from time to time noticed a number of lowly occupations monopolized by the free negroes. Such were the sawing of

[6] The report of the Society in 1797 mentions a " Committee of Inspection " to superintend the moral conduct of negroes and to protect them; a " Committee of Guardianship " to put out children with suitable persons " during a moderate term of apprenticeship or servitude " for the purpose of learning some trade; a " Committee of Education "; and a " Committee of Employ " to assist free negroes who were out of work. *Min. Third Conv. Abol. Societies*, 31-32.

[7] " Die freigelassenen Negern blieben seitdem fast alle bei ihren vorigen Herren, denen sie für Lohn als freie besser dienten, als zuvor, da sie noch in der Knechtschaft, so mild diese auch war, gehalten wurden." Ebeling, IV, 220. " In Pennsylvania, the Quakers have freed their slaves. Those who have been manumitted have taken mostly to field labour. They make good labourers, and live reputably and well. Many of them are much attached to their old masters. Some, who had given all their slaves their liberty, and now employ them at day wages, find their farms answer better and more profitably than before. They are employed in the culture of corn, maize, tobacco, and every species of husbandry." *A letter from Capt. J. S. Smith . . . on Free Negroes* (1786), 39.

[8] MS. John Wilson's Cash Book, June 30, 1768; Mar. 4, May 18, 1776; *Pa. Packet,* June 30, 1790; *Phila. Gazette,* July 8, 1807; July 18, 1808; Sept. 5, 1809.

[9] MS. John Wilson's Cash Book, Mar. 26, 1774; Feb. 6, 1775.

[10] Brissot de Warville, *Mémoire,* 28, 29. In 1806 some are mentioned who " halten kleine Läden," though the author is referring generally to the Middle States. *Nachrichten . . . von einem Rheinländer,* 17. As early as 1771 license to keep a public house was denied to " Sarah Noblitt (husband negro . . .)." *Pa. Mag.,* XXII, 127.

fire-wood and the carrying of baggage.[11] In 1800 a report of the Pennsylvania Abolition Society declared
that the free blacks of Philadelphia were employed in
various ways, some being mechanics and a still larger
number seamen.[12] It is true that both immediately after
1780 and also throughout the years following the large
majority found employment either as house-servants
or in menial labor, for to such work they had been accustomed previously ;[13] nevertheless the few who began
to seek work of a higher grade increased after a while
to a large number who engaged in a variety of occupations, either independently or hiring themselves to

[11] " For half a dollar a chord." Wansey, *Journal of an Excursion to
the United States of North America in the Summer of 1794*, p. 164.
" When our boat arrived " (Phila.) " we were inundated with porters,
the greater part of whom were blacks, . . . they had tin plates on their hats
or breasts, upon which were written their names and residences." Fearon,
*Narrative of a Journey . . . through the Eastern and Western States of
America* (1817), 134, 135. See also W. T. Harris, *Remarks* (1817), 30;
America and the Americans, by a Citizen of the World (1830), 220.

[12] *Min. Sixth Conv. Abol. Socs., Phila.*, 1800, p. 6.

[13] Twining, *Travels in America 100 Years ago*, 33, 34, 36 (1795);
Michaux, *Travels to the Westward of the Allegany Mountains*, 26 (1802);
Views of Society and Manners in America . . . By an Englishwoman, 340
(1820). Clara v. Gerstner, speaking of the independent spirit of servants
in Philadelphia, says: " die Neger dagegen zeigen mehr Gehorsam und
Ergebenheit . . . und werden daher von Vielen den Weiszen als Diener
vorgezogen." She says that the wages of a servant are three dollars a
week, of a chambermaid one dollar and a half, and that they have free
every other Sunday evening and also one free evening a week. *Beschrei-
bung einer Reise durch die Vereinigten Staaten von Nordamerica in
den Jahren 1838 bis 1840*, pp. 445, 446 (1840). Very many negroes were
employed as waiters. " Alle Diener waren Schwarze. Auch die Musik
wurde von Schwarzen gemacht; denn weisse Musikanten spielen niemals
öffentlich." *Reise Sr. Hoheit Bernhard, Saxe-Weimar Eisenach*, I, 223
(1825). "All the waiters at the hotels are *black*, and all the chamber-
maids brown." Maxwell, *A Run through the United States during the
Autumn of 1840*, II, 168 (1840). " The chimney-sweeps here are young
negro boys. As they glide through the streets in quest of employment,
they have a peculiar and melodious cry, slightly resembling a Tyrolese
' yoddle.' " Combe, *Notes on the United States of North America during a Phrenological Visit in 1838-9-40*, II, 190 (1839).

others.[14] Of these some achieved solid and substantial success.

As far back as 1779 a negro, John, figured on the assessment list for eight acres and one horse.[15] Before the end of the eighteenth century colored people in Philadelphia owned nearly one hundred houses.[16] In 1806 there is mention of a negro who was managing with much ability a farm at Merion near Philadelphia.[17] Twenty years later a number were prosperous enough to attract notice.[18] In 1832 James Forten, a sail-maker of Philadelphia, was rated at over one hundred thousand dollars, while the widow of Bishop Allen was supposed to have twenty-five thousand.[19] Later, several negroes of the same city were considered rich and well educated;[20] and before the Civil War the colored people in

[14] In 1838 there were negro bakers, blacksmiths, carpenters, dress-makers, hair-dressers, plasterers, milliners, shoe-makers, tailoresses, tanners, etc. Some of them were in business for themselves. *Register of the Trades of the Colored People in the City of Philadelphia*, 3. In 1847 an exhaustive investigation revealed the occupations of 3358 negro men and 4249 negro women. Of the men there were 1581 laborers, 557 waiters and cooks, 286 mechanics, 276 drivers, 240 sea-faring men, 166 shop-keepers, 156 hair dressers, and 96 of various occupations. Of the women there were 1970 washerwomen, 786 day workers, 486 seamstresses, 290 occupied at home, 213 at trades, 173 cooks, 156 living in families, 103 raggers and boners, 72 unclassified. *A Statistical Inquiry into the Condition of the People of Colour of the City and Districts of Philadelphia*, 17, 18.

[15] Lancaster Co. 3 *Pa. Arch.*, XVII, 525. Other instances occur. *Cf.* MS. Rec. Pa. Soc. Abol. Sl., I, 67.

[16] Average value, $200. *Min. Proceedings Third Conv. Abol. Socs., Phila., 1796*, p. 21.

[17] Sutcliff, *Travels*, 223.

[18] " In New York and Philadelphia there are many shrewd, sensible blacks. Some have amassed fortunes; and several conduct their business with considerable ability and integrity." I. Holmes, *An Account of the United States of America, Derived from Actual Observation, during a Residence of Four Years* (1823), 334.

[19] R. Purvis, *Remarks on the Life and Character of James Forten*; Garrison, *Thoughts on African Colonization*, 129 (note).

[20] Combe, *Notes* II, 63 (1839).

Pennsylvania reputed well-to-do made a fairly long list.[21]

Their collective prosperity though less striking merits notice. In 1832 negroes claimed to be paying annually $2,500 taxes, and $100,000 rent.[22] Five years later they were believed to own real estate and property worth more than $1,000,000.[23] Some of their houses were well furnished, the parlors being described as having carpets, sofas, sideboards, card-tables, mirrors, and in some cases pianos.[24] In 1847 negroes were paying over $6,000 taxes, and their real estate was valued at $400,000. At this time there were said to be more than three hundred negro freeholders in Philadelphia. They constituted about eight per cent. of the negro families in the city.[25]

That the rise was not more rapid, and that the resulting prosperity was not more generally diffused, was owing to two causes. It will be shown that after 1800 the whole problem of the negro's existence in Pennsyl-

[21]Among many others, Joseph Cassey, money-broker, Phila., $75,000; Stephen Smith, lumber merchant, Columbia, said to be the wealthiest negro in the United States; his partner, W. Whipper, Phila.; W. Riley, gentlemen's boot-maker; James Prosser, owner of a restaurant, Phila.; Henry Minton, proprietor of a fashionable restaurant, Phila.; Henry Collins, dealer in real estate, Pittsburg; Owen Barrett, manufacturer of patent medicines, Pittsburg. Delany, *Condition . . . of the Colored People of the United States*, 94-105. For the case of a negro who from slavery worked his way up to the ownership of a farm of 145 acres, see *Public Ledger*, Aug. 27, 1860. Sometimes negro immigrants from other States were assisted by their former masters. *Cf.* (Lancaster) *Inland Daily*, Dec. 9, 1854, for an instance of fifty-three freedmen from Virginia, whose former master had given them an outfit worth $15,000.

[22] Memorial to the Legislature. *Hazard's Register*, IX, 361.

[23] *Present State of the Free People of Colour* (1838), 7.

[24] *Sketches of the Higher Classes of Colored Society in Philadelphia, By a Southerner* (1841), 56.

[25] Needles, *Ten Years' Progress: or a Comparison of the State and Condition of the Colored People in the City and County of Philadelphia from 1837 to 1847*, pp. 8, 9; *Statistical Inquiry*, 14.

vania was complicated by the immigration of undesired
alien negroes, and by the increase of race prejudice.[26]
As a result old opportunities were closed to him, and his
chances instead of improving became worse. Accordingly the number of the prosperous was relatively small.
Most of the negroes in Pennsylvania as elsewhere remained in very meagre circumstances. At the bottom
of the scale there were large numbers in squalid and
starving condition. Next came the majority, who either
lived upon a very low standard, or felt the pinch of
continued poverty. Next above them came many who
had such income as could purchase moderate comfort.
At the top were a few who were really well-to-do, but
as negroes passed for wealthy men.[27] If it were possible
to ascertain the average income for all the negroes in
Pennsylvania at any period between 1830 and 1860 that
income would doubtless be seen to be exceedingly scant.
Only a minority would be found to possess anything
whatever in excess of the actual cost of their subsistence. Yet the significant thing is that in spite of all
obstacles there had begun to appear negroes who owned
their houses, paid taxes, supported their own schools,
contributed to beneficial societies, built churches, and
constituted not only a negro population but a negro
society.

The providing of schools for the negro was owing, at
least in the beginning, to the efforts of his zealous and

[26] See below, chapter IX.

[27] "They present in a gradual, moderate and limited ratio, almost
every grade of character, wealth, and . . . of education. They are to be
seen in ease, comfort, and the enjoyment of all the social blessings of this
life; and, in contrast with this, they are to be found in the lowest depths
of human degradation, misery, and want." *Sketches of the Higher
Classes of Colored Society,* 14, 15.

conscientious friends. While it is not to be expected
that the education of the negro, whether slave or free,
should have received much attention in the early years
of the colony, yet some scanty efforts can be traced. In
1722 a benevolent person let it be known that without
pay he would teach negroes to read.[28] Others seem to
have thought of this from time to time.[29] In 1740 Whitefield, then doing wonderful work in Pennsylvania, acquired land to found for negroes a free school. As yet
the time was hardly ripe for an undertaking on so large
a scale, and Whitefield's resources proving inadequate
he was compelled to abandon it.[30] In 1750 a similar attempt was made in a different manner, when Anthony
Benezet conceived the idea of an evening school, which
he opened and taught gratuitously himself. In this
undertaking he obtained notable results.[31] By 1770
much attention had been attracted ; the Quakers in many
places began educative work ; and the Friends' Monthly
Meeting in Philadelphia first appointed a committee,
and then established a school in which could be learned
the rudiments of education and also the arts of sewing
and knitting.[32] The Friends were so pleased with the

[28] "Take further Notice, There is lately arriv'd in this City a Person
who freely offers his Service to teach his poor Brethren the Negroes to
read the Holy Scriptures, etc. . . . without any Manner of Expence to
their respective Masters or Mistresses " . . . *American Weekly Mercury*, Feb. 19, 1722.

[29] "Thy Teaching Negroes to Read without Speaking to 'em (as in
thy printed Proposal) is a wonderful Faculty " . . . Alluding to Samuel
Keimer's *Compleat Ephemeris*. *Mercury*, Jan. 25, 1725-1726.

[30] *Pa. Gazette*, Nov. 27, 1740; Seward, *Journal*, 2, 10, 20, 52, 74, 80,
81; Cranz, *History of the Brethren*, 258, 259; Heckewelder, *Narrative*, 18.

[31] Vaux, *Memoirs of Benezet*, 20, 21.

[32] MS. Darby Women's M. M. M., 2 12th mo., 1775; MS. Rec. War-
rington Q. M., 7 (1787); 42 (1789); 133 (1795); also 80, 191, 204; *A
Brief Sketch of the Schools for Black People and Their Descendants
Established by the Religious Society of Friends in 1770*, pp. 4-7; *History
of the Association of Friends for the Free Instruction of Adult Colored
Persons in Philadelphia*, 3.

ECONOMIC AND SOCIAL PROGRESS   129

progress made that in the following year an additional school was opened.[33]

After a while the interest of the negroes seems to have flagged; and during the Revolution the work of education was near to being abandoned. During this period the scheme was probably saved because of the fact that Anthony Benezet took charge of it, and taught the pupils in his own house.[34] After this time the work went on prosperously. Donations were received, and interest increased.[35] In 1789 was founded the Society for "the free instruction of orderly Blacks and People of Color",[36] which undertook to do for adults what the earlier schools were doing for children. Much was accomplished by holding sessions at night.[37] Three years after this, women Friends formed a society for the education of negro women, and opened a school for them five evenings a week.[38] In 1797 there were in Philadelphia seven schools for the education of negroes, and two others were about to be opened. The usual attendance was nearly three hundred, of both sexes.[39] Two years later mention is made of another school connected with one of the negro congregations, and taught by the minister.[40] Shortly before 1805 the negroes of the city

[33] *Brief Sketch*, 9, 10. Cf. Davies, *Some Account of the City of Philadelphia* (1794), 65.

[34] *Brief Sketch*, 12, 13, 15. At his death in 1784 Benezet left part of his estate to the forwarding of this work. *Ibid.*, 16, 17; Ebeling, IV, 219; Morse, *The American Geography*, 438.

[35] *Brief Sketch*, 20.

[36] *History of the Association of Friends for the Free Instruction of Adult Colored Persons*, 3.

[37] In 1792 the night school had fifty members. *Ibid.*, 6.

[38] *Ibid.*, 10.

[39] *Min. Proceedings Fourth Conv. Abol. Socs.*, *Phila.*, 1797, p. 41.

[40] Ogden, *An Excursion into Bethlehem and Nazareth*, 90. For an account of the work of Absalom Jones at this school, and for lists of the children taught, see MS. Rec. Pa. Soc. Abol. Sl., V, 175, 177, 179.

themselves established two schools, one under the auspices of the African Episcopalians, the other under the direction of a non-sectarian association which they founded.[41]

To appreciate the significance of this work it must be remembered that most of it was done before Pennsylvania had made any provision for the education of poor children, and that white children as well as black were being taught in private schools. State assistance dates from about 1802, when an act was passed for free instruction. This was supplemented in 1804 and again in 1809.[42] These laws entitled to education all the poor children of the commonwealth. At first, however, they availed negroes but little, for one of the results of the increasing prejudice towards black people was that the officials having charge of Pennsylvania's educational work seem to have ignored them entirely. Moreover it is not probable that the white people of the state had for a moment contemplated the admission of negro children into schools for their own children;[43] hence only by the granting of separate buildings could negroes benefit by the law. Such buildings were not provided, and for some years negro education was carried on as before by individual effort and private philanthropy.[44] At last the Pennsylvania Abolition Society took up the

[41] Rep. of Pa. Soc. Abol. Sl. in *Min. Tenth American Conv. Abol. Sl.,* Phila., *1805,* p. 13.

[42] " An Act to Provide for the Education of Poor Children gratis," *Acts of Assembly, 1802,* p. 76; " An Act to Provide for the more Effectual Education of the Children of the Poor gratis," *id., 1804,* p. 298; " An Act to Provide for the Education of the Poor gratis," *id., 1809,* p. 193.

[43] I have found no evidence of such mixed schools up to 1861.

[44] *Cf.* Rep. Pa. Soc. Abol. Sl. in *Min. Fourteenth American Conv.,* Phila., *1816,* pp. 8, 9.

matter actively. A conference was arranged between their committee and the controllers, and as a result in 1820 the Society provided a building and the state undertook to supply the instruction.[45] This was the first school established by the government of Pennsylvania for negro children.[46]

Such a school seemed to augur well. It was found, however, very difficult to get additional buildings, and the facilities soon proved to be inadequate.[47] Furthermore the increasing hostility towards the negro not only made it difficult for him to get new schools, but made it sometimes seem likely that those already furnished would be withdrawn. In the constitutional convention of 1837-1838 there were some who could see no use whatever in educating the negro,[48] and at times the authorities proved very willing to take an unfavorable view of the situation. In 1842 when the attendance of the colored grammar schools dwindled, those schools were on the point of being closed, and were saved only by the prompt action of the negroes, who held meetings and increased the attendance.[49] Accordingly it was perhaps fortunate that the older private schools of the Friends were kept open. Indeed the Friends continued along with the Pennsylvania Abolition Society to make additional provision even after the state began its

[45] This because when the officials finally expressed willingness to help, they declared they had no suitable building. MS. Rec. Pa. Soc. Abol. Sl., VIII, 29.

[46] Needles, *Memoir*, 69, 70. This was the Mary Street School, which was opened about 1822. See *Address to People of Colour . . . Bethel Church, 1825*, pp. 3, 4. The *Hist. Asso. Friends Free Instruction Adult Col. Per.*, 8, gives the date as 1819. This is a slight error.

[47] Cf. *Hazard's Register*, III, 365.

[48] Cf. speech of Mr. Martin, in *Pro. and Deb. of Conv.*, III, 83.

[49] Bacon, *Statistics of the Colored People of Philadelphia*, 5.

work.[50] In 1832 they founded a pay school to instruct colored youths in such higher branches as would enable them to become teachers themselves.[51]

By this time a small coterie of educated negroes had begun founding libraries, schools, and debating societies of their own.[52] About 1840 an anonymous writer, who appears to have made an exhaustive investigation of the conditions surrounding the negroes of Philadelphia, mentioned the excellent schools, three or four in number, conducted by negro teachers, and said that the older negroes, feeling as they did in many instances their own lack of education, spared no pains to secure good teaching for their children.[53] A short time before this in a memorial to the Legislature the negroes declared that while they were thankful for public schools, yet such of them as could do so educated their children at their private expense.[54]

There is abundant evidence that all of these schools did good work. A great number of negroes learned to read and write, and some of them acquired a good education;[55] but on the whole the results were discouraging.

[50] In 1832 the Association of Friends for the Free Instruction of Adult Colored Persons was founded. Immediately it opened a school in which were taught reading, writing, and arithmetic. Five years later another school was added. *History of the Association,* etc., 18, 19.

[51] Rep. in *Min. Twenty-second Sess. Amer. Conv., Phila., 1839,* p. 8.

[52] In 1832 some negroes of Pittsburg founded the Pittsburg African Education Society. *Hazard's Reg.,* IX, 115, 116. In 1833 was established the Philadelphia Library Company of Colored Persons, and in 1836 the Rush Library Company and Debating Society. *Sketches of the Higher Classes,* 96-100. About this time they had a newspaper of their own, one of the editors being a negro. It was entitled *The Coloured American.* Combe, *Notes on the United States,* II, 190.

[53] *Sketches of the Higher Classes,* 17, 18, 25, 26, 94.

[54] *Hazard's Reg.,* IX, 362 (1832).

[55] *Cf.* MS. Rec. and Reports of Pa. Soc. Abol. Sl. for the comprehensive work done. See also Bibliography, pp. 262, 263, below.

There was scantiness and irregularity of attendance at the schools both public and private from the first, except when the facilities afforded by these schools were inadequate for the total number of possible pupils. In 1847 it was asserted that in Philadelphia considerably less than half of the negro children between the ages of five and twenty attended any school.[56] This was to be expected, since many of the parents, at the bottom of the industrial scale and often living a semi-vagrant life, found it difficult to support themselves, not to speak of maintaining children.[57] Even the attendance at the night schools, which were intended to help those employed during the day, was often lowered because of the danger which at times beset any negro who ventured at a distance from his home after dark.[58] On the whole the period prior to 1861 was characterized by lack of appreciation and by moderate results. It was also marked by public indifference and coldness on the part of the authorities, although it must be remembered that at the time the expenditure made by the state upon colored schools was much in excess of the proportion justified by that share of the taxes which negroes paid ; and that this was at a time when negroes had made themselves intensely disliked by a large part of the community. That successful results were achieved was due almost entirely to the quiet and persistent labor of the abolitionists and the Quakers. Before 1820 the undertaking was entirely in their hands. Thereafter most of

[56] *Statistical Inquiry*, 19, 22.
[57] " There are many free negro-schools in some of the cities; but there is a degree of poverty, which obliges the parents to avail themselves of the work of their children, instead of sending them to school." Grund, *The Americans in Their Moral, Social, and Political Relations* (1837), II, 321 (note).
[58] *Cf. Hist. Asso. Friends Free Instruction Adult Colored Persons*, 24.

the encouragement came from them, while they continued to do a large part of the actual work.

Next to the getting of schools it is probable that nothing contributed more to the uplifting of the negroes of Pennsylvania than the establishment of a church of their own. From participation in matters of general interest they were debarred by economic inequality, by race prejudice, and by political discrimination. They had no share also in that development which comes from public and social activity. Yet this development could be supplied to a certain extent by religious activity, for church work could afford them intercourse among themselves. Moreover, they were by nature religious and emotional. These facts go far to explain the early foundation and rapid growth of the negro church in Pennsylvania.

Far back in slavery times negroes had been found to be peculiarly susceptible to religious exhortation, especially to the preaching of itinerant ministers.[59] During this time slaves, and toward the end of the period free negroes, were admitted into some of the churches of the Episcopalians and Moravians, but as a rule not upon terms of complete membership or equality.[60] After 1780 the gradual increase of prejudice and exclusiveness on the one hand, and the rising ambition of the free negroes on the other, made it desirable for them to have

[59] See above, p. 45. "I believe near Fifty Negroes came to give me Thanks, under God, for what has been done to their Souls. Oh how heartily did those poor Creatures throw in their Mites for my poor Orphans. . . . I have been much drawn out in Prayer for them, and have seen them exceedingly wrought upon, under the Word preach'd." *A Continuation of the Rev. Mr. Whitefield's Journal* (1740), 65, 66.

[60] See above, p. 44. About 1763 William Boen, a negro, was refused admittance to the Society of Friends. He was finally admitted to membership in 1814. *Memorials Concerning Deceased Friends*, 4, 5, 7. *Cf.* also MS. Letter Book (Coll. G. Cope), 279.

churches of their own. Accordingly in 1791 some who had previously attended white churches of different denominations united to form an "African Church."[61] They began with no minister and in a school-house, but they were assisted with liberal contributions, and before the end of the century had a sacred building presided over by a minister who was a negro.[62] It was not long, however, before this "African Church" began to split up into the various denominations out of which it had been formed. The first result of this was the Colored Presbyterian Church, which was established in Philadelphia about 1800.[63] In a few years there were also established colored churches of Baptists, Episcopalians, and Methodists. It was asserted that these were the first churches in the United States to have negro ministers.[64]

In 1816 the colored Methodists of Philadelphia took part in establishing the first general organization of negro churches, when their delegates, together with those from Baltimore and other cities nearby, established the African Methodist Episcopal Church.[65] In

---

[61] " As they consist of the scattered appendages of most of the Churches in the City they have formed Articles and a Plan of Church Government so general as to embrace all, and yet so orthodox in cardinal points as to offend none." *Extract of a Letter from Dr. Benjamin Rush . . . to Granville Sharp*, 3, 4.

[62] *Ibid.;* De la Rochefoucault Liancourt, *Travels*, II, 387; Morse, *The American Gazetteer*, " Philadelphia " (1797).

[63] Rev. Wm. T. Catto, *Semi-Centennial Discourse*, etc., 18 ff.

[64] "Die ersten sind welche in den vereinigten Staaten gegenwärtig existieren." *Nachrichten und Erfahrungen von einem Rheinländer*, 16; *Phila. Gazette*, Apr. 30, 1813; Wilson, *Picture of Philadelphia, for 1824*, etc., 45, 46. They frequently imitated the churches of white people in the then popular expedient of raising money by means of lotteries. *Cf. Acts of Assembly, 1804*, p. 62; *Phila. Gazette*, Nov. 26, 1807; *General Advertiser*, Feb. 28, 1808.

[65] Bowen, *History of Philadelphia*, 161.

Pennsylvania as in other places Methodism seems to
have exerted a preponderating influence upon the religious life of the negroes, and the African Methodist
Church was soon more flourishing than any other negro
denomination.[66]

Colored churches were earliest and most prosperous
in Philadelphia. In small towns negroes continued for
a long time to attend the churches of white people, but
in the larger cities such as Pittsburg and Columbia they
had religious organizations and church buildings of
their own.[67] Many of the negro churches had a flourishing career.[68] Often they exerted a strong uplifting influence. In some of them the ministers gained a reputation through their labors and their eloquence, not a few
being recognized as the leaders of their race.[69]

[66] This was noted at an early time, and was frequently mentioned by
travellers. In 1818 Duncan found among the negroes of Philadelphia
four Methodist churches, and one each for Episcopalians and Baptists.
Travels through Part of the United States and Canada in 1818 and 1819,
I, 208. In 1825 Bernhard of Saxe-Weimar wrote: . . . " the Methodists
. . . die meisten Schwarzen, ebenfalls in grosser Anzahl hier in Philadelphia gehören zu dieser Secte." *Reise,* I, 220. In 1857 there were in Philadelphia eighteen colored churches, described by a negro as " flourishing."
They were distributed as follows: Meth. Epis., seven; Prot. Epis., two;
Meth., two; Congregational, one; Baptist, three; Presbyterian, three.
Rev. Wm. T. Catto, *Semi-Centennial Discourse,* app., 105-111.

[67] *Views of Society and Manners in America,* .53; *Hazard's Register,*
VII, 280; *Laws of Assembly, 1850,* pp. 1059-1061; *id., 1854,* pp. 335, 336.
For a negro camp meeting see *Franklin Gazette,* Aug. 26, 1819.

[68] Cf. Needles, *Ten Years' Progress,* 13.

[69] As for example Bishop Allen. The ministers occasionally gain
special mention. " Jacob Bishop (a black man), who has preached the
Gospel with *great acceptation* in various places, will deliver a discourse
This Evening, in that part of the Academy, north Fourth street, which
is occupied by the Independent Society." *Phila. Gazette,* July 3, 1805.
" We heard a sermon to-day in the Episcopalian church occupied by the
people of colour in Philadelphia. . . . The church was commodious and
comfortable, and the congregation respectable in their appearance. . . . The
service was performed, and a fair average sermon preached by the Rev.
Mr. Douglas, also a man of colour. . . . The service was read and the sermon delivered in pure good English, equal to that of any of the other
clergymen of the city, and the whole demeanour of the congregation was
becoming and devout." Combe, *Notes,* II, 62, 63 (1839). Captain

The surplus energies of the better negroes in Pennsylvania were devoted almost entirely to church work, because at first they lacked wider opportunities, and afterwards opportunity was withheld from them. It is owing to the very limited sphere in which they could move that there is almost no mention of them as participating in the affairs of their neighborhood. Except in connection with crime they are rarely spoken of in the news columns of the daily papers. On two occasions, however, they did attract some attention.

In the yellow fever epidemics of 1793 and 1797 so great was the panic that it proved difficult to get nurses for the sick or even to get the dead buried. At both these times the negroes rendered a real service, as they were much less liable to be affected by the fever. For a while they were almost the only helpers to be had. Some charged extortionate prices, and others plundered the sick and the dead, but this was by no means characteristic; and public expression of gratitude was made for their assistance.[70]

Marryat, describing the mourners in a funeral procession in Philadelphia (1838), says they were "all well dressed, and behaving with the utmost decorum. They were preceded by a black clergyman, dressed in his full black silk canonicals. He did look very odd, I must confess." *Diary in America,* I, 148, 149.

[70] Carey, *A Short Account of the Malignant Fever Lately Prevalent in Philadelphia,* 63; Letter of Margaret Haines in *Pa. Mag.,* XIX, 268; A. J. and R. A., *A Narrative of the Proceedings of the Black People, during the Late Awful Calamity in Philadelphia, in the Year 1793: and a Refutation of some Censures Thrown upon them in some late Publications,* 3-23; Rush, *An Account of the Bilious remitting Yellow Fever, As It Appeared in the City of Philadelphia, in the Year 1793,* pp. 95-97, 113; T. Condie and R. Folwell, *History of the Pestilence, Commonly Called Yellow Fever, which Almost Desolated Philadelphia, in . . . 1798,* p. 104. Some of the nurses charged as much as five dollars a night. Carey, *Short Account,* 63. " Sie ziehen nähmlich dem Verstorbenen seine Kleider aus, und schmücken sich mit der Beute. Eine Dame in Philadelphia theilte mir die Bemerkung mit, dasz die Neger niemals so gut gekleidet waren, als nach dem gelben Fieber." Buhle, *Reisen,* 18, 19 (1798). Compare the indignant denial by A. J. and R. A., *Narrative.*

Again in 1814 after the capture of Washington by the British, when Philadelphia was thrown into a panic of fear and hastily took measures for defense, the negroes did good service. Members of the Vigilance Committee conferred with the leading colored men of the city, and as a result of their interview it is said that twenty-five hundred negroes assembled in the State House Yard, and then worked ceaselessly for two days throwing up trenches.[71] For this they received a vote of thanks.[72] It was even proposed to raise a "Black Legion," but the plan was not approved.[73]

After this time negroes at no period participated in public affairs, and thereafter when they attracted attention it was only because of measures which were being taken against them, or because of their doings among themselves. Frequently they had their own meetings and conventions, and on several occasions showed in striking manner their consciousness of race solidarity. In 1807 some negroes led by James Forten and Absalom Jones met in a school-room to prepare resolutions thanking God that it was no longer lawful to import slaves into the United States.[74] In 1830 at a public meeting they passed resolutions praising the government of Pennsylvania, and commending the American Colonization Society.[75] In the next year a con-

[71] Nell, *Services of Colored Americans, in the Wars of 1776 and 1812,* pp. 24, 25. Cf. *American Daily Advertiser,* Sept. 3, 1814.

[72] Nell, *ibid.*

[73] Minutes of the Committee of Defence, in *Mem. Hist. Soc. Pa.,* VIII, 47; *J. of S., 1814-1815,* p. 56. Negroes were debarred from the Pennsylvania militia. See below, p. 182, note 47. During the Revolution there is mention of one negro recruit. MS. Misc. Papers, Aug. 12, 1780. James Forten served in the American navy. He was captured, and confined in a prison ship. Nell, *Services,* 23.

[74] *Phila. Gazette,* Dec. 30, 1807.

[75] *Hazard's Register,* V, 143, 144.

vention of negroes met at Philadelphia to consider laws
passed in some of the states abridging the liberties of
their race, and to urge emigration to Canada.[76] This
convention, the chief purpose of which was to improve
the condition of the blacks, and which included delegates from a number of states, marked the first movement of importance on the part of negroes in the United
States.[77] In 1841 they assembled a state convention to
consider the disfranchisement of their race, and to pass
resolutions denouncing it, while in 1848 they formed
"The Citizens' Union of the Commonwealth of Pennsylvania ", the purpose of which was to obtain complete
citizenship.[78] In 1853 they petitioned the Legislature to
secure them entire protection when they travelled in
slave-holding states.[79] In 1857 an indignation meeting
in Philadelphia denounced the Dred Scott decision, and
also the United States Constitution, as pro-slavery.[80]

The existence of a body of active and intelligent
negroes, which is denoted by this activity, is further
shown in the descriptions of negro society by an anony-

[76] *Minutes and Proceedings of the First Annual Convention of the
People of Colour . . . Philadelphia . . . 1831.*

[77] *Sketches of the Higher Classes, 70-77.*

[78] *Proceedings of the State Convention of the Colored Freemen of
Pennsylvania Held in Pittsburg for the Purpose of Considering Their
Condition and the Means of Its Improvement, Pittsburg, 1841.* *Min-
utes of the State Convention of the Coloured Citizens of Pennsylvania,
Convened at Harrisburg . . . 1848.*

[79] *J. of S., 1853,* vol. I, 161.

[80] *Pennsylvanian,* Apr. 4, 1857. For a meeting to express indignation at
the manner in which the Fugitive Slave Law was being carried out, *cf.*
Public Ledger, Feb. 4, 1857. An observer describing the negroes of
Philadelphia in 1841 said that they let pass no object of importance without a public expression of opinion in regard to it; but he added that on
account of the rivalries of the leaders to control these meetings, and
because of the abuse and bluster into which their efforts degenerated, the
meetings were usually of no benefit to the negroes, but rather a hindrance
to their cause. *Sketches of the Higher Classes, 77-91.*

mous writer in 1841. He declared that the negroes had
lectures, literary societies, and "Demosthenean insti-
tutes" for both men and women; and that they had
among them ministers, physicians, and at least one
artist. These negroes of profession along with other
well-to-do colored people formed a society large enough
to be divided into numerous distinct circles, in which
the members were often bitterly envious of one another.
They were hospitable; they visited frequently; and they
entertained in well furnished parlors with music and
refreshments. The author particularly noted their
temperateness and habits of self-restraint: they lived
within their incomes; they abstained from intoxicating
liquors; they retired at a seasonable hour. This description, if accurate, would denote considerable development of character.[81]

The great mass of the negroes of Pennsylvania were
generally described as indolent, thoughtless, prodigal,
and thriftless, though at the same time cheerful and
good-humored; fond of gaiety, music, and dancing; and
devoted to showiness and dress.[82] This last was con-

[81] *Sketches of the Higher Classes of Colored Society in Philadelphia,
By a Southerner*, 37-44, 56-62, 103, 105, 107, 109. " Unlike fashionable
people of other communities, they live mostly within their incomes."
Ibid., 54, 55. " The observance of abstinence at the parties of the higher
classes of colored society—total abstinence from all that has a tendency
to intoxicate—is worthy of remark." *Ibid.*, 62. That the author is no
indiscriminate eulogist may be seen from his strictures in various places.
Cf. pp. 41, 42, 44, 82. Combe, writing two years before, said: " I have
not been able to discover whether there is a sufficient number of rich
and well educated coloured persons in this city to form a cultivated
society among themselves. I suspect there is not; and that the most accomplished individuals of the coloured race live here as in a social
wilderness, raised by their attainments above the mass of their own
people yet excluded from the society of the whites." *Notes*, II, 64. For
a negro ball, see *Inquirer*, Jan. 16, 1830. For the intelligence of the
better class of negroes in Philadelphia, *cf.* Marryat, *Diary*, I, 148, 149
(1838.)
[82] *Views of Society and Manners*, 55, 56; De la Rochefoucault Liancourt, *Travels*, II, 386; I. Holmes, *Account of the United States*, 332.

sidered a serious failing, provoking alternately the wrath of the older white citizens, and the derision of the younger. The cartoonists made great sport of it.[83] In 1797 it was said that a negress servant would wear a ball-dress worth many weeks' wages;[84] and nearly the same criticism was repeated twenty-five years later.[85] Some of the travellers grew very merry at the expense of pompous, overdressed negroes;[86] while Watson, the kindly annalist, who loved things as they had been in days gone by, spoke on one occasion as severely as he could.[87] This fondness for excessive display was sometimes exhibited in public procession. On one occasion it precipitated a riot.[88]

[83] See the ridiculous colored prints by Charles Hunt and by I. Harris (probably about 1825), in the museum of Independence Hall, Phila. These pictures ridicule the brilliant, colored clothes of the negroes, and their aping the importance of white people.

[84] "A female negro servant, whose wages are one dollar per week, will at these balls, have a dress that costs sixty dollars." De la Rochefoucault Liancourt, *Travels*, II, 386.

[85] " Many of their females dress in the most costly and extravagant manner; and with regard to the young men, there is no want of black dandys at these splendid interviews." I. Holmes, *Account*, 332 (1822).

[86] " I recollect that, frequently at Philadelphia, when desirous of ascertaining whether the beauty of some finely dressed female was equal to her attire, I perceived under a huge Leghorn bonnet and lace cap, the black face and great white eyes of a negress. Sometimes I could hardly help laughing, so ludicrous was the contrast. The black women are, indeed, so fond of dress, and so eager to imitate the fashions of the whites, that I have seen several with their wool parted in front, drawn into a knot on the top of their heads, and ornamented with a large tortoise-shell comb. Moreover some of the negresses assume the dress of Quakers, in which they appear still more ridiculous, if possible, than in the ordinary dress of the white ladies." *An Excursion through the United States and Canada during the Years 1822-23, by an English gentleman*, 25.

[87] Watson, *Annals of Philadelphia* II, 261 (1842).

[88] See below, p. 163. A writer commenting on a negro procession, says: . . . " every one of them marched as though he were in reality a Caesar or a Pompey . . . for genuine love of fanciful finery, and love of display, commend us to the African race." *Evening Bulletin*, June 26, 1855. *Cf.* also *Harrisburg Telegraph*, June 26, 1856.

Altogether it would seem that the negroes of Pennsylvania had made considerable progress. Within fifty years after the passage of the abolition act they had adjusted themselves to the new economic situation so well that they were for the most part able to support themselves, held some property, and were in possession of schools and churches. Except in one or two particulars they were theoretically upon a plane of complete equality with the white man. Moreover they had zealous friends who believed and were disposed to maintain that negroes were in all respects the equals of white people. They might seem, then, almost to have attained the goal of their desire. But the truth is that great numbers of them, save in the possession of freedom, had gained but little. Many of them dwelt in misery and squalor. Many were poor, ignorant, and oppressed. Great numbers of them were hemmed in by hostility, and found themselves unable to rise. So far as the majority of the people of Pennsylvania were concerned, negroes were cut off, thrown upon their own resources, isolated, and shunned. The causes which underlay this racial feeling will be studied separately and at length.

CHAPTER IX.

RACE PREJUDICE AND DISCRIMINATION.

THE history of the relations between the negro and the white man in Pennsylvania is largely the history of increasing race prejudice. At first there was little of it, for although from time to time some expression in the colonial laws shows that the more far-seeing men regarded negroes in the commonwealth as undesirable, yet such was the character of slavery in Pennsylvania, the negroes being few, well treated, and never feared, that toward those who were already in the colony race prejudice remained in abeyance. During the years which immediately followed the abolition act of 1780 any such feeling as may have existed was forgotten amid the universal efforts to complete the extinction of slavery, and to help the freedmen in their struggle with new conditions. During a period which extended from about 1775 to 1800 many people in Pennsylvania were disposed to think that negroes should be treated exactly like white persons, and not a few believed that the negro would soon prove in every respect the white man's equal.[1] Some of the negroes cherished the same belief.[2] Occasionally there occurred little incidents in

---

[1] Benezet, *Short Observations*, 12; Brissot, *Nouveau Voyage*, I, 301.
[2] MS. Correspondence of Dr. Benjamin Rush, XXXIX, 41 (1791).

which the more enthusiastic saw presaged the general acceptance of their theory.[3]

Soon, however, there was a change in the attitude of an increasing number of people, and hostility and race prejudice assumed more and more definite outline. At the beginning these feelings took the form of a disdainful contempt for a people so long the white man's inferior. Among certain classes an inclination developed to regard negroes as fit subjects for insult, half rough, half playful, and even for gratuitous humiliation.[4] It was not long before there was abundant evidence on all sides that between the races there yawned a great gulf, which beyond doubt had always been there, but which earlier conditions had allowed to be kept out of mind, while now it was constantly in view, and continually made wider and wider.[5]

The lower and rougher classes of white people, who were brought into closer contact with negroes, fre-

[3] The *Independent Gazeteer*, June 23, 1792, noting the death of " Mrs. Gray, a black woman ", says that the funeral was " attended . . . by a numerous concourse of people of her own color, and a very respectable procession of white citizens "; and calls " This pleasing instance of total indifference to complexion " " a happy presage of the time fast approaching, when the important declaration in holy writ will be fully verified, that ' God hath made of one blood, all the nations of the earth.' "

[4] In 1809 a traveller remarked that in Philadelphia the boys seemed to look upon themselves as privileged to insult the negroes indiscriminately, and that they did this with the manifest approbation of their elders. " A Stranger in the United States," in *Phila. Gazette*, Nov. 24, 1809.

[5] " There exists a penal law, deeply written in the *minds* of the whole white population, which subjects their coloured fellow-citizens to unconditional contumely and never ceasing insult. No respectability, however unquestionable,—no property, however large,—no character, however unblemished,—will gain a man, whose body is (in American estimation) cursed with even a twentieth portion of the blood of his African ancestry, admission into society!!! They are considered as mere Pariahs—as outcasts and vagrants upon the face of the earth! " Fearon, *Narrative*, 167, 168 (writing of Phila., 1818). *Cf.* also " Hampden," in *Norristown Herald*, Dec. 22, 1824.

quently committed acts of brutality and insolence utterly disgraceful. Thus in 1819 three women stoned a negress to death.[6] In 1825 several young men entered a negro church in Philadelphia, and just as the minister was concluding his sermon, threw a mixture of pepper into the stove. The suffocating fumes and the cries of fire caused a panic among the congregation in which some members were trampled to death and many injured.[7] In Philadelphia it often happened that harmless negroes were set upon and beaten in the streets, or struck with missiles, or cut with knives, when they were molesting no one.[8] Occasionally some horrible act of cruelty was committed, as it would appear, merely for the sake of the sport.[9] As a rule the perpetrators went unpunished ; but if a negro offended, the authorities smote him heavily. In the application of the laws there was constant discrimination, so that in the Constitutional Convention of 1837-1838 it was openly declared that the negro had small chance of being treated in courts like the white man, or of being pardoned as soon after conviction.[10]

[6] *Phila. Gazette*, June 30, 1819.

[7] *Democratic Press, Phila. Gazette*, Nov. 21, 1825.

[8] As scattered examples *cf. Phila. Gazette*, Nov. 28, 1835; *Pennsylvanian*, Nov. 3, 1845; *U. S. Gazette*, July 1, 1846; *Inquirer*, Jan. 24, 1848; Nov. 2, 1848; Apr. 8, 1854; *Spirit of the Times*, July 7, 1849; *Bulletin*, Jan. 1, 1853; July 16, 1855. Sometimes the negro driven to bay turned upon his persecutor. *Cf. Phila. Gazette*, Nov. 25, 1825.

[9] For a later example of this, see *Pennsylvanian*, June 21, 1850, which contains a notice of some wretches who, while heating pitch, seized a negro boy and thrust his legs into the boiling liquid.

[10] Mr. Earle said: . . . " if any one said so, then all he had to say was that it was contrary to his opinion." *Pro. and Deb. of the Conv.*, X, 38. From 1829 to 1848 the length of the average sentence of criminals in the Eastern Penitentiary and in the Philadelphia County Prison was, white persons, 2 years 8 months 2 days; negroes, 3 years 3 months 14 days. Of the white criminals 15% were pardoned before the end of their terms; of the negroes, 3 %. *Health and Mortality of Convicts* (1849), 7, 9; *J. of S., 1849*, vol. II, 430.

The feeling against negroes, which was strongest
in the lower classes, deepened in intensity and spread
to the more representative people of the state. It was
manifested in attempts made to effect new legal discriminations against colored people ;[11] and in their gradual exclusion from white churches and from places of
amusement.[12] In 1825 a traveller noted that in the jail
of Philadelphia County the black prisoners could not
sit on the same benches with the whites.[13] In 1838 a
negro could have access to a theatre only in a certain
part.[14]

The deepening prejudice was greatly enhanced by the
anti-slavery dissensions of the thirties. In 1831, when
the citizens of New Haven in Connecticut resolved to
oppose the establishment of a negro college there,[15] a
meeting in Philadelphia passed enthusiastic resolutions
commending their attitude in avoiding this monstrous
evil, and said that their action commanded the admira-
tion of every true lover of his country.[16] About this
time it was the custom to drive negroes away from Independence Square on the Fourth of July, since they
were considered to have had no part in the founding of
the nation.[17] In 1838 it was affirmed that the feelings

[11] J. of S., 1812-1813, p. 540; Rep. of Pa. Soc. Abol. Sl. in Min. Fourteenth Amer. Conv. Abol. Sl., Phila., 1816, p. 7.

[12] Fearon, Narrative, 167, 168; Marryat, Diary, 149.

[13] Bernhard of Saxe-Weimar, Reise, I, 227.

[14] Marryat, Diary, 149.

[15] Hazard's Register, VIII, 196.

[16] Inquirer, Dec. 1, 1831.

[17] " Whoever can call to mind a celebration of our day of Independence
in Philadelphia five and thirty years ago, may remember that the part
of the day's exercises which the boys took upon themselves was to stone
and club colored people out of Independence Square, because ' niggers
had nothing to do with the fourth of July.' " Why Colored People in
Philadelphia Are Excluded from the Street Cars (1866), 23.

of the white people were 'such that annihilation would result to the negro, if an attempt were made to let him vote.[18] In 1837 and 1838 it was repeatedly said by representative men in the most public places that negroes were and must remain an inferior and degraded race.[19] It was felt that they had made no progress, that they could make none, and that they should not be allowed to make any.[20]

The attitude of the public was such as to cause grave apprehension on the part of the negro's friends. In 1839 the Yearly Meeting of the Quakers at Philadelphia directed particular attention to the rising tide of prejudice.[21] About this time George Combe, the phrenologist, desiring that a certain negro hear one of his lectures, was compelled to get him into the hall by stealth, and keep him lurking near the door, so that no notice might be taken of his presence.[22] The same writer states that so great was the prejudice and aversion felt even by educated and humane people, that they would shrink back from the gates of Heaven if they saw a

[18] Speech of Mr. Sturdevant. *Pro. and Deb. of the Conv., 1837-1838,* IX, 328. Also *ibid.,* 349.

[19] *Ibid.,* IX, 328; *Present State . . . Free People of Color . . . Philadelphia* (1838), 4.

[20] In his speech on negro suffrage, Jan. 20, 1838, Mr. Sterigere said: " The field of industry, enterprize and science has been equally open to them.—And what instances of successful industry or enterprize, and intellectual superiority have the 40,000 negroes of this state produced? None worth notice." *Pro. and Deb. Conv.,* X, 86.

[21] "We also desire that the attention of Friends may be particularly directed towards those people of colour who reside among us, and are nominally free. This class of our fellow-men are the objects of a cruel prejudice, which there is reason to fear is rather increasing among us, and they are subjected to numerous disabilities which are very unfavorable to their moral and religious improvement." *Extract from Min. Yrly. M., April, 1839.* Broadside in H. S. P., TW* 78, vol. 2.

[22] *Notes on the United States,* II, 48, 49.

negro within.[23]   The intensity of this feeling, which
now extended from the highest to the lowest ranks of
society, was a matter of wonder to nearly every for-
eigner who visited the state.[24]

After 1840 it was admitted that no career was open
to the negro, and that he had little chance to rise.[25]
James Forten, richest and most honored among the
colored people of Philadelphia, found that he was unable
to obtain any advancement for his two sons, well edu-
.cated though they were.[26]   By some it was now asserted
that education could bring the negro no adequate recompense, since he would merely find himself possessed of
attainments that could neither be used nor rewarded.[27]
There was now less disposition to give him schools;
and for a while there was absolute unwillingness to
admit negro youths into the Philadelphia House of
Refuge.[28]   All the while the newspapers reflected the
general spirit.   Only at intervals was there a note of
protest or an offer to help.[29]   As a rule the feeling was
one of cynicism and disgust.   In 1851 the *Evening Bulletin* maintained that the negro had not been raised by

[23] *Notes on the United States*, II, 63, 64. He adds, " Only the
warmly philanthropic view them as men, and treat them with real regard."

[24] *Sketch of the Internal Condition of the United States of America*,
by a Russian (1826), 30. Capt. Marryat, *Diary*, 149, says: " Singular
is the degree of contempt and dislike in which the free blacks are held
in all the free States of America. They are deprived of their rights as
citizens; and the white pauper who holds out his hand for charity (and
there is no want of beggars in Philadelphia) will turn away from a
negro, or coloured man, with disdain " (1838).

[25] *Cf. Sketches of the Higher Classes of Colored Society*, 64.

[26] Lyell, *Travels in North America in the Years 1841-2*, etc., I, 164,
165 (1842).

[27] *Sketches of the Higher Classes*, 95, 96.

[28] *Cf.* series of letters in protest in *Pennsylvanian*, Jan. 10, 11, 14, 15,
1845.

[29] *Cf.* editorial in *Inquirer*, Mar. 27, 1848.

freedom; that he had made no progress; that in Pennsylvania he filled the jails and the alms-houses; and that the quarters in which he dwelt were pest-holes from which diseases spread. In Pennsylvania he was of right a hewer of wood and a drawer of water. If he desired to rise it would be well for him to go elsewhere. He deceived himself if he thought that he could remain there and ever escape from his servile condition.[30] By this time it had even become difficult for his friends to raise money for charitable purposes.[31] At the time, therefore, when the Civil War burst upon the country pro-slavery advocates could with some reason point to the treatment of the negro in states like Pennsylvania, and could feel that De Tocqueville was right when he said twenty-five years before, that race prejudice was stronger in those states which had abolished slavery than in those states where it still remained.[32]

These hostile and bitter feelings, which were such a travesty of the high hopes of the negro's friends, and such a tragic sequel to the auspicious beginning made by the liberators eighty years before, were the result primarily of two causes: first, the enormous influx of poor and untrained negroes from the South; and secondly the obvious worthlessness of so many of the negroes both refugee and native. In the background there was always that essential, primitive aversion which the race of one color seems to feel for the race

[30] Editorial in *Evening Bulletin*, Jan. 21, 23, Feb. 11, 1851.

[31] *Cf. The Appeal of the Religious Society of Friends . . . on Behalf of the Coloured Races* (Phila., 1858). This appeal asks: "Under the same neglect and pernicious treatment, would not the whites have exhibited equal degradation?"

[32] Nichols, *Forty Years of American Life*, II, 227-241. De Tocqueville, *Démocratie en Amérique*, II, 292, 294.

of another, and which during the last thirty years before the Civil War was increased by the fury against
"abolitionism" and the fear of disunion. Yet the two
most real and specific causes which any white man
living in Pennsylvania between 1800 and 1861 would
have advanced to explain his prejudice, were the immigration and the increase of negroes, and the increase
of negroes' crime.

Whether it would have been possible for black people
in Pennsylvania to gain full sympathy and to enjoy
such measure of equality as they deserved, supposing
that the state had had to deal only with its native
population, cannot now be known. The kindly relations at first existing between the races would have lent
enduring interest to such an experiment. But un-
fortunately Pennsylvania lay on the frontier against
slavery, with its great hordes of negroes bond and free.
As slavery in the South became more rigid, and as
laws of greater stringency against the free negro were
passed there, Pennsylvania always seemed like a haven
of liberty for runaway slaves and oppressed freedmen,
so that from the beginning of the nineteenth century
there commenced a steady stream of immigrants and
fugitives which diminished little in volume during the
next sixty years.[33] Many of these refugees were

[33] " Negroes are very numerous. This is the first city of refuge at
which they arrive after making their escape from the south." Finch,
Travels in the United States and Canada, 75 (writing of Phila., 1833).
" There is no State in the Confederacy more exposed to the incursions
of the refuse black inhabitants of others, than Pennsylvania . . . Accordingly they are daily flowing in upon her—occupying the time of her criminal courts—filling her jails and poor-houses, and sauntering through her
towns and villages in misery and want; . . . " Denny, *Political Grade of
the Free Coloured Population*, 8, 9.

wholly unfitted to maintain themselves, and became a burden upon the community wherever they went.[34]

The alarm which Pennsylvania felt over pauper negroes was evident in 1804, when an attempt was made to lay a tax on all free negroes in order to provide a sum for the maintenance of such of them as thereafter became chargeable.[35] In 1806 the Friends lamented the deterioration in character of the colored people in Philadelphia, and affirmed that the constant influx of runaways was the cause.[36] In 1815 two representatives from Philadelphia caused the appointment of a committee to consider the preventing of all immigration of negroes. A bill was introduced, which was supported by a number of petitions, but it did not become a law.[37]

The negro refugees showed a tendency to huddle together in the cities and the large towns. In these places they depressed the wages of the negroes already dwelling there, and by causing a surplus of unskilled labor gave rise to crowds of loitering, mischievous beggars, a nuisance to the community wherever they

[34] The preamble to a resolution of the House, 1824, says: " constant migrations of emancipated negroes from other states, who being in most cases deprived of the benefits of education or moral instruction, become an useless and not unfrequently a burthensome addition to her population." *J. of H., 1823-1824,* p. 824.

[35] *J. of H., 1804-1805,* pp. 114, 115. Cf. also *J. of S., 1804-1805,* pp. 256, 257, 278, 320.

[36] Rep. Pa. Soc. Abol. Sl. in *Min. Eleventh Amer. Conv. Abol. Sl., Phila., 1806,* p. 13. " Freed from the shackles, but not from the vices of slavery, those victims of inhumanity thronged our streets in search of pleasure or employment. Some indeed embrased the opportunities which everywhere presented, of obtaining an honest support. But too many served only to swell the list of our criminals and augment the catalogue of our paupers." *Min. Twelfth Amer. Conv. Abol. Sl., Phila., 1809,* p. 16.

[37] *J. of H., 1812-1813,* pp. 216, 432, 567, 588, 589; *id., 1813-1814,* p. 101. The bill was opposed by abolitionists and negroes.

stayed.[38] In 1813 the mayor, aldermen, and citizens of
Philadelphia petitioned the Legislature for relief, asking that free negroes be taxed to support their poor,
that a strict registry be kept of them, and that they be
obliged to make satisfaction for crime by servitude.
The petition stated that in Philadelphia there were four
thousand negroes not recorded.[39] Following upon this
in the next year a bill was prepared authorizing the
imprisonment at hard labor of such idle and disorderly
persons.   The bill passed the House, but was lost in
the Senate.[40]

While Philadelphia continued to ask for relief other
cities were suffering also. In 1803 there was a carefully
organized conspiracy among the negroes of York to
burn the town.[41] Fires were started in several places,
but the citizens did not realize their danger until eleven
buildings had been destroyed and six attempts made to
cause a general conflagration. Then numerous arrests
followed; after which crowds of negroes armed and
made ready to break open the jail. For a few days
there was a reign of terror; business came to a stand-
still; the place was patrolled by armed guards; and the

[38] " On they come with all the accumulated depravity which they have
been long accustomed to; such as lying, pilfering, stealing, swearing,
deceit, and a thousand meaner vices, the fruits of slavery. When they
arrive, they almost generally abandon themselves to all manner of debauchery and dissipation, to the great annoyance of many of our citizens."
Branagan, *Serious Remonstrances . . . Consisting of Speculations and
Animadversions, on the Recent Revival of the Slave Trade,* etc. (1805),
68. The author is speaking of runaways from the South.

[39] *J. of H., 1812-1813,* pp. 481, 482.

[40] *J. of H., 1813-1814,* pp. 84, 264, 448, 458, 493, 494, 495, 498; *J. of S.,
1813-1814,* pp. 417, 504.

[41] This seems to have originated in revenge for the imprisonment of a
negress convicted of poisoning. *Cf.* Prowell, *History of York County,*
788.

governor was besought to send help.[42] In the end quiet
was restored, and twenty of the miscreants punished
for arson.[43] In 1820 Harrisburg was infested with so
many idle persons, and there occurred so many fires
supposedly incendiary, that a vigilance committee was
organized, after which numbers of negroes left at
once.[44]

It is not surprising, then, that there was a constant
stream of petitions from all over the state asking the
Legislature to prevent immigration of negroes. Frequently the Legislature considered a bill to this effect,
but never passed it.[45] That no action was taken seems
to have been owing to the horror which the people of

[42] The sources are a number of letters in Miscellaneous MSS., 1738-
1806. York and Cumberland Counties, 263, 265, 267. One letter says:
" For days past, we have been alarmed by the hourly cry of Fire." Another, " Excuse this Scrawl—I am worn out."

[43] Prowell, *History of York County*, 788.

[44] *Phila. Gazette*, May 31, 1820. At this time Harrisburg found it
necessary to require every negro arriving in the town to register within
twenty-four hours in a book kept by the mayor. *Ibid.*

[45] *Cf. J. of H.*, *1819-1820*, pp. 341, 511; *J. of H.*, *1831-1832*, vol. I, 48, 58,
118, 283, 307, 338, 710, 907, 918, 932, 945, 983, 996; *J. of S.*, *1831-1832*,
pp. 797, 814; *J. of H.*, *1832-1833*, vol. I, 23, 87, 91, 100, 109, 127, 136, 144,
150, 158, 186, 261, 275, 372, 645; *J. of S.*, *1832-1833*, p. 9; *Inquirer*, Feb.
8, 1833; *J. of H.*, *1834-1835*, vol. I, 383; *J. of H.*, *1838-1839*, vol. I, 850;
J. of S., *1838-1839*, vol. I, 368, 569, 607, 666; *J. of H.*, *1842*, vol. I, 122;
J. of H., *1843*, pp. 886, 887, 907; *J. of H.*, *1852*, vol. I, 21, 59, 106, 142,
170, 191, 248. The law proposed in 1852 would have put a fine upon all
citizens of Pennsylvania who in any way encouraged a negro or mulatto
to emigrate into the commonwealth. *Cf.* (Harrisburg) *Whig State Journal*, Jan. 29, 1852. For memorial against it, *cf.* broadside TW* 78, vol.
II, H. S. P.; *J. of S.*, *1852*, pp. 76, 302, 313, 384, 398, 406, 421, 453, 510,
587, 700, 863; also numerous petitions against the law asked for; *J. of H.*,
1853, vol. I, 58, 140, 161, 167, 534, 550; *J. of H.*, *1854*, p. 101; *J. of H.*,
1855, pp. 60, 63, 90; *J. of S.*, *1855*, pp. 62, 181; *J. of H.*, *1856*, p. 180;
J. of H., *1857*, pp. 221, 302, 379, 385, 467; *J. of S.*, *1857*, pp. 111, 250, 405;
J. of H., *1857-1858*, p. 347; *J. of S.*, *1857-1858*, p. 167; *J. of S.*, *1859*, pp. 225,
391; *J. of H.*, *1860*, pp. 124, 209, 237, 265, 280, 327, 375, 440, 481, 771-
774, 835; *J. of S.*, *1860*, pp. 77, 121, 260, 303, 304, 406. *Cf.* also *Pro.
and Deb. Conv.*, *1837-1838*, I, 191; II, 199-202.

Pennsylvania had of slavery. However much they came to dislike the negro, they hated slavery more, and accordingly could never bring themselves to close their doors to the fugitive.[46] There were many, also, who believed that negroes would be peaceable and industrious if given a chance. It was for the latter reason that in 1833 the Legislature would not put a stop to the bringing in of negro servants.[47]

Nevertheless adverse sentiment continued. In 1850 a petition asked that freedom of movement be taken from negroes.[48] In the same year it was asserted that they were an insufferable burden, that they showed nearly every form of destitution and depravity, and that they afforded a scene which might well give rise to the worst apprehensions.[49] That there was some basis for such fears, may be seen from the fact that as far back as 1834 twelve per cent. of the paupers in the Philadelphia almshouse were negroes, of whom many had come from Delaware, Maryland, and Virginia.[50] In 1847 a partial enumeration of the negroes of Philadelphia showed that nearly half of them had come from outside the state.[51]

---

[46] See *J. of H.*, *1860*, pp. 771-774.

[47] *J. of S.*, *1832-1833*, vol. I, 486.

[48] *J. of H.*, *1850*, vol. I, 759.

[49] *Pennsylvanian*, Dec. 11, 1850.

[50] *Hazard's Reg.*, XV, 157.

[51] The *Statistical Inquiry* made in that year showed that the total number of negroes in Philadelphia was 20,240. Of those whose birth-place was ascertained 8,900 or 57.3% were natives of the state, 6,632 or 42.7% came from other places. The *Inquiry* says that "the free coloured population is constantly augmented from the emancipated and fugitive slaves of the South". This explained how the increase of the negro population of the city was maintained in the face of a much higher death rate than that prevailing among the white people. *A Statistical Inquiry*, 6, 9, 10.

The second cause of race prejudice in Pennsylvania
was the apparent deterioration in character of the negroes there, and the immense increase in the number of
their crimes. In colonial days negro criminals had not
been lacking; but either because of stricter control then,
or because of better disposition, negroes had never attracted special attention because of their evil deeds,
nor as a class seemed abnormally vicious. For a generation after slavery had come to an end no great
change could be noticed; and though from time to
time some serious complaints were made, generally the
charge was that negroes were saucy, or that they
were not improving as fast as the efforts made for
them would warrant.[52] Afterwards, however, an immense change was apparent.

Thus in the winter of 1821-1822 the streets of Philadelphia became dangerous by night and unsafe by
day.[53] The newspapers were forced to lay special stress
upon the situation,[54] and the governor in his message
of the following winter said that the records of the
criminal courts furnished incontestable evidence that
within the past five years crime among the people of
color had increased faster than they had increased in
numbers.[55] In 1823 the grand jury of Philadelphia
presented the great number of tippling-houses, dram-

[52] Branagan, *Serious Remonstrances*, 68, 69 (note); *Phila. Gazette*,
July 22, Aug. 1, 1805; Dec. 3, 1806; Jan. 20, Feb. 15, 1808; *General Advertiser*, Jan. 21, 1806; Weld, *Travels through the States of North
America, and the Provinces of Upper and Lower Canada during the
years 1795, 1796 and 1797*, p. 36 (1795); *Min. Sixth Conv. Abol. Socs.,
Phila., 1800*, pp. 6, 7.
[53] *National Gazette*, Nov. 23, 30, 1821; *Phila. Gazette*, Nov. 24, 1821,
Feb. 11, 1822. *Cf. ibid.*, Feb. 14, 18, 1822.
[54] *Cf.* "Justitia" in the *Phila. Gazette*, May 12, 1822.
[55] 4 *Pa. Arch.*, V, 386. In 1821 there were sent to the Philadelphia
penitentiary 113 negroes and 197 white people. *Cf.* Rep. of the Visiting
Committee, *Phila. Gazette*, Oct. 18, 1822.

shops, and cheap dancing-halls in the alleys of the negro quarters, and recommended a law making it more difficult for negroes to become domiciled in Pennsylvania.[56] This condition of affairs was not characteristic of Philadelphia only, though most evident there; it was a matter for alarm in widely different parts of the state.[57] In Harrisburg in 1836 it was necessary for strangers to be careful in passing through the by-streets, for they were infested with worthless negroes ready to commit any crime.[58]

The disproportionate criminality of negroes attracted much attention. In some years their crime was four times as great as their numbers warranted.[59] The jails, the prisons, the penitentiaries were crowded with them.[60] Again and again the leading men of the state referred to this fact.[61] In 1836 a committee of the Sen-

[56] *Phila. Gazette*, Mar. 20, 1823.
[57] Cf. *Doylestown Democrat*, Jan. 24, 1825; *Phila. Gazette*, Apr. 28, 1825 (Norristown); *Upland Union* in *Phila. Gaz.*, Jan. 26, 1826; *Reading Chronicle* in *Phila. Gaz.*, July 28, 1827; *Butler Repository* in *Inquirer*, July 19, 1830; *Germantown Telegraph* in *Phila. Gaz.*, Oct. 29, 1835.
[58] *Harrisburg Republican* in *Phila. Gazette*, May 9, 1836. In 1842 the people of Harrisburg petitioned that the town council might have additional powers to deal with the colored population. *J. of S.*, 1842, vol. I, 1006.
[59] Cf. tables for the years 1823, 1824, 1825, 1826, printed in the *Phila. Gazette*, Mar. 5, 1828.

Ct. Quar. Sess.				Oyer and Terminer				Mayor's Court			
White		Black		White		Black		White		Black	
M.	F.	M.	F.	M.	F.	M.	F.	M.	F.	M.	F.
169	134	110	117	7	3	7	6	201	59	135	101
183	140	116	104	12	7	9	4	144	57	77	61
158	86	89	121	11	5	6	0	213	50	87	52
184	98	95	124	10	1	7	3	133	34	56	49
694	458	410	466	40	16	29	13	691	200	355	263

Cf. also *Hazard's Register*, I, 244, 247.
[60] Cf. *Hazard's Register*, III, 214; *Health and Morality of Convicts*, 3.
[61] Cf. *Hazard's Register*, II, 356; J. R. Tyson, *Discourse before the Young Men's Colonization Society of Pennsylvania*, 15.

ate reported that the prisons and the poor-houses were filled with negroes, and that in a few years the disparity of crime would be absolutely intolerable.[62] Meanwhile brawls occurred, the streets were unsafe, houses were broken into, men and women were insulted.[63] It is altogether useless to attempt to catalogue these crimes. It is sufficient to say that the newspapers continually record them.[64] In 1837 the records of the Eastern Penitentiary for seven years showed that negroes committed thirty-six per cent. of criminal deeds in Philadelphia.[65] At this time they constituted nine per cent. of the city's population. During the next ten years the figures showed no change for the better;[66] while during the ten years thereafter other sources show that there was little improvement.[67] It was on the strength of such evidence as this that just before the Civil War a proslavery writer asserted that in Pennsylvania freedom had caused the negro to deteriorate, and that he had

[62] *J. of S., 1835-1836*, vol. I, 680.

[63] *Cf. Phila. Gazette*, July 19, 1837; *Inquirer*, Aug. 11, 1837; *Columbia Spy*, Oct. 28, 1837; (Harrisburg) *Chronicle*, Mar. 1, 1837.

[64] See for example, *Dauphin Guardian*, Jan. 5, 1808; *Franklin Gazette*, Dec. 6, 1819; (York) *Independent Republican*, July 3, 1821; *U. S. Gazette*, Feb. 15, 1828; July 19, 1837; *Phila. Gazette*, Dec. 23, 1829; June 27, 1832; Jan. 9, 1836; Jan. 9, June 23, Oct. 23, 1837; Jan. 2, 11, 13, Feb. 6, 11, 25, Mar. 5, May 26, June 12, 1841; *Greensburg Gazette*, May 6, 1825; (Lancaster) *Anti-Masonic Herald*, Nov. 19, 1830; *Inquirer*, June 26, 1830; Nov. 21, Dec. 29, 1831; Apr. 28, Dec. 25, 1834; June 20, 1837; Sept. 5, 1848; *American Sentinel*, Jan. 12, 1836; *Pennsylvanian*, July 29, Aug. 20, Nov. 30, Dec. 21, 26, 1836; Feb. 25, Sept. 10, 1842; Sept. 7, 1843; Jan. 8, 1850; Feb. 24, 1857; *Crawford Democrat*, Jan. 9, 1838; *Spirit of the Times*, Mar. 22, 1849; *Bulletin*, Aug. 15, 1851; *Public Ledger*, Apr. 27, 1857; *North American*, Mar. 7, 1857; (Greensburg) *Herald*, Mar. 30, 1859; (Harrisburg) *Daily Patriot*, Sept. 6, 1859.

[65] *Present State of the Free People of Color*, 17.

[66] *Statistical Inquiry*, 28; *J. of S., 1849*, vol. II, 430.

[67] *Cf.* Tenth Annual Rep. Phila. Co. Prison, in *Pennsylvanian*, Mar. 11, 1857.

there revealed such characteristics as to make evident
his need for supervision and restraint.[68]

It was in vain that such friends as the negro still had
pointed out that a great part of all this crime was committed by fugitive slaves and illiterate freedmen from
the South, and that even in Pennsylvania, since the
negro often lacked opportunity and lived in the midst
of poverty and want, he was continually beset with
temptations which he had not yet learned to resist.[69]
These arguments were not accepted. For most people
it was sufficient that the deeds were done by black
men.

In addition there was another cause of an entirely
different nature. If great numbers of negroes fell into
disrepute because of their poverty, idleness, and crime,
many more were disliked because of their efficient industry and their successful competition with white
laborers. After 1780 the more reliable negroes began
to monopolize certain occupations, and as time went
on, what with their own improvement, what with the

[68] Nichols, *Forty Years*, etc., II, 239. *Cf.* also Watson, Annals
(author's MS), 534: "The Slaves of Philada were a happier class of
People than the free blacks of the present day generally are, . . . who taint
the very air by their vices & exhibit every sort of wretchedness and pro-
fligacy in their dwellings." For a rather favorable judgment as to the
conduct of the negroes in Pennsylvania, see *Remarks of Dr. J. R. Burden, of Philadelphia Co. . . . on the Abolition Question*, etc. (1838), 8, 9.

[69] "First, their necessities, then their want of education, and then the
temptation of the dram-shop, lead them step by step to a life of indolence
and crime; and the criminal records of all the courts are therefore greatly
swelled by the offences of the free coloured population." Buckingham,
Eastern and Western States, II, 25, 26 (1842). At this time, the author
says, the proportion of the negroes to the whole population was 1:33,
the proportion of their crime to that of white people, 1: 3. *Ibid.* In
1847 it was asserted that of the negro criminals 33.7% were from free
states, 66.3% from slave states. Needles, *Ten Years' Progress*, 12, 13.
Cf. Statistical Inquiry, 28. For the relative numbers of negroes and
white people in Pennsylvania at different times, see Appendix.

continual assistance of the Pennsylvania Abolition Society, they were able to make their competition felt. In 1834 white men in Philadelphia demanded that for certain work negroes should not be employed.[70] In 1838 it was asserted that the domestic servants there were all negroes, that negro women were beginning to displace white seamstresses, and that further immigration of Southern negroes would certainly depress the wages of white laborers and artisans.[71] In magnitude this cause of prejudice was less than either of the others; but it was based on a deep seated belief, which found expression at frequent intervals.[72]

Since therefore the constant influx of negroes was accompanied both by the economic pressure of the good, and the crime and lawlessness of the bad; since in spite of every discouragement men saw new negroes coming every year; since they saw wages depressed and the labor market overstocked; since they witnessed the unwise provocation on the part of impudent negroes and the continued series of graver crimes, robberies, burglaries, murders, and assaults; it is not difficult to understand how some sudden happening, or some act of exceptional atrocity, could cause wild outbursts of

---

[70] *Niles's Register,* XLVI, 441. Niles thought " This is going a ' considerable length.' "

[71] " Twenty years ago the poor man had no hesitation in placing his daughter in a respectable family as a servant; . . . The fashion became general to have colored servants. They could be obtained at lower wages, and the white girl, who had respect for herself, could not put herself on an equality with colored servants: few places were left where white girls could be employed. Unable to get employment as servants, the needle is the next resort; so many are thrown on that means of subsistence that prices are reduced; even here colored females, to a limited extent, enter into competition." Dr. Burden, *Remarks* (1838), 10.

[72] *Cf.* (Harrisburg) *Key Stone,* June 10, 1851.

passion such as were witnessed in Philadelphia and elsewhere in the years from 1832 to 1849.

The first negro riot in Philadelphia occurred in 1834. Previous to that time there had been occasional disturbances between negroes and white men,[73] but in that year many signs foreboded graver trouble. At this time "abolitionism" had awakened extreme wrath in all the Middle States, and the slightest provocation, in some instances the mere sight of a negro, had been sufficient to bring about an explosion in the Eastern cities. During July there was a disturbance at Newark, and a terrible riot at New York.[74] These events had been seized upon by the Philadelphia papers, which solemnly warned abolitionists not to come to the city, and at the same time admonished the negroes not to provoke a disaster which seemed to be in the very air. In spite of these warnings the disaster came on August 12.[75]

A crowd of men and boys began by demolishing a notorious resort. After this a mob surged down through the negro quarters committing violence of every kind, while great crowds of negroes and white men fought with clubs and stones. On the next day a mob ruined the African Presbyterian Church, after which they attacked negro houses promiscuously, ripping up the beds, destroying the furniture, and beating negroes in dreadful fashion. In such barbarous frenzy were the rioters that in one house they hurled a corpse out of its coffin, and in another they threw a dead baby on the floor. On the next day the police, at first almost power-

[73] U. S. Gazette, Oct. 10, 12, 1832; Phila. Gazette, Oct. 10, 1832.

[74] Newark Daily Advertiser, July 12, 1834; New York Journal of Commerce, July 12, 1834; New York Commercial Advertiser, July 12, 1834.

[75] Cf. Pennsylvanian, July 11, 14, 1834; U. S. Gazette, July 11, 12, 1834; Inquirer, July 14, 15, 16, 28, 1834; Phila. Gazette, July 14, 1834.

less, gradually put a stop to the violence ; but not until a church in Southwark had been entirely destroyed, and a battle with armed negroes had with difficulty been averted. During these three days a great deal of property owned by negroes was destroyed ; while the negroes themselves were completely terror-stricken.[76] A committee of citizens, who were appointed to enquire into the cause of this trouble, reported that the rioters had deliberately destroyed property in order to make negroes go away ; that they were moved to their hatred because they believed that negro labor was depriving them of work ; because negroes had notoriously shielded their criminals ; and because negro churches, owing to their noise and disorder, had come to be regarded as a nuisance to the neighborhood.[77] The better people of Philadelphia deplored the violence and injustice which had been perpetrated ; yet within a year like scenes were enacted again.

In 1835 an attempt to murder a gentleman was made by a half-witted negro. Immediately the public mind became much excited, and in spite of efforts to preserve order, a huge mob collected and rioted through the streets. Everywhere the negroes fled, such as were overtaken being shamefully beaten. A row of negro houses was attacked, and one being set on fire the firemen were not allowed to come near it. As showing the temper of the people, it was said that many respectable

---

[76] *Hazard's Register*, XIV, 126-128; *Phila. Gazette*, Aug. 14, 15, 19, 1834; *U. S. Gazette*, Aug. 15, 1834; *Inquirer*, Aug. 14, 15, 18, 19, 20, 1834; *Niles's Register*, XLVI, 413, 435. On August 20 there was again a disturbance, though a slight one. See *Inquirer*, Aug. 22, 1834. At Columbia there were several disturbances, one of which was serious. See *Columbia Spy*, Aug. 23, 30, Oct. 2, 1834; *Hazard's Register*, XIV, 143, 175; *Phila. Gazette*, Aug. 25, 1834; *Inquirer*, Oct. 7, 1834.

[77] Report in *Hazard's Register*, XIV, 201-203.

citizens swelled the crowd of spectators, while the in-
activity of the police was a matter of comment.[78]

The next disturbance, which occurred in 1838, was
directed less against the negroes than against the "abolitionists ". On May 14 of that year there was opened
in Philadelphia a place of assembly called Pennsylvania
Hall. It was afterwards said that this hall had been
erected as a place for the discussion of various subjects,
but during the four days of its existence the exercises
consisted almost entirely of speeches by noted anti-
slavery advocates on slavery and abolition.[79] During
these days the public mind was much inflamed by reports that the black and the white delegates walked to
the hall arm in arm, and that they sat together without
any distinction.[80] Meanwhile men were seen prowling
around the building, and occasionally stones were
hurled through the windows, so that appeals were
made for protection; but the authorities dallied, until
on the night of May 17 a mob gathered. The mayor
asked the crowd to be orderly; but the tone of his
speech was such that immediately upon his departure
the building was set on fire and burned to the ground.
On the next day it seemed as though pandemonium had
broken loose.[81] When night came there was fighting in

[78] *Hazard's Register*, XVI, 36-38; *Phila. Gazette*, July 13, 14, 15, 16,
17, 18, 1835; *Sentinel*, July 14, 15, 1835; *Pennsylvanian*, July 15, 16,
1835; Isaac Parrish, *Brief Memoirs of Thomas Shipley and Edwin P.
Atlee*, 8-11.

[79] Cf. *History of Pennsylvania Hall, Which Was Destroyed by a Mob*,
3-137.

[80] *Sentinel*, May, 19, 1838; Buckingham, *Eastern and Western States*,
II, 94. For a somewhat similar occurrence about 1793, cf. *Diary* of the
Chevalier de Pontgibaud, who calls it a " gratuitous insult to the manners
and customs which prevail in the country "; quoted in Sachse, *The
Religious and Social Conditions of Philadelphia, 1790-1800*, p. 18.

[81] *History of Pennsylvania Hall*, 140.

the streets between negroes and white men, and a mob set fire to the colored orphan asylum and attacked a colored church. Quiet was presently restored, but the attitude of Philadelphia was sufficiently shown in that the authorities declared that the mob had been composed of strangers, and that none were recognized.[82] The trustees of the hall made a claim for damages, but their claim was dragging its way through unsympathetic commissions as late as 1840, and was still before the courts in 1847.[83]

In 1839 there was a disturbance at Pittsburg, in which several negro tenements were pulled down;[84] but there was nothing of great consequence until in 1842 there was another serious outbreak in Philadelphia on the occasion of a negro procession. It was a time not only when race feeling was running high, but when thousands of laborers were out of work. Nevertheless on August 1 the negroes of the city rashly undertook to celebrate the abolition of slavery in the West Indies by an ostentatious parade, in which they carried suggestive emblematic banners. Almost immediately an attempt was made to break up the procession, and for two hours the streets were the scene of a violent battle with bricks and stones, in which many people were wounded. In the afternoon immense crowds had collected; houses occupied by negroes were pelted with stones; and when two boys passing an alley were fired

[82] *Ibid.*
[83] 5 *Pa. State Rep.* (Barr), 204-210. On the whole subject of this riot, see *U. S. Gazette*, May 16, 18, 19, 21, 22, 1838; *American Daily Advertiser*, May 19, 22, 1838; *Pennsylvanian*, May 18, 19, 20, 21, 24, 1838; *Sentinel*, May 18, 19, 20, 1838; *History of Pennsylvania Hall, Which Was Destroyed by a Mob, Phila., 1838*; Sturge, *A Visit to the United States in 1841*, p. 42; Sleigh, *Abolitionism Exposed*, preface.
[84] *Pittsburg Advocate*, in *Phila. Gazette*, May 6, 1839.

upon, negroes were dragged out and frightfully beaten, and boys and old men were hunted down like noxious animals.[85] That night the large, new African Hall was burned by incendiaries, as was also the Colored Presbyterian Church. On the morrow negro families could be seen fleeing for their lives; and quiet was only restored with the aid of troops and extra police. The newspapers now spoke with less sympathy than before, and the grand jury laid the blame upon the procession.[86]

For some years after this event there was comparative quiet, interrupted only by minor disturbances,[87] but in 1849 on election night the "Killers of Moyamensing" led a raid upon the blacks of St. Mary Street. There ensued a fierce fight with firearms, in which many people were wounded, and in the course of which a great fire broke out. When the engines appeared the rioters kept them away. Again it was necessary to summon military aid.[88]

These disgraceful occurrences, which at one time gained for Philadelphia, particularly, an evil reputation, had their immediate causes in various things. Thus, it is certain that "abolitionism" brought on the upheavals of 1834 and 1838; that the attempt upon the life of a well known man caused the one in 1835; that a period of depression and unemployment greatly contributed to the one in 1842; and that excitement attending the election caused the one in 1849. Notwith-

[85] *Phila. Gazette*, Aug. 8, 1842.
[86] *U. S. Gazette*, Aug. 5, 1842. For this riot, see *Pennsylvanian*, Aug. 2, 3, 4, 1842; *U. S. Gazette*, Aug. 2, 3, 4, 5, 1842; *Phila. Gazette*, Aug. 2, 3, 4, 8, 1842.
[87] See for example Reed *v.* Bias (1844), 8 Watts and Sergeant 189-191.
[88] *Spirit of the Times*, Oct. 10, 11, 12, 13, 17, 19, 1849. This riot was partly caused by reason of a negro who was living with a white wife. *Ibid.*, Oct. 11.

standing this, a careful study of each one of these riots makes inevitable the deduction that the deep, underlying cause which made every one of them possible, and which prepared them long before they burst forth, was a fierce, and at least among the lower classes, an almost universal, hatred of the negro himself.

The most logical development of this dislike for the negro was seen in the persistent efforts made to get him out of the state. In Pennsylvania the scheme of colonization had its origin in kindly efforts made to send the negro to a country which he could call his own. As far back as 1817 the question was agitated, and in that year the negroes of Philadelphia held a meeting to consider it. The attitude adopted in this meeting they maintained consistently for the next forty years. They were contented, they said, with their present situation. In Pennsylvania they enjoyed the protection of just government and laws, while in Africa they would be separated from their friends. There, too, they could not but anticipate hardships. Hence they respectfully asked that they should not be urged to go.[89] Among white people, however, the idea became very popular, and was sanctioned in numerous meetings held throughout the state.[90] Strong efforts were made to get the Legislature to appropriate money for transportation,[91] so that the negroes protested in great alarm. Some of the newspapers supported them; while Garrison,

[89] Appendix, I-IV, of *Min. Special Meeting Fifteenth American Conv. Abol. Sl., Phila., 1818. Cf.* Garrison, *Thoughts on African Colonization,* pt. II, 9.
[90] M. Carey, *Letters on the Colonization Society,* 18, 19.
[91] *J. of S., 1826-1827,* pp. 363, 394; *id., 1827-1828,* pp. 116, 133, 275; *J. of H., 1827-1828,* pp. 106, 117, 142, 148, 156, 179, 180, 192, 201, 209, 231, 268, 436, 609; *Inquirer,* Dec. 1, 1831; *J. of H., 1831-1832,* vol. I, 66, 143, 153, 174, 175.

addressing a colored assemblage at Philadelphia, told them to abandon all thoughts of colonization, and maintain their rights as they would defend their lives.[92] The negroes solemnly remonstrated against the use of coercive measures to further their departure.[93] At a convention held in 1833 they proclaimed that in Pennsylvania they were born, and in Pennsylvania they would live and die.[94]

After 1830 the dominant idea was that the removal of the negro would not only be good for the negro, but very good for the white man. This feeling, which had existed from the start, and which had been growing for some years,[95] gathered great force in the troublous times of Philadelphia's riots. In 1836 the Young Men's Colonization Society petitioned the Legislature for assistance in carrying out its work, and in that year and the years following petitions that such aid be granted came from all parts of the state.[96] At this time a committee of the Senate recommended that in view of the great increase in the numbers of negroes, and their undesirable character, this aid be granted.[97] On one occasion it seemed likely that a substantial appropriation would be made; but the plan came to nothing.[98]

---

[92] *Phila. Gazette,* Dec. 9, 1819; Sept. 16, 1824. In 1831 and 1832 the negroes issued protests at Columbia, Harrisburg, Pittsburg, and Lewistown. *Cf.* Garrison, *Thoughts,* etc., pt. II, 31, 34, 40, 49; *Liberator,* July 9, 1831; Garrison, *An Address Delivered before the Free People of Color, in Philadelphia, New York,* etc. (1831), 16, 17.

[93] *Min. Second Conv. Improvement Free People of Color,* (1832), 8.

[94] *Inquirer,* Apr. 30, 1833.

[95] *Cf. Tour through Parts of the United States and Canada by a British Subject,* 29.

[96] *J. of S., 1835-1836,* vol. I., 338, 795; *J. of S., 1835-1836,* vol. I., 213, 240, 248, 260, 266, 278, 291, 332, 352, 371, 389, 405, 442, 678, 721; *J. of H., 1836-1837,* vol. I, 240, 241, 310, 344, 371, 406, 437, 467, 513, 547, 579, 641, 671, 770, 900, 959; *J. of H., 1837-1838,* vol. I, 219, 262, 324, 351, 423, 532, 586.

[97] A minority dissented. *J. of S., 1835-1836,* vol. I, 679-682.

[98] *Pro. and Deb. Conv. 1837-1838,* vol. X, 274; *J. of S., 1837-1838,* vol. I, 616.

Meetings continued to be held for the purpose of devising plans for sending negroes away; numerous colonization societies were formed; and more drastic measures were considered. In 1840 it was proposed to lay a tax upon all free negroes in the state in order to assist them in getting out of it.[99] In 1850 citizens of Lehigh County asked the authorities to expel all negroes and persons of color from the state.[100] This may be said to have marked the culmination of such efforts, for although the Pennsylvania House of Representatives continued to deal with the question, and though the newspapers gave it editorial support, the efforts diminished in strength and in number, and accomplished substantially nothing. Indeed the project had been impracticable from the first. Not only was it contrary to what was held to be right by some of Pennsylvania's best citizens,[101] but it had also to encounter physical obstacles of such stupendous magnitude, obstacles involved in the removal and transportation of many thousands of unwilling people, that the scheme was then, as since, looked upon as hopeless if not impossible; a matter less to be expected than desired.

It may therefore be seen that the residence of the negro in Pennsylvania was a cause of irritation constantly increasing. Efforts were made to keep him from entering the state; efforts were made to get him to go out. That neither of these designs proved

---

[99] *African Repository*, VIII, 125, 283; XI, 185, 347, 348; XIV, 63; J. of H., *1840*, vol. I, 347, 508, 614, 622, 623, 680; J. of S., *1840*, p. 275.
[100] J. of S., *1850*, vol. I, 454, 479.
[101] Not by the majority, however. "The belief is common to the mass of whites in the north, that the blacks are living among them merely by sufferance, and that, without the shadow of wrong, they might become subject to general deportation " . . . *The African's Right to Citizenship*, etc. (Phila., 1865), p. 6.

possible of accomplishment served only to render his presence more obnoxious. It will now be possible to understand more clearly the attempts that were made to abridge his rights and curtail his privileges: especially the memorable contest over the suffrage in the years 1837 and 1838.

CHAPTER X.

THE SUFFRAGE.

IT has been shown that the rise of the negro in Pennsylvania was gradual; that before he became free he mounted up through successive stages of servitude; and that on gaining freedom his status for a long while was not that of the white man. After 1780, when the free negro received civil equality, he might seem to have finished his ascent; but later, when the question of his political status was agitated, it was seen that his citizenship was not yet complete, and that he had not the full rights of a freeman, because he could not vote. Since in Pennsylvania the franchise depended upon the paying of taxes, the political rights of the negro could not be a pressing issue in the early stages of his economic rise. As a matter of fact they provoked almost no discussion until the famous controversy in 1837-1838.

In the spring of 1837 a Convention assembled to draft a new constitution for the state. The question of negro suffrage does seem to have been attracting attention at this time,[1] but when the article of the constitution relating to the qualifications of an elector was reached, it was proposed in the Convention to limit the

---

[1] There had been little, if any, notice of it in the papers.

franchise to white men.[2]   An interesting discussion
followed in which some took the ground that a negro
holding property might vote,[3] others that he never had
had such a right.[4]   The prevailing comment was that to
allow him the franchise would be inexpedient and undesirable, that it would conduce to social equality, and
that it would bring ruin upon the negro's head.[5]   After
a while, however, a new clause was adopted which did
not specifically exclude negroes.[6]   Shortly after the
Convention was adjourned for the summer.[7]

During these months the discussion had attracted little popular attention.   Outside of the Convention it does
not seem to have created any noticeable interest.   In
the fall, however, the question was suddenly brought
into the field of politics, when it assumed an importance
which it was destined not to lose for the next thirty
years.

In October, 1837, in Bucks County a defeated candi-

---

[2] " In elections by the citizens, every freeman of the age of twenty-
one years, having resided in the State two years next before the election, and within that time paid a State or county tax, which shall have
been assessed at least six months before the election, shall enjoy the
rights of an elector." Constitution of 1790, art. III, sect. I, Poore,
Federal and State Constitutions, II, 1551. For the debate see *Pro. and
Deb. Conv.,* I, 164, 191, 233, 270, 293; II, 470, 472.

[3] *Ibid.,* II, 476, 478, 479.

[4] *Ibid.,* III, 91.

[5] *Ibid.,* II, 477, 478, 549.   "Every negro in the State, worthy and
worthless—degraded and debased, as nine-tenths of them are, will rush
to the polls in senseless and unmeaning triumph.   The chimney sweep
and the boot black will eat the fruits of liberty with the virtuous
mechanic, laboring man, farmer, and merchant." *Ibid.,* II, 540, 541.
" There are some wards of the city, in which I find, if the Constitution
give them the right, that they will be able, not only to carry the wards,
but to distribute all the offices." Mr. Martin, Phila., *ibid.,* III, 83. Also
ibid., III, 84, 89.

[6] *Ibid.,* III, 91.

[7] The Convention reassembled at Harrisburg on October 17.   On November 23 it removed to Philadelphia.

date for a local office laid claim to his opponent's seat
on the ground that negroes had voted for his opponent,
and that this was contrary to law.[8] That the question,
in spite of its apparent suddenness, was not entirely
new at the time, is shown by the magnitude of the
forces set in motion. The Democratic organization in
Bucks County, feeling its power threatened, held a
meeting at once, and resolved to try three methods of
excluding the negro vote: to petition the Legislature, to
take the matter before the courts, and to have the ob-
scure phrase in the constitution so amended as to exclude negroes indubitably.[9] Meanwhile the newspapers
related and magnified the affair. It was asserted that
negroes had gone to the polls armed; that they had
threatened to shoot down whoever questioned them;
and that they had been incited to this by members of the
Abolition Society.[10] In addition it was made plain that
negroes had voted in a number of localities.[11] This
awakened astonishment in Philadelphia, where there
was a greater number than in any other place, but
where, it was said, no negro had ever cast a vote.[12]

[8] *Sentinel*, Nov. 11, 1837.

[9] *Pennsylvanian*, Oct. 30, 1837; *Sentinel*, Nov. 7, 1837; Davis, " Negro
Suffrage in Pennsylvania," *Era Magazine*, XII, 385 (1903). Also *Sentinel*, Nov. 11, 1837.

[10] *Bedford Gazette*, Nov. 17, 1837; Davis, *ibid.* Among those accused
of inciting the negroes was one whose name became ominous in the South
many years later. " Thaddeus Stevens!—a man who has taught the
NEGROES to contend for the rights of a white man at the polls! by his
zealous support of the accursed doctrines of ABOLITION." *Bedford
Gazette*, Nov. 17, 1837.

[11] *Pennsylvanian*, Oct. 30, 31, 1837.

[12] The *Pennsylvanian*, Oct. 30, 1837, said that while both parties at times
procured votes from other States, nevertheless, although there were
25,000 (*sic*) negroes in Philadelphia, " no person has ever been found so
base and unprincipled as to lead Negro voters to the polls, as such votes
would be rejected as illegal by all parties."

In December Judge Fox of the Bucks County Court, to which the case had been brought, handed down a decision that the complainant had been legally elected His opinion displayed much learning and ability, and was substantially the basis of similar opinions thereafter. He declared that the right of negroes to vote depended upon the interpretation of the constitution, which said that in elections by the citizens all "freemen" under certain circumstances should have the privilege. The negro, he said, was not a freeman in Pennsylvania, and had not been from the first.

Judge Fox asserted that among the fundamental principles of Penn's government these two were of the most importance: the right of freemen to choose an Assembly and to be chosen to it, and the right of trial by jury. But negroes could not have participated in the early Assemblies, since the members were to have all the rights and privileges of free born subjects of England, and such as were usual in the King's American plantations; while on the other hand almost immediately after the issuing of Penn's charter of privileges, which guaranteed trial by jury to freemen, there was passed a law for the trial and punishment of negroes, of such effect that a negro could be hanged on the summary judgment and sentence of a special court.[13] Thus

13 In 1701 it was proclaimed that the freemen should choose an Assembly which " shall have all other Powers and Privileges of an Assembly, according to the Rights of the free-born Subjects of England, and as is usual in any of the King's Plantations in America." Charter of Privileges, Poore, *Federal and State Constitutions*, II, 1538. According to the " Laws agreed upon in England " " every Inhabitant in the said province, that is or shall be a purchaser of one hundred acres of land or upwards, his heirs and assigns, and every person who shall have paid his passage, and taken up one hundred acres of land, at one penny an acre, and have cultivated ten acres thereof, and every person that hath been a servant or bondman, and is free by his service, that shall have taken up his fifty

it was certain that at the establishment of Pennsylvania
the negroes who were slaves had neither of these most
important rights of citizenship. Furthermore the law
for the regulation of free negroes passed in 1725-1726
was such that it could not be supposed that negroes
even if free were freemen under the charter and laws
of Pennsylvania; for although they might be free from
the control of a private master, yet they occupied an
inferior status in relation to the government. White
men were governed by one code of laws made by themselves, negroes by another code made by the white men.
It was plain, therefore, that a free negro was not a freeman as the term was understood by the provincial law-
makers. In 1776 the first state constitution provided
that elections should be by every freeman,[14] and as it
made no provision for free negroes, it left their status
unchanged.[15] The act for the abolition of slavery,
passed in 1780, gave negroes no political rights, since
the Assembly had no power to do this.[16] The constitution adopted in 1790 made no change.[17] In 1790, said
Judge Fox, Pennsylvania had taken the Federal Constitution as a model. In 1789, when this Constitution

---

acres of land, and cultivated twenty thereof, and every inhabitant, ar-
tificer, or other resident in the said province, that pays scot and lot to the
government, shall be deemed and accounted a freeman " . . . *Laws of
the Province of Pennsylvania, 1682-1700*, p. 99. Also *ibid.*, 246, 247.

[14] " Every freeman of the full age of twenty-one years, having resided
in this state for the space of one whole year next before the day of
election for representatives, and paid taxes during that time, shall enjoy
the right of an elector " . . . Sect. 6, Poore, II, 1542.

[15] " The Convention of 1776, in making a frame of Government, acted
as if no such beings as negroes were in existence." *Opinion of Judge
Fox.*

[16] " The Legislature could not give the negro political power. They
could not bring within the words of the Constitution a class of men not
comprehended by the Convention which framed it." *Ibid.*

[17] Poore, II, 1551.

was adopted, only five of the states had done anything
to abolish slavery, yet the Constitution said that the
citizens of one state should be entitled to all the privileges of the citizens of another. Was it likely that the
Southern states would have adopted the Constitution
if they had thought that free negroes from the North
could have citizenship within their borders? Moreover, by the state constitution the right to bear arms
was guaranteed to citizens;[18] and negroes had not been
allowed to do this. The Federal naturalization law
passed in 1802 expressly confined to white people the
right of becoming citizens.[19] As to Pennsylvania herself, in the terrible crisis of 1776 she would not have
taken the dangerous step of giving negroes the right to
vote. In 1790 things were left as before. The best
proof that it had never been the intention to let negroes
be freemen was that in Philadelphia, where they were
most numerous, they had never had the franchise.
Therefore, he said, in Pennsylvania the negro was not
a freeman, and had not the right to vote.[20]

During the weeks between the October meeting of
protest and the rendering of Judge Fox's decision the
whole question had attained a publicity, and awakened
an interest, which were manifest in the numerous petitions sent to the Constitutional Convention when it

[18] " That the people have a right to bear arms for the defense of
themselves and the state " . . . Constitution of 1776. Poore, II, 1542.
[19] "An Act to establish an uniform rule of Naturalization," etc., . . .
" any alien being a free white person, may be admitted to become a citizen
of the United States, . . . on the following conditions," . . . Stat. at
Large of the U. S., Seventh Cong., sess. I, ch. 28. Cf. ibid., Eighteenth
Cong., sess. I, ch. 186 (1824).
[20] Opinion of the Hon. John Fox . . . against the Exercise of Negro Suffrage in Pennsylvania (Harrisburg, 1838). It should be remarked that
during the debates in the Convention it was said that formerly Judge Fox
had himself led negroes to the polls. Pro. and Deb. Conv., X, 48.

reassembled. Many of these favored the negro, but the majority were against him.[21] On the sixteenth of November a petition from citizens of Bucks County was presented praying for a constitutional provision specifically excluding negroes from the right of suffrage.[22] The question was thus reopened for debate.

The arguments that followed were long, and some of them were able. In character some were historical and legal, others ethical and sentimental. While it was upon the legal arguments that Pennsylvania rested her case, yet she was brought to her decision largely through reasons of prejudice and expedience. The arguments may be grouped as follows:

The negro ought not to have the suffrage because it was contrary to the law, and because it would be bad policy. In the first place he had never been a citizen in the full sense of the term either under the colonial laws, or by the first constitution, or because of the act of 1780, or by reason of the constitution then in force.[23] That he was partly a citizen was true so far as he was a free negro, but this involved only rights civil, not political. The mere possession of freedom did not make him a freeman, nor make it possible for him to become

[21] *Pro. and Deb. Conv.*, VII, 295; VIII, 113, 117, 161, 162, 193, 267; IX, 40, 83, 114, 155, 224, 257, 293, 339; XI, 1. *Ibid.*, V, 414, 443; VI, 370, 371; VII, ؟, 117, 272, 295, 357, 384; VIII, 40, 91, 92, 113, 117, 161, 162, 241, 267; IX, 41, 83, 114, 218, 224, 225, 257, 293, 294, 339; X, 29, 193; XI, 1. Mr. Sterigere, speaking Jan. 18, 1838, said that after the adjournment of the Convention in July preceding, he passed through half the counties of the state, that everywhere by people of both parties the opposition to negro suffrage was almost unanimous, that a mass of petitions had come in, that the newspapers were against it, and that numerous public meetings had been held. *Ibid.*, IX, 357.

[22] *Pro. and Deb. Conv.*, V, 414.

[23] *Ibid.*, IX, 325, 363. *Ibid.*, V, 422, 424; IX, 326, 348, 363; X, 20, 103.

one.²⁴ That this view had been consistently accepted was shown by many laws of Pennsylvania, of many other states, and of the United States.²⁵ In the second place it was most inexpedient to allow the negro to vote,

²⁴ Mr. Cummin, who used the word " citizen " where most of the members used " freeman ", said that a man might be free and yet not a citizen; that citizens paid taxes and were enrolled in the militia, and in time of war marched in the service of their country; but that it " has never been supposed nor contended by any one, that they " (negroes) " are eligible, as citizens, to civil, military, or judicial stations under the government of this state. They are still freemen in regard to some personal rights, and the rights of property." *Ibid.*, V, 422. Mr. Sturdevant said that according to the constitution of 1776 freemen were to be trained and armed for the defence of the country (*cf.* Poore, II, 1542), but that negroes were not allowed to bear arms. *Ibid.*, IX, 325. Also *ibid.*, IX, 347, 358-364, 385.

²⁵ Mr. Mann said that some of the slave-holding states forbade the immigration of free negroes, which would be contrary to the Constitution of the United States if those negroes were freemen. *Ibid.*, V, 453. Mr. Cummin said: " The coloured race are a distinct people: and have always been held by our citizens at large as to be subjected to a separate and distinct law." *Ibid.*, IX, 257. Mr. Sterigere asserted that the United States naturalization laws applied only to white people; that eighteen states had expressly discriminated against the negro; that the Kentucky Court of Appeals had decided that free blacks were not citizens (citing 1 Littell 333); and that in Connecticut in 1833 Chief Justice Daggett had made a like decision (citing 2 Kent's *Commentaries*, 258, note). *Ibid.*, IX, 359, 360. It may be remarked that as regards the suffrage in the different states the constitutions adopted up to the end of the year 1838 provided as follows: (*a*) voting restricted to *free white men*—Alabama (1819), Arkansas (1836), Connecticut (1818), Delaware (1792, 1831), Florida (1838), Illinois (1818), Indiana (1816), Kentucky (1799), Louisiana (1812), Maryland (1810), Michigan (1835), Mississippi (1817, 1832), Missouri (1820), North Carolina (1835), Ohio (1802), Pennsylvania (1838), South Carolina (1778, 1790), Tennessee (1834), Virginia (1830); of these states the following had by previous constitutions given the right to all freemen or all male citizens, though this did not necessarily admit negroes—Maryland (1776), Michigan (1822), North Carolina (1776), Pennsylvania (1776, 1790), Tennessee (1796), Virginia (1776), (*b*) voting allowed to *all freemen or citizens*, not necessarily admitting negroes—Georgia (1798), Maine (1820), Massachusetts (1780), New Jersey (1776), New Hampshire (1784, 1792), New -York (1777, 1821—with higher property qualifications for negroes), Rhode Island (1777, 1786, 1793); of these states Georgia (1777) had previously restricted it to white men. Poore, *The Federal and State Constitutions. Cf. Pro. and Deb. Conv.*, IX, 380.

because the negro was an inferior being, and because
Pennsylvania would be overrun by hordes of black men
from other states if she afforded a privilege then so
unusual.[26]

In answer, it was said that the negro ought to be
allowed to vote because the law gave him this privilege,
and also because it was just that he should have it. That
he had the right was shown by the fact that for some
time he had voted unquestioned in many parts of the
state. It was probable that the right had been conferred by the constitution of 1776.[27] It had been assured
by the act of 1780, and confirmed by the constitution of
1790.[28] Finally the negro was no inferior being, but
an excellent and worthy citizen, whom it would be unjust to degrade or depress.[29] These arguments must be
examined in detail.

That the free negro had not full rights of citizenship
in Pennsylvania during the colonial period is true, as

[26] " They are also a debased and degraded portion of our population . . .
All attempts to elevate them have proved abortive. They seem to have
no desire to be elevated. The mass are ignorant and debased." *Pro.
and Deb. Conv.*, IX, 364. Mr. Martin said that if the restriction was
imposed " Pennsylvania . . . will not then be the receptacle of fugitive
slaves, or runaway negroes . . . as she now is." *Ibid.*, IX, 321. Also
ibid., III, 84; V, 445; IX, 357, 369; X, 94.

[27] *Ibid.*, IX, 329, 354.

[28] There was some hearsay evidence that the Convention which framed
the constitution of 1790 had proposed to insert " white " in the section
which contained the suffrage qualifications, but that the word had been
stricken out on the motion of Albert Gallatin. When questioned, Gallatin, who was then very old, replied: "I have a lively recollection that,
in some stages of the discussion, the proposition pending before the convention, limited the right of suffrage to ' free white citizens,' etc., and
that the word ' white ' was struck out on my motion." Letter from
Albert Gallatin to Joseph Parrish, Dec. 21, 1837, in *Pro. and Deb. Conv.*,
X, 45. It was the opinion that such action had been taken in order that
white men of dark complexion might not be excluded. *Ibid.*, X, 96; 6
Watts 559.

[29] *Pro. and Deb. Conv.*, IX, 391; X, 10, 71.

Judge Fox said. According to the laws agreed upon in England in 1682 the right of suffrage was conferred upon men who were property-holders and who were free.[20]   At this time it is extremely improbable that Penn was taking cognizance of any negroes, for their normal status at this period in the country around the Delaware was *de facto* slavery, and no record of a negro then free has survived.   A class of free negroes began to exist almost immediately after 1700, and grew steadily throughout the colonial period, but their status was one inferior and distinct.   They did not have the right of trial by jury until 1776 at the earliest; they were forbidden to marry white people; they were liable to summary regulation if they failed to work; and their children were directly subject to the state in that they were bound out to service by the state for a longer time than white children could be bound.[21]   These restrictions would seem to indicate that free negroes were debarred from the right of suffrage, even without allowing for the fact that had these restrictions not existed, the requisite property qualifications would have proved a barrier almost as great.   Nowhere has there come to light any evidence that the negro ever did vote in Pennsylvania in colonial times.   There is, however, toward the end of the period strong evidence that he did not vote.[22]

After 1776 the case becomes somewhat less clear.

[20] See above, p. 172, note 13.
[21] See above, chap. VII.
[22] Christopher Marshall, speaking of an election of burgesses, says: " This has been one of the sharpest contests . . . (that has been for a number of years)", though peaceable " except some small disturbance among the Dutch Occasioned by some Unguarded expressions of Joseph Swift, viz, that: except they were Naturalized they had no more right to a vote than a Negro or Indian " . . .   MS. Remembrancer, May 1, 1776.

On the adoption of her constitution in that year Pennsylvania made use of those ardent expressions, that all men are created equally free and independent, and that all free men of sufficient interest in the community possess the right to share in the government.[33] In the state at that time there were undoubtedly many free negroes; but it is difficult to determine whether the constitution meant that being free they might vote when they had paid the required taxes, or that being free men they might become freemen. The question was not then raised, so that the men who framed the constitution left no explicit interpretation. There are strong indications, however, that contemporaries did not interpret the suffrage provision to include negroes.

One of the clauses of this constitution lays down the fundamental right which men have of bearing arms.[34] In 1777 the militia law limited the right to white males.[35] During the early years of the Revolution numerous acts were passed limiting the privileges of citizenship to such men as were loyal to the new government. No less than six of these "Test Acts" were passed between June, 1777, and October, 1779.[36] In every one of them it was declared that the oath of

---

[33] *Cf. Journals of the House, 1776-1781*, pp. 66, 90.

[34] " That the people have a right to bear arms for the defence of themselves and the state." Poore, II, 1542.

[35] " Every male white person " . . . ". An Act to Regulate the Militia of the Commonwealth of Pennsylvania," sect. II, *Stat. at L.*, IX, 77 (1776-1777).

[36] June 13, 1777, *Stat. at L.*, IX, 111; Oct. 12, 1777, *ibid.*, IX, 148; Apr. 1, 1778, *ibid.*, IX, 239; Sept. 10, 1778, *ibid.*, IX, 284; Dec. 5, 1778, *ibid.*, IX, 303; Oct. 1, 1779, *ibid.*, IX, 405. " And be it . . . enacted . . . That every person . . . refusing or neglecting to take . . . the said oath . . . shall . . . be incapable of holding any office or place of trust in this state, serving on juries . . . electing or being elected . . . " *Stat. at L.*, IX, 112.

allegiance was to be administered to white men.[37] There seems reason to believe, then, that the constitution did not grant the right of suffrage to negroes; and that it had designedly omitted all mention of them.[38]

In 1780 the act for the gradual abolition of slavery made use of expressions which might be construed to favor the view that negroes could not vote;[39] but this instrument was merely an act of assembly, which was designed primarily to set negroes free and for its validity it would depend on the meaning of the constitution then in force.[40] It is true that the opponents of this act protested that it would allow negroes to vote; but on the other hand there appears immediately thereafter testimony that such was not the result.[41]

The constitution of 1790 again defined the qualifications required for the exercise of suffrage. It was again asserted that all men were born equally free and independent, and that every eligible freeman should enjoy the rights of an elector.[42] As to this definition also it was the opinion of those best able to decide, that the constitution took no notice of negroes, and did not

[37] " All male white inhabitants " . . . *Ibid.,* IX, 111.

[38] " The framers of this constitution unquestionably regarded them as a degraded race, and therefore took no notice of them." Speech of Mr. Sturdevant, *Pro. and Deb. Conv.,* IX, 325.

[39] " The offences and crimes of negroes and mulattoes as well slaves and servants and freemen " . . . *Stat. at L.,* X, 70. This might indicate that all negroes were regarded as in a separate class.

[40] *Cf. Pro. and Deb. Conv.,* V, 424; IX, 348, 363; X, 20.

[41] Benjamin Rush, than whom the negro had no better friend in Pennsylvania, speaking of this act, says explicitly: " It does not admit free Negroes, it is true, to the privilege of voting, but then it exempts them from taxes. A free Negro is in a safer and more honorable situation in Pennsylvania, than a Quaker who has not submitted to the test-law." *Considerations upon the Present Test-Law of Pennsylvania* (1784), 13.

[42] Poore, II, 1551, 1554.

mean to include them among voters."[43] It would seem, then, that negroes had no right to vote while Pennsylvania was a colony, nor after the adoption of the state constitutions, unless they were included in the term " freemen."

A free man was by no means necessarily a freeman. This word as used in English law had a special meaning, its connotations suggesting much more than a man personally free from servitude. Such an one had, it is true, full civil rights, and was entitled to protection of the laws and to enjoyment of his property. These rights free negroes undeniably had after the abolition act of 1780. But only such a man as had exactly the qualifications prescribed by law was a freeman, and so entitled to corporate privileges and political rights. In England for four centuries after 1430 only those men could vote for members of Parliament who had a forty shilling freehold, or were otherwise specifically qualified.[44] In some of the colonies only church members had been permitted to vote.[45] Thus mere possession of a certain amount of property or the paying of certain taxes

[43] *Cf.* decision of Chief Justice Gibson of the Supreme Court of Pennsylvania, in the case of Hobbs *v.* Fogg (1838), 6 Watts 559; *Opinion of Judge Fox*; also *Pro. and Deb. Conv.*, V, 422; IX, 325-327, 358, 369; X, 53.

[44] 8 Henry VI, c. 7. *Cf.* Maitland, *Constitutional History of England*, 175.

[45] " It was likewise ordered and agreed that for time to come noe man shalbe admitted to the freedome of this body polliticke, but such as are members of some of the churches within the lymitts of the same." *Rec. Massachusetts Bay*, I, 87 (1631). *Cf.* Osgood, *The American Colonies in the Seventeenth Century*: for Massachusetts, I, 154; for Connecticut, I, 314; for New Haven, I, 325; for Rhode Island, I, 337, 340; but *cf.* I, 358. Osgood says: " The idea of freemanship was political in its nature, . . . Individuals were admitted to the position of freemen by vote of the town, and only persons whom the town fellowship found acceptable attained to this privilege." *Ibid.*, I, 464.

was not sufficient.[46] The man so qualified, although he was free, was not by virtue of such qualifications a freeman. This he could become only by explicit legal admission either as an individual or in a class specified by law. In Pennsylvania such enactment had never been made for negroes; and therefore from the strictly legal point of view it is doubtful whether at any time down to 1838, free negroes could be freemen, and so have the right to vote.[47]

On the other hand it might seem that when the constitution of 1776 said that all free men properly qualified might vote, it included free negroes, both because it said all free men, and also because it had said that all men were born equally free and independent. In 1780 the act for the gradual abolition of slavery declared that free negroes were in all respects to be treated as free men and free women.[48] Free white men who ful-

[46] Rush, speaking in 1784 of non-jurors excluded by the test-law, said: " They complain loudly since the peace, and express the utmost anxiety to enjoy the privileges of a freeman." *Considerations upon the Present Test-Law of Pennsylvania*, 15.

[47] That this was the interpretation consistently placed upon the status of the free negro would seem to be shown by the course of Federal legislation, as well as law in Pennsylvania, since 1789. The United States laws governing naturalization, and the enrolling of a militia, had limited these privileges to white men: . . . " each and every free able-bodied white male citizen of the respective states " . . . . "An Act more effectually to provide for the National Defence by establishing an Uniform Militia throughout the United States." *Stat. at L., U. S.*, Second Congress, sess. I, c. 33 (1792). Every militia law passed in Pennsylvania since 1790 had expressly confined enrollment to white men. *Cf. Acts of Assembly*, *1793*, p. 394; *1799*, p. 427; *1802*, p. 208; *1807*, p. 205; *1814*, p. 320; *1821*, p. 263; *1822*, p. 231. " Not a black man in the union lifts even a cooks-spit to help to defend our liberties, (indeed this is an excellent piece of policy not to permit them to bear arms) " . . . Branagan, *Serious Remonstrances* (1805), 79, 80. *Cf. Pro. and Deb. Conv.*, V, 422; IX, 325, 326, 361.

[48] *Cf.* the charge by Judge Baldwin to the jury in the case of Caleb Johnson *v.* John Kinderdine, and others: . . . " the abolition act put free blacks on the footing of free white men " . . . *Hazard's Register*, XI, 343.

filled the suffrage requirements possessed the right to vote; then free negroes fulfilling the requirements might seem in like manner to have the same privilege. Circumstances which attended the passing of the statute indicate this. The abolition act did not have unanimous approval. In 1780 there were few people in Pennsylvania who supported slavery; but out of the fifty-five members who voted, twenty-one voted against the act and registered a minority protest. This protest categorically objected to the fact that by such a law negroes would receive the suffrage.[49] The constitution of 1790 reasserted the fundamental principles of human liberty expressed in 1776; and at the same time did not explicitly exclude negroes from voting. Many years later it was said that soon after the adoption of the constitution a legal opinion was given that negroes could vote.[50]

The strongest of all arguments in support of negro suffrage is the fact that negroes had been voting in Pennsylvania for a long time before the controversy arose. The practice would go far to show that they had

[49] "3rd. Because, . . . we could not agree to their being made free citizens in so extensive a manner as this law proposes; we think they would have been well satisfied . . . had these unhappy people been permitted to enjoy the fruits of their labor, and been protected in their lives and property, in the manner white persons are, without giving them the right of voting for, and being voted into offices, . . . We think that future legislatures might have added to their privileges . . . with much more propriety than they could abridge them, should they be found too extensive after being fixed by a fundamental law." *Journals of the House 1776-1781*, p. 436.

[50] In the Convention of 1837-1838 Mr. Hopkinson said that he recollected that soon after the adoption of the constitution " at a very heated election in their city, the question of negro suffrage was raised. The judges of the election were at fault and took the opinion of eminent lawyers—two of them were, Mr. Lewis, and Mr. Rawle, and Mr. H. thought that a third was Mr. Ingersoll; and they concurred in affirming the right of suffrage to the negro. It must be remembered that two of these gentlemen were members of the convention who made the constitution." *Pro. and Deb. Conv.*, X, 97. Lewis and Rawle were abolitionists.

been regarded as freemen under the constitution of Pennsylvania. This argument, which was the most convincing one urged by advocates in the Convention of 1837-1838, was challenged only from the standpoint of legality, and was not disputed as to fact. It was possible then to accumulate some evidence. A search over the period in question reveals much more.

In 1796 the Senate of Pennsylvania received a petition from citizens of Huntingdon County asking for a law to compel masters of negro servants to give them sufficient education, since many negroes were ill fitted to exercise the privileges of citizenship to which they had been admitted.[51] In 1807 when a proposed law for the regulation of negroes was being debated in the Senate,[52] two members moved to exempt from the restrictions contemplated in a certain clause such negroes and mulattoes as were legal voters.[53] In 1819 a traveller observed that every citizen could vote in Pennsylvania when he had paid the county tax.[54] Somewhat later it became a matter of comment that in elections held in different places there was a great deal of irregularity as to suffrage requirements. What constituted some of this irregularity may be learned from a message of Governor Shulze in 1826, when he asked whether negro votes were not accepted in one district and rejected in another.[55] In 1836 John Denny admitted that in parts

[51] J. of S., 1795-1796, p. 43.
[52] " An Act respecting black and mulattoe persons."
[53] Motion of Mr. Wayne of Chester Co. and Mr. Sommer of Phila. Co. to amend section II by exempting " those " (black and mulattoe persons) " who heretofore have been and now are legal voters; AND who shall hereafter become legal voters." J. of S., 1806-1807, pp. 296, 297.
[54] Johnson, Letters from the British Settlement in Pennsylvania, 125.
[55] " Is the term freeman, so construed in one district as totally to exclude, and in another freely to admit persons of colour to exercise the right of suffrage? " 4 Pa. Arch., V, 663, 664.

of Pennsylvania negroes shared in political privileges, although he believed that it was unlawful for them to do so.[56] In 1838 it became known that they had voted in at least seven counties.[57] That they had never been allowed to vote in Philadelphia was asserted in the debates of the Convention, and this seems to be true; but it was admitted that they were excluded because the officials in that city purposely failed to assess them for taxes.[58] In 1833 there appeared in one of the Philadelphia papers a very detailed account of the qualifications prescribed for the suffrage; in this nothing was said about the exclusion of blacks.[59] Hence there can be no doubt that if negroes did not generally vote in Pennsylvania, yet the practice was by no means unusual.[60]

Accordingly the questions which came for decision

[56] " In some districts of Pennsylvania that class is admitted to some share of political privileges." Denny, *An Essay on the Political Grade of the Free Coloured Population under the Constitution of the United States, and the Constitution of Pennsylvania,* 51.

[57] Allegheny, Bucks, Dauphin, Cumberland, York, Juniata, Westmoreland. Speech of Mr. M'Cahen, *Pro. and Deb. Conv.,* IX, 380. Mr. Brown, of Philadelphia, said that he believed that some hundreds voted in York County, thirty or forty in Bucks County, and many others in various parts of the state. *Ibid.,* III, 90. But it was acknowledged that " The right of the coloured taxable inhabitant to vote (if it be a right) is a very precarious one indeed; it is rarely, if ever, exercised by them." Speech of Mr. Reigart, *ibid.,* IX, 375.

[58] *Ibid.,* III, 83. On this device for the exclusion of voters, see *Phila. Gazette,* Oct. 30, 1812; *U. S. Gazette,* Oct. 9, 1832; *Pro. and Deb. Conv.,* III, 88.

[59] *Inquirer,* Oct. 7, 1833.

[60] " The right of the former " (negroes) " to exercise the privilege of voting at elections, was formerly enjoyed, in some parts of the state, but denied in other parts. As the number of the colored population, however, increased, public inquiry and opposition to its enjoyment were excited." *Report of Committee of the House, June 24, 1839* (H. S. P.), p. 5. " Persons of colour resident in the State, although free, and assessed, and paying taxes, are denied the privilege of voting. Before the amendment there were no specific words excluding them, but few ventured to claim the privilege, so inveterate is the prejudice against them." Combe, *Notes,* I, 297, 298.

before the courts and the Convention in 1837-1838, whether free negroes in Pennsylvania were legally entitled to vote, and whether it was possible for free negroes to acquire full rights of citizenship under the constitution of that state, were beset with great difficulties; and it is not easy to come to a decision now. On the one hand the negro had certainly voted for a number of years; on the other hand the practice had never been universal or unquestioned.[61] If his champions could point to the fact that he had never in so many words been excluded, those who opposed them could with equal truth assert that he had never been specifically admitted.[62] For the one it is necessary to acknowledge that in construing the vaguely comprehensive words of the constitutions of Pennsylvania there were precedents in the Articles of Confederation, and analogies in the documents of some of the states, which favored such an interpretation as would include the negro among freemen;[63] but for the other it can be said that colonial usage, and the mass of both precedent and practice in Pennsylvania, in other states, and in the United States, seemed to favor the narrower and stricter view. After all the argument can be narrowed

[61] Denny, speaking about negro suffrage, says: " This however is a mere gratuity, and often of but transient enjoyment—the suspension of a disability which the constitution imposes, through the tenderness of those who happen to be entrusted, for the time, with its local administration." *Political Grade*, 51.

[62] *Cf.* the decision in the case of Foremans *v.* Tamm (1853), in which it was remarked that as to suffrage the negroes must be content until the white people who had founded the colony " think proper to admit " (them) " into political partnership." 1 Grant 23.

[63] *Cf.* the opinions of Justices McLean and Curtis in the Dred Scott case, 14 Howard 538, 572, 582. See also Livermore, *Historical Research respecting the Opinions of the Founders of the Republic on Negroes as Slaves, as Citizens, and as Soldiers.*

down to one point. The negro in Pennsylvania was legally entitled to vote if the constitution of the state gave him that right. The constitution of 1790 gave it to freemen. If the negro was a freeman, then the suffrage was his. Upon this point every argument converges. But upon close examination it appears that the word "freeman" had a special meaning in Pennsylvania as elsewhere; and that while the privilege conferred by this word could have been granted to the negro, such grant had never been made.

This conclusion had been previously worked out by a careful writer, John Denny. Alarmed at the influx of negroes into Pennsylvania, and realizing that if they were citizens of the United States the influx was not to be prevented, and that if they became citizens of Pennsylvania they were not to be expelled, Denny began an investigation, in the course of which he concluded, substantially for the reasons afterwards given by Judge Fox and others, that a negro could become a citizen by common law, that is, hold property and be taxed, but that he was as yet an alien in regard to political privileges.[64] Previous to publication he submitted his book to John Marshall, who granted to its thesis the great weight of his approval.[65]

On the same argument was based the decision of the Supreme Court of Pennsylvania. While the suffrage question was being argued in the Convention there had come before the Supreme Court for final decision a case which up to that time had attracted little attention,

---

[64] Denny, *An Essay on the Political Grade of the Free Coloured Population under the Constitution of the United States, and the Constitution of Pennsylvania*, 13-28, 52-56, and *passim*.

[65] ' The sentiment it conveys appears to me, to be perfectly sound." Letter to the author, Oct. 24, 1834, *ibid.*, preface.

although it had been pending for some years.[66]   In October, 1835, in Luzerne County a negro named Fogg, who admittedly possessed the necessary qualifications of residence and taxable property, endeavored to vote, and was refused.[67]   When the negro sued in the County Court of Common Pleas, Judge Scott, who said that he knew of nothing in the constitution or the laws of either the United States or Pennsylvania, which prohibited a negro otherwise qualified from voting, charged the jury to bring in a verdict for the plaintiff.[68]   The case was then taken to the Supreme Court, and in 1838 the opinion of the court, as given by Chief Justice Gibson, was that a negro was not a freeman, and was not entitled to vote under the existing constitution of the state.[69]

[66] It is not improbable that a number of negroes brought the matter before the courts.   In addition to the cases mentioned there is an allusion to a decision given against James Forten in 1838.   Cf. Marryat, Diary in America, I, 150.

[67] 6 Watts 553.

[68] 6 Watts 554.

[69] " The fallacy of it " (the right of the negro to vote) " is its assumption that the term freedom signifies nothing but exemption from involuntary service; and that it has not a legal signification more specific."   6 Watts 556.   The Chief Justice asserted that freedom of a municipal corporation or of a body politic implied fellowship and participation in corporate right; that one might be free and bound by the laws of a community, and yet not be a freeman in respect of its government; that courts had refused to acknowledge that inheritance of property, or the paying of scot and lot, gave incidental right to corporate freedom; and that such freedom must be derived from prescription or grant.   Hobbs and others v. Fogg, 6 Watts 553-560.   For an excellent discussion cf. editorial in Public Ledger, July 24, 1857.   Chief Justice Gibson tried to strengthen his decision by alleging a similar decision of the High Court of Errors and Appeals of Pennsylvania, according to which the negro had been excluded from the suffrage, he said, about 1795.   He was able to find no record of this decision, but quoted from the memory of a friend.   Cf. 6 Watts 555.   Stroud, who made a thorough search afterwards, could find no record, and supposed that the idea had arisen from an indistinct recollection of the dissimilar case of Negro Flora v. Joseph Graisberry. Stroud, Laws of Slavery, 227, 228 (note).   See above, p. 82.   As to the element of doubt in the decision of the Chief Justice, cf. Goines v. M'Cand-

There can be no doubt that at this time many people, some of them like Judge Scott of very respectable attainments, sincerely believed that the negro had a legal right to vote.[70] Indeed the whole matter was so doubtful that it was afterwards asserted that the Constitutional Convention had desired to wait until the decision of the Supreme Court was given, and that the Supreme Court had deliberately withheld the decision until the suffrage article in the constitution had been changed.[71] Nevertheless there seems to be little doubt that from the standpoint of strict legality the adverse decision of the Pennsylvania Supreme Court in 1838 was correct. It is true a liberal interpretation might have been given, as in Massachusetts, and as had been the case in parts of Pennsylvania. This was not done, it would seem, because negro citizenship was not desired. The really decisive factors, in the Convention at any rate, were the general dislike of the negro in Pennsylvania, and the general prejudice against him.

As the weeks wore on these feelings had come to be uppermost in the minds of a great many of the members of the Convention. Interspersed with the legal arguments there came an ever increasing volume of impassioned defense and violent abuse, of pleading, ridicule and scorn. It was said that the negro was peaceable, law-abiding, and progressive; that he was a worthy citizen, and loved his state; and that his rights

---

less, 4 *Phila. Rep.* 257. "The decision thus made was virtually ratified not long afterwards, as that which the people of this State meant should be the supreme law, if it was not so already, by the introduction of the word ' white ' before the term freemen . . . in our present constitution."

[70] "There are a great many in Pennsylvania who believe that every one born in this State, has a right to vote." Speech of Mr. Dickey, *Pro. and Deb. Conv.*, X, 66.

[71] Letter of " Senex," in *Pennsylvanian*, Apr. 17, 1857.

were sacred in the sight of God and man. It was just
as fiercely urged that he had made no progress, and
was unable to make any; that he was an inferior and
degraded being; that he was naturally lawless and idle,
and so filled the jails and the poor-houses; and that to
allow him to vote would do irreparable injury to Pennsylvania, since it would attract to the state vast hordes
of lawless negroes to swell the crowds already settled
there.[72] After a while it became evident that the question would be decided largely in accordance with these
arguments; and on January 20, 1838, the amendment
that only white freemen could vote, was carried by a
vote of 77 to 45.[73] At the October elections the new
constitution was ratified.[74] From this time no negroes
voted in Pennsylvania until after the Civil War, and
the constitution was not changed until 1873.[75]

This definite settlement of the question in 1838, which
met with very general and hearty approval[76] was yet

[72] *Cf. Pennsylvanian,* Jan. 21, 1838.

[73] *Pro. and Deb. Conv.,* X, 106. A comparison of the names of the
members who voted, with a list of the Democratic members of the Convention shows that at least fifty-seven Democrats voted for the amendment. Cf. (Carlisle) *American Volunteer,* Mar. 1, 1838. For the amended
article, *cf. Pro. and Deb. Conv.,* XIII, 239, 240; Poore, II, 1560. 1561.
Mr. Scott tried unsuccessfully to have added an amendment that suffrage
might be extended to eligible negroes at any time after 1860 by a law
passed at any two successive annual sessions of the Legislature. *Pro.
and Deb. Conv.,* X, 106, 107. Mr. Dunlap wanted such an amendment
that those who could not vote should not be taxed. *Ibid.,* X, 111. After
a long discussion this was lost 36 to 86. *Ibid.,* X, 125. Mr. Merrill's
proposition to give a vote to native negroes properly qualified was lost
26 to 91. *Ibid.,* X, 128.

[74] 113, 971 for, 112, 759 against. *Ibid.,* XIII, 260, 261.

[75] " Every male citizen," etc. Poore, II, 1583.

[76] " We are at least tolerably sure that nine tenths of the people of
Pennsylvania are opposed to granting equal political privileges to the negro race—such, we are positive, is the case with that proportion of the
people of the city and county of Philadelphia." *Pennsylvanian,* Jan. 20,
1838. Cf. *Pennsylvanian,* Jan. 21, Mar. 6, 1838; *American Daily Advertiser,* Oct. 1, 1838; *Crawford Democrat,* Jan. 30, 1838; *Harrisburger
Morgenröthe,* Feb. 1, 1838; (Carlisle) *American Volunteer,* Mar. 1, 1838.

opposed by the friends of the negro, while they themselves believed that they were the victims of fatal wrong and oppression. Shortly after the assembling of the Convention the negroes of Pittsburg had sent up a petition against exclusion, stating their merits and rights.[77] This petition because of its apparently overbearing tone had aroused strong feeling in the Convention.[78] During the course of the debates other negroes sent petitions, though not a great many;[79] but after the decision had been made, and after the wide-spread discussion had brought to them keen realization of what they had lost, they and those who sympathized with them set to work with an energy which abated little during the next twenty years, and which kept the subject alive down to the time of the Civil War. They held meetings, they adopted resolutions, they argued, they issued broadsides and pamphlets.[80] In addition there was sent to the Legislature an endless stream of memorials and petitions, which at times swelled into a veritable flood.[81]

[77] *Pro. and Deb. Conv.*, III, 685-701.

[78] *Ibid.*, III, 685, 686, 693, 694-701.

[79] *Cf. ibid.*, IX, 379.

[80] See for example the *Appeal of Forty Thousand Citizens, Threatened with Disfranchisement, to the People of Pennsylvania* (1838)), which after appealing to the people of the state from the Convention which has robbed them of their rights, tells of the property they own, how worthily they have behaved, and how much progress they have made.

[81] *J. of S., 1838-1839*, vol. I, 409, 423, 452; *J. of H., 1840*, vol. I, 292, 569; *J. of H., 1841*, vol. I, 343, 472; *J. of S., 1841*, vol. I, 84, 162; *J. of H., 1842*, vol. I, 592, 593; *J. of S., 1842*, vol. I, 359, 533; *J. of S., 1842-1843*, pp. 355, 459; *J. of H., 1843*, pp. 313, 314, 489, 894; *J. of H., 1844*, vol. I, 131, 172, 213, 261; *J. of S., 1844*, vol. I, 202, 362; *J. of S., 1845*, vol. I, 178-181, 248; *J. of H., 1846*, vol. I, 39, 54, 326; *J. of S., 1846*, vol. I, 227; *J. of H., 1847*, vol. I, 415; *J. of S., 1847*, p. 447; *J. of S., 1848*, vol. I, 38, 64, 217, 240, 319, 434, 453, 467; *J. of H., 1849*, vol. I, 101, 124, 152, 242, 302, 704; *J. of S., 1849*, vol. I, 113, 133, 159, 182, 237, 266, 277, 286, 297, 322, 329, 372, 380, 402, 536, 626, 685; *J. of H., 1850*, vol. I, 88, 114, 137, 155, 377; *J. of S., 1850*, vol. I, 97, 120, 212, 389, 479, 547, 588, 707; *J. of H., 1851*, vol. I, 234, 265; *J. of S., 1851*, vol. I, 211, 246;

All this was·in vain.[82] Occasionally a proposition was
made to amend the constitution, or a bill was introduced to effect enfranchisement, but no consideration
could be gained.[83] It was thought to be an especial hardship that tax-paying negroes should be thus excluded,
but even for this no remedy was allowed. There is no
doubt that the disability was felt very keenly by those
negroes, who because of their education, their opportunities, and their ownership of property, were fully
qualified to vote.[84] They even founded an association
with the avowed purpose of winning complete citizenship by appeals to the voters of the state.[85] But they did
this to no purpose, for the majority of the people of
Pennsylvania had decided that negroes were not to be
so encouraged ; and to this decision they held unswerv-
ingly throughout the period under consideration.

And so, if from 1800 to 1838 the negro in Pennsyl-

J. of H., 1855, p. 193; J. of S., 1855, pp. 147, 371, 419; J. of H.,
1856, p. 674; J. of S., 1859, pp. 650, 736, 780; J. of H., 1860, p. 347.
This last petition was made by three thousand " native colored citizens "
of Pennsylvania.

[82] Cf. J. of H., 1846, vol. I, 54; J. of S., 1848, vol. I, 197; J. of S., 1849,
vol. I, 176; J. of H., 1850, vol. I, 559.

[83] J. of H., 1855, pp. 106, 118, 131; J. of S., 1845, vol. I, 178; J. of S.,
1855, p. 147; J. of S., 1859, p. 415.

[84] " The conviction . . . that they are politically disfranchised, and that
they are to remain a degraded caste, has sunk into the depths of their
hearts, quenching every noble aspiration, repressing every manly effort,
and crushing their spirits to the earth." Report on Colonization by Select
Committee of the House, Legislative Documents, 1854, p. 582. See also
the bitter complaint of the negroes of Philadelphia about disfranchisement,
where they say that the Reform Convention " robbed us of those rights
we had enjoyed under the Constitution for 47 years " . . . ; and in which
they say that now they are a prey to tyranny, that they are assaulted, insulted, and dragged before magistrates. Memorial of Thirty Thousand
Disfranchised Citizens of Philadelphia, to the Honorable Senate and
House of Representatives (1855), 1, 2.

[85] Minutes of the State Convention of the Coloured Citizens of Pennsylvania, Convened at Harrisburg, etc. (1849), 22, 23.

vania was the object of continually increasing prejudice and discrimination, after that year his condition was worse, because of his definitely recognized position of semi-citizenship, and because politically he was helpless and null. It was now seen that they who in 1780 predicted that Pennsylvania was giving to her new negro citizens privileges too many and too great, and who said then that the state would one day lament such liberality, were so far correct, that at the end of fifty-eight years many believed that these privileges should be taken back, while most people asserted that the grant had never been made.

CHAPTER XI.

Discrimination and Depression.

The definite denial of suffrage to the negroes of Pennsylvania was the most conspicuous as well as the most successful attempt to keep their status distinct and lower than the white man's, but it was not the only attempt made. Similar efforts were directed toward preventing intermarriage of the races, reducing the legal rights of negroes, and abridging their privileges. Although most of these efforts failed of accomplishment, none were without influence in depressing the condition of the colored people, and all are significant of the hostile feelings prevalent in the state.

Against intermarriage a long fight was waged. During colonial times mingling of the races in Pennsylvania had been forbidden by a stringent law,[1] but this law was one among others affecting the negro which was repealed in 1780.[2] Shortly after that year a few cases of mixed marriage are mentioned, and in 1788 there are said to have been two such couples at Pittsburg, one of them occupying a respectable position.[3] In 1805 Thomas Branagan complained that intermarriage had become common, that many white women were seduced by negro men who then married them, and that mulatto

[1] 1725-1726. See above, p. 30.
[2] See above, p. 78, note 40, and p. 79.
[3] " Cette famille est une des plus respectables de cette ville." Brissot de Warville, *Nouveau Voyage,* 33, 34 (note).

children by white women were numerous.[4] These statements were no doubt exaggerations, but there was
probably some basis for them.[5]

After a while a strong feeling was aroused, so that
in 1821 a petition was sent to the Legislature, asking
that mixed marriages be declared void, and that it be
made a penal act for a negro to marry a white man's
daughter.[6] In 1834 such a marriage provoked a riot at
Columbia; while in 1838 the subject caused a vehement
outburst in the Constitutional Convention then assembled.[7] Three years later a bill to prevent intermarriage
was passed in the House, but lost in the Senate.[8] From
time to time thereafter petitions were sent to the Legis-

[4] " There are many, very many blacks, who . . . begin to feel themselves
consequential, . . . will not be satisfied unless they get white women for
wives, and are likewise exceedingly impertinent to white people in low
circumstances." Branagan, *Serious Remonstrances*, 70, 71.

[5] " I solemnly declare, I have seen more white women married to,
and deluded through the arts of seduction by negroes in one year in
Philadelphia, than for the eight years I was visiting " [West Indies and
the Southern States]. Branagan, *Serious Remonstrances*, 73. " I know
a black man who seduced a young white girl . . . who soon after married
him, and died with a broken heart; on her death he said he would not
disgrace himself to have a negro wife, and acted accordingly, for he soon
after married another white woman." *Ibid.*, 74, 75. " There are perhaps
hundreds of white women thus fascinated by black men in this city, and
there are thousands of black children by them at present " . . . *Ibid.*, 73.
Also *ibid.*, 68, 69, 73, 74, 75, 102. *Cf.* advertisement in *Somerset Whig*,
Mar. 12, 1818; also article "A Negro Wife Wanted," in *Union Times*,
Aug. 15, 1834.

[6] Petition from Greene County saying that many negroes have settled
in Pennsylvania, and that " they have been able to seduce into marriage,
the minor children of the white inhabitants " . . . *J. of S., 1820-1821*, p.
213. *Cf. American Daily Advertiser*, Jan. 23, 1821.

[7] *Columbia Spy*, Oct. 2, 1834, in *Inquirer*, Oct. 7, 1834. In the Convention Mr. Woodward said: " Shall we then amalgamate with them,
marry and intermarry with them . . .? God forbid it." *Pro. and Deb.
Conv,.* X, 23. *Cf. Remarks of Dr. J. R. Burden*, 11, 12.

[8] *J. of H., 1841*, vol. I, 83, 193-194. The marriages were to be declared
void, and a penalty of $500 was to be imposed. (Gettysburg) *Adams
Sentinel*, Feb. 1, 1841.

lature, but no action was taken; the obnoxious marriages continuing to be reported, and even being
encouraged by some extreme advocates of race equality.[9]   Nevertheless what the law left undone was
largely accomplished by public sentiment and private
action.[10] As time went on marriages of white people
with negroes came to be considered increasingly odious,
and so became far less frequent. When a case occurred,
it was usually followed by swift action and dire
vengeance. The fact that a white man was living with
a negro wife was one of the causes of the terrible riot
in Philadelphia in 1849.[11]

In melancholy contrast with the feeling against mixed
marriages was the lack of spirit manifested in the struggle against an evil which was far more widespread and,
to thoughtful people, no less alarming. Public opinion
would not tolerate the marriages of white people with
blacks, yet all the while illicit and clandestine inter-
mingling was going on, until toward the end of the
period it had assumed enormous proportions.   In
colonial times the law had tried to check amalgamation;
but the large number of mulattoes bears mournful testimony to its failure.[12] When after 1780 the restrictions
had been removed, and when through immigration
from the South the number of negroes had become much
larger, there was a very great increase in the evil.[13]

[9] J. of H., 1860, p. 237; J. of S., 1860, p. 121; North American, June 29,
1859; American Sentinel, Oct. 25, 1838.

[10] Cf. (Harrisburg) Pennsylvania Telegraph, Mar. 9, 1842.

[11] See above, p. 164, note 88.

[12] See above, p. 31.

[13] " In Philadelphia alone there are fifteen or twenty thousand blacks
and mulattoes, numbers of them children of white women of easy virtue."
Branagan, Serious Remonstrances (1805), 45. Cf. J. of H., 1802-1803, pp.
259, 260; U. S. Gazette, Nov. 10, 1832.

There is one decisive proof of this: mulattoes were
numerous in Pennsylvania throughout the whole period.
In 1860 it was estimated that they made up one-third
of the entire colored population of the state.[14]

Meanwhile there was a tendency to maintain that the
negro's political inferiority involved an abridgment of
his legal rights.   Shortly before 1853 a certain negro,
Tamm, had occupied vacant land in the commonwealth,
admittedly with the intention of making it his home
and raising a family there.   To this land he acquired a
title by preemption; but a short time afterwards he was
ejected by Foremans, a white man, who asserted that a
negro could gain no title to such land, since, not being
a citizen, he was not included in the meaning of the act
of Assembly allowing it.   The negro then sought legal
redress, and in the Court of Common Pleas of Lycoming
County got a favorable verdict.   The case was appealed,
but in 1853 the Supreme Court decided without hesitation that although negroes had no political rights in the
state, this did not deprive them of civil rights, and that
as regarded the acquisition and preemption of land they
had full power.[15]

If the courts would not sustain the exclusion of the
negro from legal rights, public opinion and individual
action were able to put beyond his reach many of the
privileges in which he might have shared.   This was
evidenced by his practical exclusion from theatres and
churches.   It was particularly evident in the treatment
he received as to the use of the street cars.

These cars began running in Philadelphia in 1858.[16]

[14] Negroes, 37,807—66.33%; mulattoes, 19,142—33.67%.   How many
of these mulatoes had emigrated into Pennsylvania it is impossible to say.
[15] Foremans v. Tamm, 1 Grant's Cases, 23-26.
[16] See Public Ledger, Jan. 20, 1858.

The rules of the Company allowed negroes to ride only on the front platform.[17] In June, 1859, a mulatto on entering a car was ejected; after which he sued for damages. A nominal award was given him in order that the matter might be appealed. This was done; but in 1861 the District Court of Philadelphia decided that in view of the different treatment which had been accorded the two races in Pennsylvania, especially since 1838, a passenger railroad company might lawfully refuse to allow negroes to enter its cars, and that it might expel them when they did so enter.[18] Thereafter this policy was sustained by an overwhelming popular sentiment, and in spite of the active efforts of a few, the exclusion was continued until 1867, when by an act of Assembly such discrimination was forbidden.[19]

The actual condition of the negro in Pennsylvania during eighty years of freedom had in some respects steadily improved; in others it had steadily grown worse. In 1780 some six thousand freedmen had set out to solve the problem of the advancement of their race, having at the start little besides their freedom and the substantial good wishes of the community in which they lived. In the next three generations many negroes from the South had joined them. Of Pennsylvania's native negroes many, of the newcomers some, had risen to independence, comfort, and even prosperity. If their condition in 1861 be contrasted with that of their ancestors who first had been brought to America,

[17] Cf. Inquirer, Oct. 31, 1860.

[18] Goines v. M'Candless, 4 Phila. Rep., 255-258; Public Ledger, Jan. 21, 1861.

[19] Laws of Assembly, 1867, pp. 38, 39. It seems likewise to have been the practice to segregate negroes on the steamboats running on the Delaware River. See advertisement in Public Ledger, Mar. 21, 1851.

the difference is seen to be immense. In the time inter-
vening they had been lifted up through entire stages
of human progress; they had been made civilized
Christian men and women. If their condition be contrasted with that in 1800, it is evident that in material
prosperity, in culture, and refinement, the difference is
still very striking. But on the other hand there was
much to counterbalance this progress. Gradually even
the very best negroes had come to be regarded as of an
alien race, and as an outcast and degraded people with
whom no intimate association was possible. This feeling, which had taken possession of all but the Friends
and the anti-slavery advocates, had given birth to a
prejudice which was widespread and persistent, and
which tended always to depress the condition of negroes. Accordingly of political rights now they had
nothing. If they were citizens of Pennsylvania they
were not completely or undoubtedly so. Before the
courts of law they still had the same rights as the
white man, and they were tried in the same way, but
their chances of getting exact justice were smaller, and
their punishment was more frequent and severe. The
law did not forbid them to intermarry with white
people, but public feeling made this almost impossible.
From theatres, from churches, from public meetings,
and from the street cars, they were virtually excluded.
Even schools were now grudged them. Moreover the
better avenues of employment were closed to them, and
it had become difficult for them to apprentice their
children. In ordinary times they were the object of
petty tyranny and dislike. In moments of excitement
their lives were not safe upon the streets.

If, however, the contrast in condition between earlier and later times be made not with regard to the better and more prosperous negroes, but with regard to the great mass of lowlier ones,—the unfortunate, the unsuccessful, the immigrants, the late comers, the criminal, the vicious,—it will be seen that in point of magnitude the race question had become pressing and acute, and that the condition of these negroes was deplorable, and far worse than that of the slaves of former days.

This result was due in the first place to the difficulty which an ignorant and untrained people always have in sustaining themselves in economic competition with a people of greater training and efficiency, who have, moreover, the ownership of the property and the means of production. It was due in the second place to the idleness and thriftlessness of the negroes themselves.[20] It was due in the third place to the overcrowding of negroes, and to their congestion in cities. And finally it was due to the hatred and prejudice which surrounded them, and which effectually cut them off from any chance to compete with white people on equal terms.[21]

[20] It had been anticipated that after they were free the negroes of Pennsylvania would either be industrious, or because of economic pressure be driven from the state. Letter to the clergyman, in *Pa. Packet*, Jan. 1, 1780. The experience of many years, however, showed that owing to their much lower standard of living they were able to flock to the cities, and swarm in vicious idleness and hopeless misery. W. Cobbett, *A Year's Residence in the United States of America*, 265, speaking of the negroes of New York, Philadelphia, and Boston, says: " There is, besides, a class of persons here of a description very peculiar; namely, the *free negroes*. Whatever may have been the motives, which led to their emancipation, it is very certain, that it has saddled the white people with a heavy charge. These negroes are a disorderly, improvident set of beings; and the paupers *in the country* consist *almost wholly* of them " (1818).

[21] Cf., for example, *The Mysteries and Miseries of Philadelphia*, 18, for the manner in which the lowly negroes were drawn into court for trivial reasons, in order that corrupt lawyers and magistrates might profit.

In cities their condition was particularly bad.[22] During the period from 1837 to 1847, when a special study was made of this question, it was learned that in the winter time many lived in cellars and squalid shanties, and that they were sometimes found frozen to death,[23] and that in numerous instances they died of intemperance, exposure, and want of nourishment.[24] During

[22] " There are hundreds as wretched in Philadelphia, and more so in the winter time, than slaves in the West Indies. No person can conceive the wretchedness they exhibit in the environs of this city, while the work-house and bettering-house are crowded with them." Branagan, *Serious Remonstrances,* 76. "In the winter they are a public charge, and in the summer they spend in debauchery all their earning. Last winter several hundreds would have perished in this city, had it not been for the liberality of the citizens ";... *Ibid.,* 68, 69. *Cf. J. of H., 1841,* vol. II, 540; *Public Ledger,* Feb. 7, 1851.

[23] *Cf. Spirit of the Times,* Jan. 13, 1849.

[24] " Many were found dead in cold and exposed rooms and garrets, board shanties five and six feet high, and as many feet square, erected and rented for lodging purposes, mostly without any comforts, save the bare floor, with the cold penetrating between the boards, and through the holes and crevices on all sides; some in cold, wet and damp cellars, with naked walls, and in many instances without floors; and others found dead lying in back yards, in alleys, and other exposed situations ... These cases were principally confined to the lowest and most degraded of the coloured population, whose occupations were ragging, boning and prizing. Hundreds are engaged in those occupations ... many of whom, unless provided for, must become victims of death through their habits and exposure, should the coming winter be at all severe. Most of them have no home, depending chiefly upon the success of their pursuits through the day, either in earning or beggary, (and I may add stealing,) sufficient to pay their grog and lodging. For food they depend mostly upon begging, or gathering from the street what is thrown from the houses or kitchens of others ... Lodgings are obtained from a penny to six-pence a night according to the extent of the accommodations, with or without an old stove, generally without a pipe, a furnace or fireplace, so that a fire may be had if they have means to pay for a few sticks of wood, or some coal; and were it not for the crevices and openings admitting fresh air, many would be suffocated (a few have been) by smoke and coal gas. It is no uncommon circumstance to find several sitting around on the floor, with an open furnace in their midst burning coal. Those places are mostly back from the street, not observable in passing, reached through narrow alleys, or by a back entrance ... wherein each story is subdivided into numerous small rooms, ofttimes made to accomodate as many as can be stowed into them, without regard to colour or sex. Such articles as

these years there was also much suffering among the
lowest classes of the white people, but it was asserted
by one well informed that this suffering existed nowhere in the same degree as in the courts and the alleys
of Moyamensing between Fifth and Eighth, South and
Fitzwater streets, where the negroes of Philadelphia
were largely congregated.[25]

The conditions amidst which the colored people of
Philadelphia were living were often such as to make
impossible any normal increase in their numbers. That
they did increase at all was owing very largely to the

an old bed, a carpet, or even straw upon the floor, are not often seen. . . .
Notwithstanding their degraded occupation, yet it is possible for them to
earn from ten to fifteen cents per day. There are numerous places for the
disposal of their rags, bones, etc., but there are far more numerous places
(and constantly increasing) for the disposal of their hard earned (or ill-
gotten) pennies; namely at small shops, stocked with a few stale loaves of
bread, a few potatoes, a small quantity of split wood, some candles, a
few dried and stale herrings, etc., exposed to view, serving too often as a
cloak; whilst behind and under the counter, concealed from the eye,
are kegs, jugs, bottles and measures, containing the poison, some at 4
and 5 cents a 'pint, and which is the great leading cause of the misery,
degradation and death of so many." Letter from N. B. Leidy, coroner,
Dec. 18, 1848, in *Statistical Inquiry*, 34-36. For the tendency of the negroes of Philadelphia to crowd together in narrow courts and alleys, for
the miserable cellars that rented for 1½ cents a night, for the effects of
the cheap liquor sold for a cent a glass, and for a general picture of
poverty, misery, and squalor, see *ibid.*, 32, 35-39. For the high death-
rate among negroes in Philadelphia, see *Hazard's Register*, XIII, 96;
Niles and Russ, *Medical Statistics; or a Comparative View of the Mortality in New York, Philadelphia, Baltimore, and Boston for a Series of
Years*, Tables VI and VII, where the rate from 1820 to 1826 is shown
to have varied between 1:39.45 and 1:27.84 for white people, but between
1:24.62 and 1:14.62 for negroes. See also explanation of Table XIII.
In 1837 the mortality among white people was 1:54, among negroes 1:33-
35. This excess was due largely to bad housing and poor ventilation,
consumption and diseases of the chest being the most effective causes.
Present State Free People of Color (Phila., 1838), pp. 35-38. In 1853
there is a similar description of miserable living, and of the filthy, crowded
lodgings called " cribs." *The Mysteries and Miseries of Philadelphia,
as Exhibited and Illustrated by a late Presentment of the Grand Jury,
and by a sketch of the Most Degraded Classes in the City* (Phila., 1853.)
[25] Coroner's letter in *Statistical Inquiry*, 36.

hordes of fugitives and freedmen who came up from the South. A partial enumeration of the negroes of Philadelphia in 1847 showed that more than forty per cent. were not natives of the state. Nothwithstanding such accessions it was matter of comment at this very time that their increase was much slower than that of the white people.[26]

It was this influx of people, to a great extent undesirable in character and lacking in economic efficiency, which complicated the situation. There was at Philadelphia and elsewhere all of that magnified misery which is now caused by the rush of foreign immigrants into the tenement quarters of our Eastern cities. There was the inevitable displacement of white people from some of the lower forms of labor. There was the immense difficulty involved in the sheer uplifting of these negroes from the status in which they had been born to that of the people whose state they had invaded. There was, in spite of the good intentions of many of these negroes, the inevitable failure to find sufficient employment, and the still more inevitable deterioration of character, degenerating into a life of vicious idleness and crime. There were finally the political complications in which Pennsylvania became involved with her sister states of the South.

Less and less after 1800 did Pennsylvania desire to have negroes, yet more and more did they come; so

[26] The enumeration showed 8,900 natives of Pennsylvania, 56%, 6,632 not natives, 41%, 510 whose birth place was not ascertained, 3%, out of a total of 16,042. " It thus appears that 42.7% (*sic*) of the coloured population of Philadelphia has been born out of the State; and this fact, taken in connection with the slow increase as compared with that of the whites, shows not only a very great immigration, but very great drains, by deaths and removals, of the population thus poured in upon us." *Statistical Inquiry*, 10.

that unavoidably a burden fell upon the state, and at times to the white people the situation seemed unbearable. And so as a natural climax there comes at the very end of this period what doubtless would have caused astonishment to the liberators sixty years before. In the course of the year 1860 there were sent to the House numerous petitions asking that either the immigration of negroes into Pennsylvania be forbidden forever, or else that laws permitting slavery be passed again.[27] These petitions are preserved in a volume rarely opened now, but it is well to recall them, for such extreme requests did not represent the dominant feeling in the state. The committee to whom they had been referred, replied in a paper worthy of comparison with the old protest of 1688, a paper which for dignity and eloquence is as glorious as any in the archives of the state.

It is true, this report says, that old, broken down, and undesirable negroes do crowd into the state from other places; but is Pennsylvania to drive such miserable people out? Many of them do commit crimes; they do fill the penitentiaries; but the negroes at fault are not those native to the state. It is the slavery from which they have come, that makes them as criminal as they are. And is it slavery that the petitioners desire in Pennsylvania? Let them consider what they ask. Eighty years ago Pennsylvania took measures to abolish slavery; Virginia, among other states, did not. At that time Virginia was far richer and far greater than Pennsylvania. But Virginia has retained the slavery for which they now ask, with the result that Philadelphia alone has come to be worth more than all of Vir-

[27] *J. of H., 1860*, pp. 124, 209, 237, 265, 280, 327, 375, 440, 481, 835.

ginia. Of such evils, they said, slavery is the cause. Therefore they resolved that to grant the prayers of the petitioners˙would be inexpedient, impolitic, and unjust."

To this had it come, that in Pennsylvania less than a century after abolition there were men who wished slavery reestablished. If it be granted that this was only an outburst of feeling extreme and not general, it is nevertheless certain that since the beginning of the century, and particularly throughout the last thirty years before 1861, the history of the relations of the white man to the negro in Pennsylvania is a history of prejudice, dislike, and aversion, checkered with outrage and oppression; so that not alone was the negro no real citizen, but such as he was allowed to be, he was always a citizen undesired.

---

[28] Report in *J. of H., 1860*, pp. 771-774. For the opposite effects of slavery and freedom in Virginia and Pennsylvania see *An Impartial Appeal to the Reason, Interest and Patriotism, of the People of Illinois, on the Injurious Effects of Slave Labour* (1824), 12.

CHAPTER XII.

ABOLITIONISM AND ANTI-SLAVERY.

PREJUDICE against negroes in Pennsylvania was not felt by all the white people of that state, for if the negro had bitter enemies he had also sincere well wishers and powerful friends. It was for this reason that although hostile laws were frequently contemplated, they were always vigorously opposed. It was also owing to this that although many attempts were made to prevent negroes coming to Pennsylvania, or to get those already there to go away, these projects having the support of great numbers of men both lawless and law-abiding, the results were always insignificant in the end. On the other hand such work was done and such laws were passed that negroes from the South found Pennsylvania a place of refuge particularly attractive. That all this was so resulted from the earnest efforts and vigorous propaganda of the abolitionists and the anti-slavery workers.

Abolitionism and anti-slavery were in many respects different. The first may almost be said to have originated in Pennsylvania, and the society formed by its adherents was the original and pattern of all abolition societies elsewhere. Such was not the case with anti-slavery, whose inspiration came largely from outside the state. Abolitionism exercised a powerful influence in Pennsylvania from 1775 until 1861, although the period of its dominance in the work against slavery was before

1833. After that time the efforts made by its supporters did not diminish either in magnitude or importance, but they now began to be overshadowed by the more striking and vigorous anti-slavery work, which was inspired largely by what was being done in New England. The first was earnest, efficient, and conservative; the second hasty, violent, and radical. In many respects one shaded off gradually into the other, for numbers of abolitionists became violent anti-slavery men, and anti-slavery men frequently called themselves abolitionists. Yet, as the guiding principles of the two were distinct, in this chapter they will be treated separately. The abolitionists desired to put an end to slavery first in Pennsylvania, then elsewhere, if possible; and they were willing to accomplish their task by the slow method of labor and persuasion, acting always within full sanction of the law. The anti-slavery men desired the same, and were also willing to work and persuade; but impatient at the scant success of their fellow workers, they would have destroyed slavery at any cost, whether of law, of state rights, or of constitution.[1]

---

[1] This analysis is different from that which is usually given. Professor A. B. Hart, than whom no one is more competent to speak, considers anti-slavery to have flourished before abolitionism, and ascribes to abolitionism the attributes which I ascribe to anti-slavery; while Miss Alice Dana Adams has written an excellent monograph whose title, " The Neglected Period of Anti-Slavery in America (1808-1831)," is a direct contradiction of the statement which I have given above. Professor Hart's view is made clear in his volume *Slavery and Abolition* (*American Nation*, XVI) where after devoting a chapter (XI) to the "Anti-Slavery Movement (1624-1840)," he asks " Why did the anti-slavery movement, which had been going on steadily for half a century, apparently die down in 1829 . . . ? " (p. 170). He continues: " The rise of abolition was coincident with a change in the attitude of the public mind " . . . (p. 172), and then analyzes each movement. " Such men " (anti-slavery) " were eager to be rid of slavery in their own community, and deprecated it wherever it existed, not so much out of sympathy with the oppressed negro, as from the belief that slavery was an injury to their own neighbors and constituents, and that

As abolitionism in Pennsylvania was orderly in its methods so was it slow and continuous in its development. It began at the end of the seventeenth century, when Pastorius and his associates drew up their protest, and when the Keithian Quakers wrote their

---

the influence of the slave power in national affairs was harmful. Most of the northern anti-slavery people disclaimed any intention of interfering with slavery in the southern states . . . their principle was that slavery and the slave-holding power should remain where they were." " Very different in their outlook were the abolitionists . . . Every abolitionist was . . . heart and soul opposed to slavery as it existed; he was bent on persuading or coercing the master to give up his authority . . . He wished to get rid of slavery speedily, root and branch, cost what it might " . . . " Antislavery was a negative force, an attempt to wall in an obnoxious system of labor so that it might die of itself; abolition was a positive force, founded on moral considerations, stoutly denying that slavery could be a good thing for anybody, and perfectly willing to see the social and economic system of the south disrupted " (pp. 173, 174).

There is no doubt that anti-slavery and abolitionism were similar in many respects, and if the names were merely arbitrary, descriptive epithets to be applied by the modern historian, either name might be affixed to either movement, and then properly qualified. But Professor Hart's choice of these names cannot be entirely justified, since it is partly in violation of contemporary usage. In 1775 was founded the " Pennsylvania Society for the Abolition of Slavery," etc., and shortly afterwards there were " abolition " societies in Delaware, New Jersey, New York, and in other neighboring states; local " abolition " societies sprang up everywhere; and for more than forty years the principal organizations assembled in the " Conventions of Delegates from the Abolition Societies Established in Different Parts of the United States," etc. Yet this is the period which Professor Hart describes as " Anti-Slavery." After 1830 a great change took place and new and more radical movements were started. In 1832 the " New England Anti-Slavery Society " was founded; in 1833 the " American Anti-Slavery Society; " while state and local organizations calling themselves " anti-slavery " societies were instituted in numerous places. All this Professor Hart himself describes (p. 183), yet he calls the movement " Garrisonian Abolition " (chap. XI,) and designates the members of these societies as " abolitionists." His explanation is that the first movement, anti-slavery, was sustained by men who were antagonistic to slavery; the second, abolitionism, by those who were resolved to act more strenuously and abolish slavery altogether. The truth seems to be just the contrary. Abolition flourished in the earlier period when men had good reasons to believe that all slavery could be abolished; anti-slavery in the later years when abolition in the South was seen to be impossible, and when nothing remained but to fight against

pamphlet.[2] The efforts to accomplish the abolition of
slavery, which were continued by the Quaker abolitionists and by the organized movement within the Society
of Friends,[3] were largely successful by 1780, so that
thenceforth the more important task lay rather with
the growing body of free negroes than with the lessen-
ing number of slaves. It was largely to assist free negroes, and particularly to protect them from being kidnapped, that the Pennsylvania Abolition Society was
founded.

In 1775 an Indian woman was purchased in New Jersey by a Virginian. Her owner brought her to Philadelphia, where she asserted that she and her children
were free. Then Israel Pemberton and other citizens
of the place became interested, and fought for her liberty in the courts. The matter lingered for two years
until finally she was adjudged a slave; but the case
made a deep impression on those who conducted it, and
they resolved to organize so as to prevent such things
in the future. 'Such was the origin of the first abolition
society in the United States.[4]

The Society was instituted in 1775, but the troublous

the slavery which was firmly intrenched. After all the problem resolves
itself into a correct choice of terms. Before 1830 the opponents of
slavery were members of abolition societies rather than abolitionists or
anti-slavery advocates. Since, however, they described their organizations
as " abolition," and since their principal object was the abolition of slavery
and the slave-trade, it seems more proper to call them abolitionists than
anti-slavery men. After 1830 the members of the new societies called
their organizations " anti-slavery; " but in popular usage the older idea
survived, so that " abolitionist " and " abolitionism," loosely applied
as epithets of hatred or reproach, gained their widest currency in the later
period.

[2] See above, pp. 65, 66.
[3] See above, pp. 69-77.
[4] " This is the first case on the minutes of the society, and appears to
have given rise to its formation." MS. Rec. Pa. Soc. Abol. Slavery, IV, 35.

events of the years succeeding caused a cessation of all work until the end of the Revolutionary War. In 1784 it was reorganized, and thenceforth its work was continuous and unceasing.[5]   The Society itself was new, but its work differed little from what had been done before it was founded. As most of that work had been done by Friends, so most of the Society's members were and continued to be Friends.[6]   Their organization had simply acquired corporate form under which they now began to labor more effectively. Its official title was "The Pennsylvania Society for Promoting the Abolition of Slavery, for the Relief of Free Negroes Unlawfully Held in Bondage, and for Improving the Condition of the African Race." In each of these departments it was equally active.

The most successful and constructive part of its work, and withal the quietest, was the assisting of free negroes to better their condition. It is not too much to say that the greater part of the progress made by the negroes of Pennsylvania was directly due to the efforts of this Society and its sympathizers. They obstructed adverse legislation.[7]   Often they helped the negro to purchase his freedom, or gave bond that he would not become chargeable to his former master.[8]   They gave him recommendations, found employment for him, and saw

[5] MS. Rec. Pa. Soc. Abol. Slavery, IV, 35. *Cf. Act of Incorporation and Constitution of the Pa. Soc. Abol. Sl.*, etc., 13.

[6] " The style generally was that used by the Society of Friends as a majority of its members always belonged to that denomination." William J. Buck (describing how he wrote his) History of the Pennsylvania Abolition Society (MS.), 2.

[7] Cf. MS. Rec. Pa. Soc. Abol. Sl., IV, 91; VII, 107, 119, XI, 63; *J. of H., 1812-1813,* pp. 566, 567; *J. of S., 1812-1813,* p. 540; *J. of S., 1822-1823,* p. 435; *J. of S., 1831-1832,* p. 250.

[8] See above, pp. 61-63.

that he was well treated.[9] In 1789 the ·Society organized visiting committees to enquire into the negro's problems and help him to solve them.[10] It was in the Society's schools that the negro was first taught.[11] So well did they do their work, and so far did their fame spread, that on several occasions Southern masters about to free their slaves bequeathed them to the Society, and sent them to Pennsylvania.[12] In conducting this part of its work the Society collected statistics and information about the negro which are among the most valuable in existence.[13]

In the relieving of free negroes unlawfully held in bondage it was no less energetic and almost as successful. The drastic laws against kidnapping in Pennsylvania were very largely due to its efforts;[14] and the enforcement of these laws lay in its hands to an even greater extent. Through its vigilant committees of correspondence it was able to get quick intelligence about any negro who was carried off; it was unwearied in its efforts to restore him to liberty, and relentless in running the offender down. To punish the kidnapper it spared no time and no money. It would follow him any distance, engage the best counsel, and stop at

[9] *Cf.* MS. Rec. Pa. Soc. Abol. Sl., III, 254; *Min. Sixth Conv. Abol. Soc. Phila., 1800,* p. 7; Buck, MS. Hist. Pa. Abol. Soc., I, 111.

[10] MS. Rec. Pa. Soc. Abol. Sl., VI, 41, 45, 47.

[11] *Cf.* MS. Rec. Pa. Soc. Abol. Sl., V, 83, 89; VII, 51, 53, 55, 57; VIII, 209, 211, 213.

[12] *Ibid.,* VII, 7, 81, 163, 259; VIII, 277. Also VI, 63, 75.

[13] See bibliography, MSS., " Records of the Abolition and Anti-Slavery Societies ", pp. 262-264.

[14] See above, pp. 117-118. *Cf.* MS. Rec. Pa. Soc. Abol. Sl., VI, 266; IX, 1; *J. of S., 1811-1812,* pp. 109, 186, 214; *J. of H., 1818-1819,* p. 238; *J. of H., 1831-1832,* vol. I, 283; " Report of the Delegates to Harrisburg 3 mo. 30th. 1826," MS. in Misc. Coll., Box 10, Negroes; MS. Min. Pa. Abol. Soc., 1825-1847, pp. 520-522, 533-535.

nothing to secure conviction.[15] Believing that many
negroes were kidnapped under sanction of the fugitive
slave laws it tried hard to have Pennsylvania give fugitives trial by jury.[16] Kidnapping continued to occur despite everything that could be done, but it was kept
within bounds largely by the abolitionists.

After all, however, the fundamental idea upon which
the Society was founded was the abolition of slavery,
and it was to this that the members devoted their greatest effort. First they tried to procure the total destruction of slavery in Pennsylvania. It was due in great
part to them that the abolition act of 1780 was made
more thorough in 1788.[17] From them and from their
adherents came most of the petitions asking that all
slaves be set free at once.[18] They endeavored to have
the courts declare slavery illegal.[19] They tried hard
also to secure abolition of the extra years of service for
the negro servants who were children of slaves.[20] Failing to accomplish these things they sought to attain
their object as far as possible by enforcement of the
existing laws with utmost thoroughness and vigor. The
clause of the abolition act which required slaves to be
registered was liable to many technical violations, and
its requirements had often been carelessly fulfilled.[21] To
this the Society gave special heed, and for years its

[15] Cf. MS. Rec. Pa. Soc. Abol. Sl., III, 105, 107, 109, 113, 130, 150,
218, (for a case prosecuted in Jamaica), 164, 174, 258; VI, 21, 264; VII,
35, 95, 99; IX, 69, 75, 122; and numerous references in VII and VIII.
[16] Pro. and Deb. Conv. 1837-1838, III, 778; VIII, 117; J. of H., 1836-1837,
vol. I, 349; J. of S., 1836-1837, p. 206; J. of H., 1838-1839, vol. I, 198;
J. of S., 1838-1839, vol. I, 323; J. of S., 1840, vol. I, 275.
[17] See above, p. 81.
[18] See above, pp. 83-84.
[19] See above, pp. 82-83. Also MS. Rec. Pa. Soc. Abol. Sl., IV, 19; V, 141.
[20] Ibid., I, 23.
[21] See above, pp. 81-82.

members were tireless in following up all possible cases, in bringing them to trial, and fighting them to the highest courts.[22] In this work they employed the best legal talent they could get,[23] and in furtherance of it made the earliest compilation of Pennsylvania's slave legislation.[24]

From slavery within Pennsylvania the abolitionists soon extended their hostility to slavery beyond the state's limits. First of all they attacked the slave-trade. In 1787 they prepared a memorial to be sent to the Federal Convention then about to assemble in Philadelphia asking that this trade be brought to an end.[25] In the following year when they asked the Pennsylvania Legislature to put a stop to the traffic from Philadelphia, their request was heeded, and a law passed.[26] About this time began the practice, so largely extended afterwards, of circulating broadsides, pamphlets, and pictures. In 1789 they tried to arouse feeling by the distribution of a horrible picture showing negroes crowded between a slaver's decks.[27] They continued to investigate alleged violations of the law at Philadelphia

[22] MS. Rec. Pa. Soc. Abol. Sl., I, 35, 197; VI, 159, 161; MS. Rec. of Manumissions, Book A, 242; MS. Min. Acting Committee (Pa. Soc. Abol. Sl.), 1784-1788, *passim*.

[23] MS. Rec. Pa. Soc. Abol. Sl., V, 43, 267; VI, 119.

[24] *Ibid.*, IV, 143. See bibliography, p. 263.

[25] " It is with deep distress they are forced to observe that the peace was scarcely concluded before the African Trade was revived " . . . MS. Rec. Pa. Soc. Abol. Sl., I, 83, 85.

[26] Act of 1788. See above, p. 81. The committee to which a later petition was referred, reported: " Your Committee cannot help here observing that the very iniquitous practice which has heretofore taken place in this State of equipping and fitting out Vessels for the African trade, has not yet been prevented by any efficient law." MS. Rec. Pa. Soc. Abol. Sl., I, 240.

[27] *Ibid.*, II, 5. " Plan of an African Ship's lower Deck, with Negroes, in the proportion of not quite one to a Ton." It had appeared in the *American Museum*, May, 1789.

for many years.[28] In 1812 they sent a secret agent to New York and to Rhode Island to gather information about the slave-trade there.[29]

Active hostility against slavery outside of Pennsylvania was both the cause and the effect of the diligence of the Pennsylvania Abolition Society in helping to found similar societies in other states. If not the parent she was at least the foster-mother of most similar societies elsewhere. In some cases the very origin of the earliest abolition societies was due to her inspiration,[30] while to many she gave advice, encouragement, and assistance.[31] With all she maintained constant and immense correspondence.[32] When in 1795 the New York Abolition Society felt that advantage would be gained by holding an abolition convention, it proposed to the Pennsylvania Society that the meeting should be held in Philadelphia.[33] Some idea of Pennsylvania's primacy in the abolition movement may be had from the fact that out of twenty-four conventions held between 1794 and 1829 twenty were held in Philadelphia.[34]

[28] MS. Rec. Pa. Soc. Abol. Sl., VI, 109, 111, 113, 123.

[29] Ibid., VII, 97. This had engaged their attention in 1788. Cf. ibid., I, 143, 171, 175, 177, 179.

[30] For example the New Jersey Abolition Society, 1792. Cf. Needles, Memoir, 40.

[31] MS. Rec. Pa. Soc. Abol. Sl., III, 230, 242; IV, 37; VI, 71.

[32] Among numerous instances of letters to abolition societies and to abolitionists, cf. ibid., I, 115, 121, 125, 129, 131, 137, 159, 161, 163, 165, 193; II, 219, 253; III, 55, 81, 83, 87, 116; IV, 41, 45, 55; VI, 214, 230; VIII, 179.

[33] MS. Rec. Pa. Soc. Abol. Sl., III, 248.

[34] Conventions were held at Philadelphia in 1794, 1795, 1796, 1797, 1798, 1800, 1801, 1803, 1804, 1805, 1806, 1809, 1812, 1816, 1817, 1819, 1821, 1823, 1825, 1827; at Washington in 1829. Adjourned meetings were held at Baltimore in 1826, 1828; and a special meeting at Philadelphia in 1818. Cf. Min. of Conventions of Delegates from Abolition Societies, etc., 1794-1837.

From opposing slavery in many different localities the abolitionists began to oppose it in the United States as a whole. In 1790 they sent to the Federal House of Representatives a memorial containing a strong appeal for the abolition of slavery and the slave-trade, but Congress could do little.[35] In 1794 the Convention at Philadelphia issued a stirring address, "To the Citizens of the United States," [36] and in 1809 one to the clergy.[37] Meanwhile the Pennsylvania Society opposed the Federal statute of 1793 concerning runaways, and began to fight the return of fugitive slaves.[38] The abolitionists were bitterly against the extension of slavery into Florida, or Missouri, or any new state.[39] They undertook to circulate in the South literature showing the impolicy of slavery and the advantages of emancipation.[40] Their memorials to the legislature and to Congress continued down to the Civil War.[41]

This work, however irritating it may have been to the slave-holders and the people of the South, had this character largely because of its thoroughness and persistence, not because it was violent or illegal. Very rarely did any member of the Society break the law, or

[35] " They earnestly entreat your serious attention to the Subject of Slavery; that you will be pleased to countenance the Restoration of liberty to those unhappy Men . . . that you will devise means for removing this Inconsistency from the Character of the American People . . . and that you will Step to the very verge of the Power vested in you, for discouraging every Species of Traffick in the Persons of our fellow Men." MS. Rec. Pa. Soc. Abol. Sl., II, 85.

[36] Of slavery they said: " It is inconsistent with the safety of the liberties of the United States. Freedom and Slavery cannot long exist together." *Ibid.*, IV, 15.

[37] " To the Clergy, and Pastors, thro'out the U. States." *Ibid.*, VI, 238.

[38] *Ibid.*, III, 285; also VI, 276, 283; VIII, 143.

[39] *Ibid.*, VI, 272; VIII, 267.

[40] *Ibid.*, IX, 156.

[41] *Cf. ibid.*, XI, 104 (1860).

desire that it should be broken. Some few favored immediate abolition of slavery in the South, but this feeling was not general.[42] On the contrary the leaders on several occasions denounced this as unwise and deprecated its consequences.[43] The furthest the Society would go was to distribute literature constantly,[44] and at times to favor not buying the goods of those who owned slaves [45]

On the whole, then, the work of the abolitionists in Pennsylvania during this period may be said to have been quiet, continuous, and successful. It was almost undisturbed by dissensions within the Society,[46] it was carried on by some of the most respectable and influential people of the state,[47] and awakened little opposition. It did much to elevate the negro, it put a stop to the slave-trade from Philadelphia, it checked kidnapping, and in Pennsylvania it drove slavery to the wall.

---

[42] In a declaration of principles in 1819 the Society proclaimed that " the practice of holding and selling human beings as property, . . . ought to be *immediately* abandoned," but " Resolved that while this Society deprecate physical resistance to established Law they hold it to be their " (duty) " by every lawful and constitutional means to seek the amendment of whatever in the constitution or Laws upholds the barbarous and oppressive system of Slavery in the United States." MS. Rec. Pa. Soc. Abol. Sl., VIII, 235 (1819).

[43] *Cf.* letter of committee of the Pa. Soc. Abol. Sl., to Arthur Tappan and others in New York, Oct. 7, 1833; " We hold it to be *unwise,* to urge by a National Convention, the principles of *immediate emancipation,* before the people at large, are properly informed of our meaning of the terms." MS. Rec. Pa. Soc. Abol. Sl., X, 205. *Cf.* also T. I. Wharton, *Memoir of William Rawle* (very prominent in the Society), 26, 27; " He had too much . . . ' *Common* sense ' . . . to suppose that emancipation was likely to be brought about by denunciation and abuse, or that it can ever be effected with safety to either race, except by the gradual progress of opinion in the communities in which it exists; " . . .

[44] MS. Rec. Pa. Soc. Abol. Sl., II, 7, 25, 37, 53, 55, 79, 95, 245; III, 1, 5, 124.

[45] *Ibid.,* IV, 261; VIII, 175; X, 27. *Cf.* also the Constitution of the " Free Produce Society of Pennsylvania."

[46] *Cf.* however, MS. Rec. Pa. Soc. Abol. Sl., VIII, 243, 251 (1820).

[47] *Cf.* various lists of members.

In the South, however, it had accomplished almost nothing. By 1830 this was evident, and many people tiring of the slow and orderly methods of the Quakers and the older abolitionists resolved to fight against slavery by any means in their power.

The increasing hostility in Pennsylvania against Southern slavery becomes marked after 1830, but the transition notwithstanding was gradual. After this time the Pennsylvania Abolition Society continued on its plodding course as before, but whereas previous to 1830 it had dominated the contest against slavery, it now dropped into a subordinate position, and its more hasty and impetuous members joined the anti-slavery movement. The influence of Garrison and the New England enthusiasts became more and more marked. The campaign that followed was vigorous, sensational, and uncompromising.

In 1833 Edwin P. Atlee issued a pamphlet in Philadelphia in which he said that gradual abolition had been effective only in some of the states, and that now immediate overthrow was necessary. He attacked the Constitution of the United States on the ground that it perpetuated slavery.[48] In the next year the Philadelphia Anti-Slavery Society was founded for the purpose of exterminating slavery ; it sought above all abolition in the District of Columbia ; and intended to oppose the admission of any more slave states.[49] In the year following the Young Men's Anti-Slavery Society of Phila-

---

[48] He urged " total abolition. Not gradual, but immediate." Atlee, *An Address to the Citizens of Philadelphia, on the Subject of Slavery,* 9.
[49] *Constitution of the Philadelphia Anti-Slavery Society* (Phila., 1834). Its first annual report (1835) said: " *Resolved,* As the sense of this Society, that it is the bounden duty of every good citizen of the United States to aid, as far as in him lies, to procure the amendment of whatever, in either the Constitution or Laws, upholds the monstrous oppression of Slavery and the Domestic Slave trade." *First An. Rep.,* 1.

delphia declared that slavery was contrary to the precepts of Christianity, dangerous to the liberties of the country, and ought to be abolished.[50] New societies sprang up rapidly in Philadelphia and elsewhere,[51] and one inflammatory declaration followed another.[52] It was not long before candidates for office began to be interrogated as to their stand on the slavery question,[53] while slave products were boycotted,[54] and immediate abolition was fiercely urged or else disunion.[55]

[50] *Constitution, By-Laws, etc. Young Men's A-S. Soc., Phila.*

[51] Many of these societies are known through petitions which they sent to the Legislature. Chester Co., A-S. Soc. (*J. of H., 1840*, vol. I, 508); York Springs A-S. Soc. (*ibid.*, I, 542); Clarkson A-S. Soc. (*ibid.*, I, 101); A-S. Soc. of Eastern Pa. (*J. of H., 1841*, vol. I, 153); Caln, Chester Co. A-S. Soc. (*ibid.*, I. 171); Union, Chester Co. A-S. Soc. (*ibid.*, I, 418); Colerain, Chester Co. A-S. Soc. (*ibid.*, I, 419); Fallowfield, Chester Co. A-S. Soc. (*ibid.*, I, 521); Phila. Female A-S. Soc. (*J. of S., 1849*, vol. I, 159). *Cf.* also J. H. Wert, " Old Time Notes of Adams County," nos. XIII to XV, in *Harrisburg Star and Sentinel*, Apr. 12-16, 1905.

[52] " Let the reader imagine a combination of the very worst features of all the endless forms of cruelty that have ever been devised, from the barbarities of the uneducated savage to the tortures of the Spanish Inquisition, and he may then have some idea of the condition of slavery in the United States." *Address of the Members of the Philadelphia Anti-Slavery Society to their Fellow Citizens,* 13, 14. " Resolved:—That we regard American Slavery, both in principle and practice, to be a violation of the law of God, and contrary to the spirit of the Constitution and institutions of our country " . . . , MS. Min. Junior Anti-Slavery Soc., 24 6 mo., 1836. *Cf.* also *Address to the Citizens of Pennsylvania* (by the convention at Harrisburg for the formation of a state anti-slavery society, 1837); *Address of the State Anti-Slavery Society to the Ministers of the Gospel in the State of Pennsylvania* (1838). The Eastern Section of the Pa. A-S. Soc. issued a pamphlet in German, *Was ist Aufhebung der Sclaverei (Abolition)*?

[53] *Cf. The Doctrines of the " Abolitionists " Refuted, etc.* (1840), by J. Washington Tyson.

[54] *Address to Abolitionists* (Phila., 1838); *American Free Produce Journal, Circular* (Phila., 1842).

[55] " It is the duty of Pennsylvania and of the South, to do to others as they would that others should do to them. It is their duty to let other States secede from the Union, much as they may regret it, if the only means of preventing it is to assist in inflicting a wrong upon others, which they would not undergo themselves for the sake of any political union that ever existed." " We ought instantly to grant to all men the enjoyment of their inalienable rights." *The Duty of Pennsylvania Concerning Slavery* (1840), 4, 5.

The difference between the new and the old method is made strikingly evident by the sudden fury which the anti-slavery people drew upon themselves. The abolitionists had formerly incurred hostility, though never very much ;[56] but from about 1834 there was condemnation of the new kind of abolitionism throughout the state.[57] In some places speakers were forbidden to lecture ;[58] and the activity of such advocates together with hatred of the negro was the direct cause of the burning of Pennsylvania Hall and of the riot at Philadelphia in 1838.[59] Beginning with the political campaign of that year, when Governor Ritner was accused of being an "abolitionist,"[60] this name was made one of the vilest terms of opprobrium that could be used against an opponent.[61]

The notoriety which Pennsylvania anti-slavery in common with that of other states of the North gained at this time, is shown in the furious protests which came from the South, demanding the passage of laws to check it.[62] The indignation in Pennsylvania itself

---

[56] *Cf.* for example MS. Rec. Pa. Soc. Abol. Sl., III, 148 (1792).

[57] *Marietta Advocate,* June 5, 1834; *Columbia Spy,* July 12, 1834; *Reading Democratic Press,* Feb. 14, Oct. 3, 1837; *Upland Union,* Oct. 2, 1838. " No where is the plan of instant abolition more deeply deprecated than in this Commonwealth." *Marietta Advocate,* July 31, 1834. *The Luzerne Union,* June 1, 1853, speaking of William Lloyd Garrison, said: " If this notorious individual had dealt out to him his just deserts, he would probably long since have been placed in a lunatic Asylum."

[58] *Cf. Marietta Advocate,* July 31, 1834.

[59] See above, p. 162. *Cf.* also *Address of the Eastern Executive Committee of the State Anti-Slavery Society, to the Citizens of Pennsylvania* (1838); *The Little Western against the Great Eastern,* etc. (1838); *Pro. and Deb. Conv., 1837-1838,* XI, 297.

[60] *Carlisle American Volunteer,* Mar. 1, 1838; (Harrisburg) *Pennsylvania Reporter,* 1838, *passim; Upland Union,* Oct. 9, 1838.

[61] *Cf.* (Harrisburg) *Key Stone,* July 1, Sept. 3, 1851.

[62] From S. C., N. C., Ga., Ala., Va., Ky., Miss. See *J. of H., 1835-1836,* vol. II, 195-199; 200-204, 387-390, 547-548, .613-614, 710-713, 760-762; *J. of S., 1835-1836,* pp. 110, 187, 438, 574, 704. These protests came from the state legislatures.

was so great that the Legislature was asked to suppress the evil.[63] The anti-slavery enthusiasts were acknowledged to be a public nuisance,[64] but the Legislature had already concluded that while their arguments might be harmful, it would be unwise to prohibit their utterance.[65] For a while anti-slavery continued to be condemned;[66] the leaders of the older abolition movement discountenanced it;[67] and special protection from mob

[63] A law was asked to punish as vagrants " idlers . . . prowling through the country calling themselves abolitionists, without any visible means of support, stirring up discord and dissension among the people " . . . *J. of H., 1836-1837,* vol. I, 770.

[64] Resolution of the House, *J. of H., 1837-1838,* vol. I, 291.

[65] *J. of H., 1835-1836,* vol. II, 804-806.

[66] Sleigh, *Abolitionism Exposed* (1838); *Abolition A Sedition, By a Northern Man* (1839), where the methods of the American A-S. Soc. are contrasted with the quiet work of the Quaker abolitionists.

[67] *Cf.* the remarkable letter of William Rawle, one of the presidents of the Pa. Soc. Abol. Sl., read before the Pa. Constitutional Convention, Feb. 5, 1838. " The objects of this association were temperate, legitimate and correct—they were substantially confined to the limits of our own state—much individual good was done—coloured people suffering by reason of fraud or unlawful violence were relieved—the pursuits of them by persons falsely claiming rights to their service were judiciously repelled—their youth were educated—their industry assisted—in sickness they were aided—and in the hour of death they were solaced and supported.

" In all this no offense was given to the citizens of other states. Their boundaries were respected, and their laws and constitutions not attempted to be violated. A belief was entertained that an abhorrence of slavery would gradually work its way, and that it was the duty of the society patiently to wait the event.

" It was not till the year 1833, that some well meaning men, chiefly north of our city, exhibited indications of dissatisfaction with the slow progress that had been made in the work of general emancipation. Societies were formed with the express object of producing—if possible—an immediate and total extinction of slavery throughout the United States, not by force, but by reasoning, and by endeavouring to convince the holders of slaves that their conduct was inconsistent with morality, religion, and even their own interest."

" It appeared to me that however fair and promising in the abstract, this course might be, it could not be long pursued without exciting jealousy, suspicion, and dissatisfaction, on the part of the slave-holders of the southern states. Conviction was less likely to be produced than opposition." *Pro. and Deb.,* XI, 287, 288.

violence was sharply refused.[68] It was the opinion of conservative people that the results of the movement were disappointing, and that in Pennsylvania it had increased the prejudice against the negro race.[69]

After 1839 there was a reaction, and gradually opposition to anti-slavery decreased. On the one hand the work, if not less vigorous, was at least less conspicuous, while on the other radical feeling in Pennsylvania slowly increased.[70] After 1850 the trend of national affairs made many converts, and what was regarded in Pennsylvania as the aggression of the Southern slave power caused numbers of men to become more active against Southern slavery.[71] This is seen in nothing more clearly than in the rise of the Society of Progressive Friends.

It has been shown that in Pennsylvania warfare against slavery was from the first carried on by the Friends. They had most to do with destroying it, and they had formed the backbone of the old Abolition Society. After 1833, however, the leadership fell to the more aggressive anti-slavery societies, owing to dissatisfaction with the conservative methods of the elder organization. This dissatisfaction was felt by many of

---

[68] *Cf. Report of the Committee on the Judiciary Relative to the Abolition of Slavery in the District of Columbia,* etc. (1839), 10.

[69] *Cf. Remarks of Dr. Burden* (1838), 8, 9; Letter of W. Rawle quoted in *Pro. and Deb.,* XI, 288.

[70] In 1838 the abolitionist tone of Governor Ritner's message had astonished the state. *Cf.* (Wilkesbarre) *Republican Farmer,* Aug. 8, 1838, which declared that Ritner's encouragement had made abolitionism a force in Pennsylvania. Thaddeus Stevens was blamed for this conversion. *Bedford Gazette,* June 22, 1838.

[71] " If the abolitionists just now have unusual popularity and power, it is because the Democrats have gratuitously violated pledges, invaded human rights, and shed human blood." *Harrisburg Telegraph,* Sept. 25, 1856.

the Quakers themselves.[72] After 1840 the members of
some of the Quaker Meetings began silently dividing
into two parties, one favoring the quiet, traditional
methods, the other desiring active participation in the
new anti-slavery movement. In most cases this split
went no further than animated discussions in the meetings; but in 1845 the Western Quarterly Meeting held
at London Grove was broken up by Stephen S. Foster,
an ardent advocate who urged immediate emancipation.[73] He had many followers, and for some years one
of the meeting houses was used by them after the sitting of the conservative Friends was over.[74] After
a while, however, the doors were locked upon them,
and a definite secession took place.[75] In 1853 they and
others like minded met in Kennett Square and founded
the Society of Progressive Friends.[76] Thereafter there
were no more vigorous opponents of slavery than they,
none more outspoken and bitter in denouncing it.[77]

Although abolitionism incurred some odium and anti-
slavery often encountered active hostility, yet both were

[72] One of the most picturesque of these was Isaac T. Hopper. *Cf.* L. M.
Child, *Life of Isaac T. Hopper,* 314; H. Simpson, *The Lives of Eminent
Philadelphians, Now Deceased,* 548-563.
[73] Edith Pennock, " Early History of the Pennsylvania Yearly Meeting
of Progressive Friends," *Proceedings of, 1891.*
[74] *Ibid.*
[75] It began among the Hicksite Friends, who had themselves formerly
seceded from the Orthodox Quakers. MS. by Edith Pennock in possession
of the author.
[76] Edith Pennock, in *Proceedings Pa. Yr. M. Pro. Friends, 1891,* p. 12.
[77] " American Slavery, the master crime of our country and of the age."
Pro. Pa. Yr. M. Progressive Friends, 1853, p. 31. " That gigantic system
of robbery and wrong, American Slavery " *Ibid., 1856,* p. 43. " Henceforth, the duty of the North is plain. It is at once to repent of its iniquity,
and to withdraw from its present alliance with the South . . . It is to pro-
claim the American Union a wild and guilty experiment . . . pandering to
all the demands and necessities of the Slave Power, and sure, if not abolished, to bring destruction upon the whole land." *Ibid., 1857,* 14. *Cf. ibid.,
1858,* p. 35.

able to exert great influence in Pennsylvania, because
after all they only expressed in radical manner ideas
widely held there. After 1780 the dislike of the people
for slavery came by degrees to be almost universal in
the state. This feeling was the cause of the numerous
protests against the slave-trade, against the extension
of slavery, and against slavery in the District of
Columbia. Even in the Legislature men were bold and
outspoken, and restrained, when at all, only by the
desire not to offend the South.

Pennsylvania's hostility to slavery intruded into
national politics in 1804, when Bard, one of her representatives, moved in Congress that negroes imported
into the United States should be taxed ten dollars each.[78]
Two years later the Legislature instructed the representatives of the state to press for a constitutional
amendment putting an end to the slave-trade at once.[79]
Similar expressions continued until the traffic was forbidden in 1808.[80]

Opposition to the extension of slavery began at the
time of the Missouri Compromise, when Pennsylvania,
in common with other northern states, passed strong
resolutions, which if fruitless at least showed her attitude clearly.[81] Later, after the Compromise had passed,

[78] *Annals of Congress*, 8 Cong., 1 sess., 820, cited in Channing, *Jeffer-
sonian System*, 105.

[79] *J. of H., 1805-1806*, pp. 434, 435.

[80] " The General Assembly look forward with Confidence, that as soon
as that period arrives, the Congress of the United States will promptly
exercise their power, to wipe off that foul stain which has long tarnished
the American character." Resolution of Mar. 19, 1807. *Acts of Ass.,
1806-1807*, p. 301. *Cf. J. of S., 1807-1808*, pp. 174, 203, 212.

[81] Extension of slavery was declared to be a policy " which, if adopted,
would impede the march of humanity and freedom through the world;
and would transfer from a misguided ancestry an odious stain and fix
it indelibly upon the present race " . . . *J. of H., 1819-1820*, p. 52. The
resolution was adopted unanimously. *Ibid.*, 97, 98. *Cf. J. of S., 1819-1820*,
pp. 7, 64, 69, 75, 77.

a blow was aimed at the very root of the trouble, for in 1824 the House resolved that it was expedient that the several state governments should cooperate with the government of the United States so as to procure gradual abolition throughout the Union. This was to be done without any infringement of state rights.[82] A similar resolution passed the Senate in the following year,[83] while the sentiment of the people was shown in numerous petitions.[84]

An object sought far more persistently was the abolition of slavery and the slave-trade in the District of Columbia.   During the entire generation before the Compromise of 1850 petitions were sent to the Legislature asking that Congress be urged to bring this about.[85] In 1828-1829 the Legislature passed almost unanimously a resolution instructing Pennsylvania's congressmen to work for abolition in the District;[86] and when in 1831 the State Senate, replying to a petition from the American Convention for the abolition of slavery, said that nothing more could be done, it de-

[82] J. of H., 1823-1824, pp. 825, 968.

[83] J. of S., 1825-1826, pp. 77, 78, 152, 155.

[84] J. of H., 1826-1827, vol. I, 317, 392, 433, 444, 459, 480, 509; J. of S., 1826-1827, pp. 553, 669; J. of S., 1827-1828, p. 133.

[85] J. of H., 1827-1828, vol. I, 179, 239, 256, 330, 414, 495, 682; J. of H., 1830-1831, vol. I, 140; J. of H., 1836-1837, vol. I, 435; J. of H., 1837-1838, vol. I, 45, 97, 134, 161, 187, 219, 237, 264, 388; J. of S., 1837-1838, vol. I, 130, 139; J. of H., 1838-1839, vol. I, 127, 160, 222, 232, 251, 262, 309, 344, 376, 377, 394, 417, 432, 455, 468, 572; J. of S., 1838-1839, vol. I, 368, 404, 409, 420, 423, 441, 452, 527; J. of H., 1840, vol. I, 366; J. of H., 1842, vol. I, 149. These petitions came from all parts of the state, a large proportion from anti-slavery societies. Many contained the signatures of women.

[86] Laws of Ass., 1828-1829, p. 371; J. of H., 1827-1828, vol. I, 610, 798; vol. II, 891, 892; J. of S., 1828-1829, pp. 152, 166, 168, 169, 172. 'Cf. Speech of Mr. Miner . . . on the Subject of Slavery and the Slave Trade in the District of Columbia, etc. (1829).

clared bitterly that slavery at the Federal capital was a foul stain upon the character of the nation.[87]

Meanwhile the Legislature continued to be memorialized about the spread of slavery into new territory,[88] the domestic slave-trade was reviled,[89] and the bitterest reproach that could be cast upon a candidate for public office was that he was a slaveholder or a dealer in slaves.[90] Sometimes a voice was raised in favor of the South, asserting that it should not be blamed for the system which it had inherited, and of which it could not get rid;[91] but as a rule condemnation was hearty and general.[92] Therefore when in 1846 David Wilmot urged his famous Proviso in Congress, it may be seen that whatever his motives were, he had behind him a large part of the people of his state.

There is reason to believe that before 1850 a majority of the people of Pennsylvania were hostile to slavery anywhere. Most of them believed that they had no right to interfere with Southern problems, and strongly desired to avoid offending the South,[93] so that at times rabid anti-slavery leaders were dejected.[94] After 1850,

[87] *J. of S., 1830-1831,* pp. 460, 461.

[88] For example *J. of S., 1838-1839,* vol. I, 314, 423; *J. of S., 1850,* vol. I, 548. *Cf. Bradford Reporter,* Jan. 5, 1847.

[89] *Cf. Westmoreland Intelligencer,* Jan. 24, 1834.

[90] *Cf. Harrisburg Argus,* July 26, 1828, which accuses Gen. Jackson, with *York Gazette,* Oct. 24, 1828, which reviles Henry Clay.

[91] *Philadelphian,* Feb. 19, 1835.

[92] " It need not be concealed, and it cannot be denied that in Pennsylvania, we, with a unanimity unequalled on any other subject, regard slavery as a national curse and a national disgrace." J. X. McLanahan, *Speech . . . on the Slave Question* (1850), 6.

[93] This is obvious in almost every Pennsylvania newspaper down to the very outbreak of the Civil War. *Cf.* for example the calm discussion of the Dred Scott decision in the *Public Ledger,* Mar. 10, 19, 1857.

[94] *Cf. ibid.,* Mar. 30, 1857, for report of an address made by a mulatto from Massachusetts.

however, the rapid movement of national events, the repeal of the Missouri Compromise, the troubles in Kansas, the Dred Scott decision, all made new converts, and all made existing anti-slavery feeling stronger. Beyond all of these things the law of 1850 embittered feeling, and made more acute a question that had long been a source of trouble. This was the question of fugitive slaves.

CHAPTER XIII.

FUGITIVE SLAVES.

IN the treatment of the Pennsylvania negro after 1800 there is seemingly a strange contradiction, for he was the victim of violent prejudice at the same time that he received the liveliest sympathy and aid. During the whole period, while funds were being raised to ship negroes to Africa, while the Legislature was overwhelmed with petitions for their exclusion, while one race riot followed another, and while everything was done to convince the world that Pennsylvania desired no negroes, or at least no more of them, there was witnessed the curious spectacle of action on the part of the state, which betrayed an apparent desire to have them after all. From 1830 to 1860 almost never was assistance refused to a fugitive slave from the South, even when he was known to be such; and during this time it was with the greatest difficulty that a master could recover his property. In the course of this conduct men and women of Pennsylvania went any length of risk and self-sacrifice to assist runaways. Toward the end of the period the state was brought to the threshold of nullification. All this was for the most part the outcome of the abolitionist and anti-slavery movements, which at last overran the entire state.

In her earlier history Pennsylvania was involved in no difficulties with neighboring states because of fugitives, since she then had numerous slaves of her own,

many of whom ran away. Accordingly when advertisements appeared in the Philadelphia papers about negroes who had fled from Virginia or Maryland, they
generally appeared intermingled with similar advertisements inserted by masters of the city and county nearby.[1]
The legislation on the subject while negative was of a
friendly character. The abolition act of 1780 distinctly
affirmed that its provisions covered no fugitive,[2] and
after the first law was made against kidnapping it was
decided that it gave no relief to a runaway slave.[3] Hence
fugitives from the South like runaways in Pennsylvania were detained in the county jail, where the local
authorities might lodge them on suspicion, and where
they were kept pending the arrival of the owners. Advertisements to inform owners were inserted in the
newspapers, and masters might get their slaves on
proving ownership and paying the costs. If no claimant appeared, a negro who had been detained was sold
or set free at the discretion of the local court.[4]

The increasing activity of the Quakers and the abolitionists made it impossible for such conditions to last,
since the people who were so eager to help the former
slaves of Pennsylvania began also to pity the fugitives
from states nearby. Even as early as 1792 complaint
was made that certain persons were seducing and har-

[1] Phila. newspapers *passim*, also many notices in the early papers of the
border counties, as (York) *Pennsylvania Herald, Harrisburg Courant,
Lancaster Intelligencer.*

[2] *Stat. at L.*, X, 71.

[3] *Laws of Pennsylvania* (Dallas), II, 587; 2 Dallas 224-228 (1795).

[4] See above, p. 49. Cf. *Pa. Gazette*, Feb. 18, 1801. The earlier spirit
is revealed in a letter from President Muhlenberg to Governor Randolph
of Virginia, asking whether a certain fugitive was owned there, and saying
that he " will . . . with pleasure restore him to his owner." 1 *Pa. Arch.*,
XI, 249, 256.

boring slaves from Virginia.[5] In 1804 a traveller
speaks of a Friend, a tailor of Philadelphia, who used
to sit at his front window, and leave his work whenever
he saw a negro whom he thought to be a runaway. If
such proved to be the case, he would help him to reach
the interior parts of the state.[6] Meanwhile news began
to reach the negroes to the southward that they had a
fair chance of being assisted to their freedom if they escaped across the line.[7] The result of the aid given by
individuals together with an increasing sentiment which
made the existing laws both inadequate and difficult of
enforcement, was that great numbers of slaves fled
north into Pennsylvania and found refuge there. Such
proportions did this movement assume that in 1813 a
petition to the Legislature said that there were four
thousand runaway negroes in Philadelphia alone.[8] At
the same time they were spoken of as undesirable in the
extreme.[9] The increasing difficulty of getting slaves
back to the South is in no way so evident as that, although the number of fugitives was continually growing, their masters ceased advertising for them in the
papers. After 1820 such advertisements were rare.

While the loss occasioned by this fleeing from service
was felt in all the neighboring Southern states, the one

[5] *J. of S., 1791-1792*, p. 74.

[6] " Where he would be sure to find employment." Sutcliff, *Travels in
Some Parts of North America*, 58.

[7] " The slaves in this state " (Virginia) " generally supposing they may
obtain their freedom by going into Pennsylvania makes it highly probable
that he is in some part of that state." Advt. for a runaway, *Pa. Packet*,
Oct. 22, 1789.

[8] *J. of H., 1812-1813*, p. 417.

[9] *Ibid. Cf.* also 3 Sergeant and Rawle 6 (1817): " These runaway
slaves are often guilty of riots, violent assaults and batteries, and other
offences, which, though not felonious, are dangerous to the peace of the
commonwealth." *Cf. J. of H., 1818-1819*, p. 139.

which naturally suffered most damage was Maryland. In 1801 she asked Pennsylvania for assistance, but reply was made that the matter was covered by the Federal fugitive slave law of 1793.[10] In 1817 Maryland formally complained that Pennsylvania encouraged her runaways, and in the next year her General Assembly passed a resolution requesting that the executives of the two states endeavor to find a remedy.[11] Nothing was done; but meanwhile the stream of fugitives increased to such an extent that in the year following even the inhabitants of Philadelphia asked the Legislature to interfere.[12]

In 1822 the Governor of Maryland transmitted a resolution of the Legislature of his state which declared that the encouragement given to runaways by citizens of Delaware and of Pennsylvania had caused such serious injury to owners, and that harboring them had increased so alarmingly, that it would be criminal to keep silence any longer. It asked that the respective Legislatures endeavor to prevent this.[13] A committee of the Pennsylvania House, to which this communication was referred, declared that it did not believe that the laws of the commonwealth were adequate.[14] In the next year another long communication from Maryland related that her people were beginning to view Pennsylvania as a hostile state; that some of her citizens had recently been murdered when attempting to recover

[10] J. of H., 1800-1801, pp. 350, 416; J. of S., 1800-1801, p. 231.

[11] J. of H., 1816-1817, pp. 524, 525, 577, 578, 627.

[12] J. of H., 1818-1819, p. 139.

[13] 4 Pa. Arch., V, 371-373, 386, 387; J. of H., 1821-1822, pp. 1067-1069; J. of S., 1821-1822, pp. 739-741.

[14] They did not give the protection " which in good faith we are bound to give." J. of H., 1821-1822, pp. 1115, 1116.

their slaves across the line;[15] and that the people of
Pennsylvania had interposed every possible obstacle,
going so far as to encourage negroes to resist by tell-
thing them that they had the right to put pursuing
owners to death.[16] Finally in 1826 Maryland sent three
commissioners to negotiate with the Legislature of
Pennsylvania about how best to facilitate the recovery
of runaways, and also how to prevent their absconding.[17]
Thus as early as this time the Federal law respecting
fugitives had come to have so little effect, that it was
necessary for these two states practically to arrange a
treaty.[18]

In the capture and return of fugitive slaves the procedure at this time in force was that ordained by the
United States law of 1793.[19] This law declared that any
owner, his agent, or attorney empowered, might reclaim
a runaway wherever found; but that in so doing he
must take the fugitive before the judge of a Circuit

[15] 1821. Cf. Niles's Weekly Register, XIX, 336. This case affords an
excellent illustration of the hazard encountered by pursuing masters. A
runaway negro from Maryland had established himself in Chester County.
He had lived there for some time when late one night his master attempted to enter his house, saying that he had a warrant to search for
stolen goods. The negro killed him and one of his companions. At the
trial it was shown that the negro was a runaway, but it was asserted that
under the curcumstances he had some right of self defense. He was not
returned to Maryland, but was sentenced to seven years in the penitentiary for manslaughter. Cf. Pa. Mag., XIII, 106-109.

[16] J. of S., 1822-1823, pp. 233, 234. In Philadelphia in 1824, when an
alleged runaway was remanded to jail, one hundred and fifty armed negroes attempted his rescue. For this seven of the ringleaders were sent
to prison. Democratic Press, Sept. 7, 1824; American Daily Advertiser,
Sept. 8, 1824; Niles's Reg., XXVII, 32. For a similar incident, cf.
Greensburg Gazette, Jan. 28, 1825.

[17] 4 Pa. Arch., V, 627-629.

[18] Cf. 4 Pa. Arch. VIII, 291.

[19] "An Act respecting fugitives from justice, and persons escaping
from the service of their masters." U. S. Stat. at L., 2 Cong., 2 sess.,
ch. 7, 1793.

Court or District Court of the United States, or before the magistrate of the county, city, or town, who, on satisfactory proof, should issue an order granting the negro to his master.[20] It imposed a penalty of five hundred dollars upon any one who obstructed pursuit, assisted a negro to escape, or harbored or concealed a fugitive; besides which the claimant might bring action for injury.[21] This law had remained comparatively unaffected by any legislation of Pennsylvania. Only in 1820, because, as it was asserted, great abuses existed, an act was passed forbidding aldermen or justices of the peace to act in fugitive slave cases.[22] On the other hand nothing had been done to give efficacy to the law, and it was now thought that this should be done.

On arriving the Maryland delegation conferred with a joint committee of the Pennsylvania Legislature, which prepared a bill designed to assist the execution of the law of the United States.[23] The work was done with swiftness and decision. Numerous petitions were

[20] " Whereas John a negro man aged about twenty-seven years of age of black complection has been claimed before me Jonathan T. Knight an Associate Judge of the Court of Common Pleas of Philadelphia County by Richard Ireland Jones of Anne Arundel County Maryland, as a fugitive from the service of him . . . and I being satisfied upon proof made to my satisfaction that the said John does owe labour and service to the said . . . Jones under the laws of Maryland . . . I have granted this certificate to the said . . . Jones, which shall be sufficient warrant to him . . . for removing said John . . . to . . . Maryland from which he fled " . . . MS. in Misc. Coll., Box 10, Negroes.

[21] Cf. Hill v. Law (1822), 4 Washington's Circuit Court Rep., 327-331; Van Metre v. Mitchell (1847), 4 Pa. Law Journal Rep., (111)-(120); 2 Wallace Jr. 311-323.

[22] See above, p. 117.

[23] " An Act To give effect to the provisions of the constitution of the United States, relative to fugitives from labor, for the protection of free people of color, and to prevent kidnapping." Acts of Assembly, 1825-1826, p. 150.

received, and the bill was thoroughly debated;[24] but in spite of strenuous opposition it passed both houses, and the Governor signed it immediately.[25]

The law of 1826 gave to slave-owners substantial help in one respect only: it permitted a claimant to place an alleged runaway in the Pennsylvania jails pending his trial. It provided that the claimant under oath must secure a warrant for the arrest, and produce evidence together with an affidavit subscribed before a justice of the peace of that locality from which the fugitive had escaped. The testimony of other interested parties was to be debarred.[26] On the other hand the act provided heavy penalties to prevent kidnapping, and to protect free people of color.[27]

This law, which was the most that the people of Pennsylvania were ever willing to do for slave-owners elsewhere, marks a turning point. Almost immediately the current began setting slowly but surely against giving any help at all. In the very next year a supplementary law was passed,[28] and after that time there is a steadily

[24] *J. of H.*, *1825-1826*, pp. 307, 310, 323, 341, 344, 345, 350, 351, 352, 358, 359, 362, 364, 365, 366, 371, 372, 374, 376-383, 384-387, 389, 625; *J. of S.*, *1825-1826*, pp. 282-284, 333, 339, 349, 350, 353, 354, 466, 468, 472, 481, 491, 494, 511. The Pa. Abolition Society protested that the law contemplated might make felons of its members. *Cf. Phila. Gazette*, Feb. 16, 1826.

[25] *J. of H.*, *1825-1826*, pp. 389, 644, 657; *J. of S.*, *1825-1826*, p. 491.

[26] *Acts of Assembly*, *1825-1826*, pp. 150-155.

[27] *Ibid.* In the end even the abolitionists were almost satisfied with this law. *Cf.* MS. Rec. Pa. Soc. Abol. Sl., IX, 202, 210, 216, 224; also MS. Min., 1825-1847, pp. 29-33.

[28] "An Act to prevent certain abuses of the laws relative to fugitives from labour," . . . "whereas, The traffic in slaves, now abhorred by all the civilized world, ought not in the slightest degree to be tolerated in the state of Pennsylvania" . . . the sale of a fugitive in the state is forbidden under heavy penalties. *Laws of Assembly*, *1827*, pp. 485, 486. *Cf. J. of H.*, *1826-1827*, pp. 26, 33, 88, 89, 100, 110, 786, 788; *J. of S.*, *1826-1827*, pp. 245, 983.

rising tide of protest against doing anything to the detriment of freedom.

There can be no doubt that this feeling was partly excited by the successful capture of a number of fugitives. In 1831 a negress was arrested, and the proof being sufficient she was taken away, the picture of despair, it is said.[29]   In 1833 there was so sad an occurrence that it was remarked that such incidents caused many people of the North to demand immediate emancipation.[30]   Two years later there was a most pathetic case, and the strong feeling evoked caused a riot in which two witnesses were injured.[31]   Several captures were effected about the time that the Constitutional Convention began sitting in 1837.[32]   During these years the same tactics began to be employed as found place in the final destruction of slavery in Pennsylvania itself.[33] The Quakers and the abolitionists used every possible legal technicality, and took advantage of every one of the law's delays.[34]   Counsel was often hired, or efforts were made to buy the captive free.[35]   Frequently the

[29] *Village Record,* quoted in *Inquirer,* July 8, 1831.

[30] Editorial in *Inquirer,* June 1, 1833. The woman was taken away from her husband and six children.

[31] *Inquirer,* June 17, 19, 1835; also editorial *ibid.,* June 24, 1835.

[32] *Inquirer,* Aug. 8, Nov. 29, Dec. 5, 1837; *Sentinel,* Dec. 19, 1837.

[33] See above, pp. 81-82.

[34] *Cf. Hazard's Register,* VII, 136; 4 *Pa. Law Journal,* (6), (7); (Harrisburg) *Pennsylvania Telegraph,* June 8, 1842. In 1835 two gentlemen from Virginia, while taking back their fugitive slaves, were arrested for travelling on Sunday. Volunteer lawyers, who had secretly arranged the matter, argued the case at such length, that the slaves, who had meanwhile been set at large by other conspirators, were never retaken. The owners got heavy damages, however. *Butler Repository,* June 23, 1836.

[35] *Inquirer,* June 17, 1835; *id.,* July 8, 1831; Aug. 8, 1837; *Public Ledger,* Jan. 27, 1851.

sympathies of the court were entirely with the fugitive.[36]

Meanwhile the Legislature was besieged with petitions asking that alleged runaways be allowed trial by
jury. Had such trial been granted there can be very
little doubt that at times few owners would have recovered slaves, however clear their title. It was probably
because the abolitionists realized the strength of popular feeling against slavery that jury trial was requested.
It was demanded insistently and continually through
session after session of the Legislature. The number
of petitions sent in was prodigious. If they received
any consideration at all, they must have distracted much
of the members' attention.[37] When the Convention of
1837-1838 was sitting one of the matters which occasioned long debate was this same thing. It was argued
with great eloquence that under existing conditions the
trial of fugitives could be a mockery of justice; and that
kidnapping was encouraged, since negroes undoubtedly
free might be tried in the same manner.[38] Some asserted that the Federal statute did not preclude granting jury trial, or at least that the United States Consti-

[36] For Robert Wharton, alderman and mayor of Philadelphia, who
during forty years never surrendered one runaway, see L. M. Child,
Life of Isaac T. Hopper, 141.

[37] Cf. *J. of H., 1835-1836*, vol. I, 336, 423, 445, 468, 492, 522, 590, 618,
648, 720, 797, 901, 1003; *J. of S., 1835-1836*, vol. I, 329, 376, 428, 482;
J. of H., 1836-1837, vol. I, 108, 132, 168, 183, 194, 199, 247, 284, 316,
344, 350, 371, 406, 437, 467, 648, 671, 800; *J. of S., 1836-1837*, vol. I, 110,
125, 137, 143, 150, 159, 171, 197, 206, 212, 224, 228, 244, 273, 279, 285,
300, 315, 372; *J. of H., 1840*, vol. I, 140, 264, 292, 344, 422, 447, 507,
613, 649, 707, 1136; *J. of S., 1840*, pp. 143, 151, 157, 182, 183, 211,
232, 259, 264, 275, 312, 446; *J. of H., 1841*, vol. I, 82, 100, 101, 171, 188,
215, 237, 263, 295, 320, 343, 418, 472; *J. of S., 1841*, vol. I, 126, 136,
211, 545; *J. of S., 1842*, vol. I, 164, 213, 217; *J. of S., 1844*, vol. I, 92.

[38] *Pro. and Deb. Conv.*, XI, 251-262, 312; XII, 43.

tution did not.[39] Such trial would probably have been granted had it not been shown that this would be virtual nullification, and defiance of the United States government.[40] The proposition was finally voted down by a decisive majority;[41] but the feeling behind the attempt was shown by the number of memorials and representations which came from every direction,[42] the majority from Friends, from abolitionists, and from women.

Meanwhile the law of 1826 became less and less popular, and various proposals were made to take away such effectiveness as it had in the returning of runaways.[43] It is probable that some change would have been made had no new factor been introduced. A powerful factor was, however, unexpectedly brought to bear.

The law of 1826 had been passed partly to satisfy Maryland, but more to put a stop to kidnapping.[44] In 1837 a certain Edward Prigg and associates, agents for a Maryland owner whose slave had escaped into Pennsylvania in 1832, took out of that state a negress, the alleged fugitive, together with her children, one of whom had been born in Pennsylvania. They did this although the magistrate before whom they appeared had refused to take cognizance of the case. Accordingly they were indicted for kidnapping in the Court of Oyer and Terminer of York County, and there ad-

[39] *Pro. and Deb. Conv.*, XI, 264, 265, 298-304; XII, 29.
[40] *Ibid.*, XI, 268-279, 282-298.
[41] 76 to 39. *Ibid.*, XI, 329; XII, 43.
[42] *Pro. and Deb. Conv.*, II, 333; III, 369, 521, 561, 567, 701, 757, 778; V, 49, 98, 270, 414, 443; VI, 69, 161, 203, 297, 340, 371; VII, 1, 2, 83; VIII, 40, 71, 91, 268; IX, 225; X, 29, 274; XI, 31, 76, 174, 211, 253, 280.
[43] *Cf. J. of H.*, *1835-1836*, vol. I, 523, 524; *J. of H.*, *1836-1837*, vol. I, 29, 81, 157, 201, 202; *J. of S.*, *1836-1837*, vol. I, 251, 447, 448, 451, 461, 466, 469, 473, 477; *J. of H.*, *1837-1838*, vol. I, 597; *J. of S.*, *1837-1838*, vol. I, 314, 538, 566, 592, 596, 597, 614-616.
[44] See above, p. 233.

judged guilty. While the case was pending Maryland asked that it be dismissed, and at the same time herself expressed discontent with the act of 1826, saying that it obstructed the return of fugitive slaves, and so violated the Federal statute of 1793. She declared that unless it were repealed she would test it before the Supreme Court of the United States.[45] Upon this the Legislature of Pennsylvania took measures to have the point decided. Temporary immunity was granted to the defendants,[46] while the case was taken to the highest court of the state, where the judgment was affirmed.[47] Prigg then appealed to the Supreme Court of the United States, his counsel pleading that the Pennsylvania act was unconstitutional. In 1842 decision was handed down that this was true in so far as the act obstructed the return of runaways, while part of the Court held that in the matter of returning fugitive slaves Pennsylvania had no power to make any law whatsoever.[48] Thus the Supreme Court was brought to declare void a law of Pennsylvania which many of Pennsylvania's people ardently desired to annul. In the natural reaction which followed, the former efforts

[45] Communication from J. Meredith, Commissioner of the State of Maryland. *J. of S., 1838-1839*, vol. II, 421-425.

[46] "An Act Relating to the Trial of Bemis and others, in York county." *Laws of Assembly, 1839*, p. 218.

[47] 16 Peters 539-541; Lewis, *Criminal Law of the United States*, 24-27.

[48] "Where Congress have exclusive power over a subject, it is not competent for state legislation to add to the provisions of Congress on that subject." "The power of legislation in relation to fugitives from labor is exclusive in the national legislature." 16 Peters 542. *Cf.* 16 Peters 622. This extreme view was restated in Kauffman *v.* Oliver (1849), 10 *Pa. State Rep.* (Barr) 514-519. On the contrary Chief Justice Taney thought that while a state must not impede the execution of the Federal law, it could assist, and should do so. 16 Peters 626-633. *Cf.* Moore *v.* The People of the State of Illinois (1852), 14 Howard 13.

were redoubled.[49] In 1847 a drastic change was made.

The act of 1847 began by reaffirming the most stringent penalties against kidnapping, in this not disturbing the work of 1826. It then went the full length of refusing to allow any officer of the state to assist in carrying out the Federal law of 1793. Under heavy penalty[50] it forbade any judge or state official to take cognizance of any case arising under that law, or to issue any warrant for removal. With delicate irony it then imposed a penalty upon any jailer who should confine in his jail a negro except where the judges aforesaid had jurisdiction. Finally it declared that if any person claiming a negro attempted to take him violently, even with the intention of bringing him before a district or a circuit judge, he should be adjudged guilty of a misdemeanor, and be subject to fine and to imprisonment in the county jail.[51]

[49] J. of H., 1842, vol. I, 536, 923; J. of H., 1843, pp. 250, 275, 499, 567; J. of S., 1842-1843, pp. 257, 268, 297, 337, 339, 501, 549, 682, 697; J. of H., 1844, vol. I, 107, 261, 330, 395, 547; J. of S., 1844, vol. I, 93, 277, 506; J. of H., 1845, vol. I, 105, 132, 179, 181, 242, 290, 649; J. of S., 1845, vol. I, 94, 97, 110, 140, 151, 159, 174, 187, 188, 201, 209, 256, 263, 277, 660; J. of H., 1846, vol. I, 25, 139, 164, 481; J. of S., 1846, vol. I, 43, 249; J. of H., 1847, vol. I, 47, 67, 68, 76, 131, 160, 207, 273, 303, 341, 355, 460; J. of S., 1847, vol. I, 52, 63, 75, 117, 125, 138, 195, 199, 217, 241, 248, 261, 280, 291, 299, 312, 397.

[50] $500-$1,000, half to go to the prosecutor.

[51] $100-$1,000, and costs; imprisonment for three months. " An Act to prevent kidnapping, preserve the public peace, prohibit the exercise of certain powers heretofore exercised by certain judges, justices of the peace, aldermen and jailors in this commonwealth, and to repeal certain slave laws." Laws of Assembly, 1847, pp. 206-208. The temper that was now coming to be predominant in Pennsylvania is shown by the fact that a section of this act annulled the old provision which allowed an owner to bring his slave into the state and keep him there for six months. Cf. above, p. 86. There is reason to believe that some of the framers of the act intended the formal abolition of slavery in Pennsylvania. Cf. statement of the Hon. T. J. Bingham, chairman of the committee which drew up the law: " Our simple design was to dissolve all connection with slavery in our State legislation." Pittsburg Journal quoted in Harrisburg

It now became almost impossible for an owner to recover his slave. Not only was he liable to be arrested on the charge of kidnapping, but even if clearly within his rights he could get no help from the state,[52] but was on the contrary threatened with punishment if he used any violence. The fact that there was now a strong feeling against him, no matter what might be the merits of his case, and this too on the part of an exceedingly militant and aggressive body of abolitionist and anti-slavery workers, rendered an attempt without some sort of violence impossible.[53] Effective and widespread activity was displayed in deliberate obstruction of recapture and in abetting escape.[54] When recourse was had to the courts of Pennsylvania the decisions handed down were such as to give scant comfort.[55] From the Southern point of view the conditions in the state after 1847 were such as to make imperative the passing of a new fugitive slave law to be vigorously enforced by the government of the United States.

Furthermore since 1800 there had been in operation a mysterious organization, which had continually aggra-

---

Telegraph, Mar. 21, 1856. He said that the Pa. Soc. Abol. Sl. and the Quakers had proposed the law, and had been consulted at every stage of its formation. *Ibid*.

[52] *Cf*. Kauffman *v*. Oliver (1849), 10 *Pa. State Rep*. (Barr) 514; Commonwealth *v*. John Clellans *et al*. (1847), 4 *Pa. Law Journal*, (92)-(100).

[53] *Cf*. Commonwealth *v*. Taylor (1850), 4 *Pa. Law Journal Rep*. (492); (speaking of the Fugitive Slave Law of 1850) " Before the passage of that act, every city, town and village of our Commonwealth was subject to riots and brawls by the efforts of citizens from the southern states to exercise their undoubted rights under the constitution and laws of the United States."

[54] *Cf*. Clellans *et al*. *v*. the Commonwealth (1848), 8 *Pa. State Rep*. (Barr), 223-229; Kauffman *v*. Oliver (1849), 10 *Pa. State Rep*. (Barr), 514-519; Commonwealth *v*. Taylor (1850), 4 *Pa. Law Journal* (480)-(492).

[55] See cases cited in note preceding; also Commonwealth *v*. Auld (1850), 4 *Pa. Law Journal* (431)-(436).

vated the feeling in the South, and which had to a great extent made it possible for such a steady stream of fugitives to find permanent freedom. In Pennsylvania the Underground Railroad had its origin.

Almost immediately after its foundation in 1787 Columbia in Lancaster County became a settling place for emancipated negroes from Maryland and Virginia, and soon also a hiding place for runaway slaves.[56] It was here that the shadowy railroad received its name.[57] Soon it had become desirable to assist the runaways farther into the interior of the state; and such work was being regularly done as early as 1804.[58] In the course of time branches of the road came to extend over many portions of the state. There were numerous routes in the western part, but the work throve particularly in the southeastern counties, where it had first been developed.[59] In York, Lancaster, Chester, and Delaware counties, where great numbers of people were willing to assist, it is said that there were more routes in proportion to the area than anywhere else in the Northern states.[60] In the earlier days strange negroes had not always been helped to escape, even by those who disbelieved in slavery, when the negroes were suspected of having run away;[61] but now devoted men and

[56] *Life of John Thompson, Written by Himself,* 100; McKnight, *Pioneer Outline History of Northwestern Pennsylvania,* etc., 317.

[57] Smedley, *History of the Underground Railroad in Chester and the Neighboring Counties of Pennsylvania,* 35; Siebert, *The Underground Railroad from Slavery to Freedom,* 45.

[58] Sutcliff, *Travels,* 58, 257.

[59] See the excellent map in Siebert, *Underground Railroad,* facing p. 113. *Ibid.,* 115, 117, 119, 120. Prowell, *History of York Co.,* 592-598.

[60] Siebert, *Underground Railroad,* 120, 121; E. H. Magill, *When Men Were Sold,* 5.

[61] *Cf.* advt. in *Pa. Gazette,* Feb. 20, 1795, which after saying " We the subscribers became bound, by an obligation, about the latter end of the year 1791, in a certain penalty, to deliver up a certain Mulatto, . . . named

women went to any length of risk and hardship to get fugitive slaves to a place of safety.[62] The Friends of Pennsylvania continued and renewed that struggle against slavery which their Society had carried on for five generations. In defiance of the law, and sometimes at great personal sacrifice, negroes were hidden and fed and clothed until they could be sent beyond the risk of recapture.[63] In this work the Friends were ably seconded by the efforts of negroes, some of whom had previously been fugitives themselves.[64] So what with the powerful public feeling and the workings of the Underground Railroad, what with the favorable legislation of 1847, there had come to be a large number of runaway negroes in Pennsylvania, some of them living in the most careless defiance of the Federal law itself.

The last period in the history of the relations of Pennsylvania with the runaway negroes of other states began with the passing of the United States Fugitive Slave Law of 1850. The unpopularity of this law was revealed in the newspaper discussion which followed its enactment. It was believed in the South that only one newspaper in the state supported it, and such was probably the case so far as Philadelphia was concerned.[65]

William Lewis, if he should be proved a slave " . . . announces that if no master appears within thirty days the subscribers are free from the obligation.

[62] From a personal conversation with Miss Grace Anna Lewis, of Media, Pa. *Cf.* Smedley, *Underground Railroad*, 168-190.

[63] Amanda G. Fogg, "Incidents of Slavery Times," etc., in *Kennett News and Advertiser*, Dec. 1, 1897; Siebert, *passim; The Friend*, LXIX, 314, 315. For heavy damages recovered by slave owners from those who had assisted fugitives, *cf.* Oliver *v.* Weakley *et al.* (1853), 2 Wallace Jr. 324-326; Van Metre *v.* Mitchell (1853), *ibid.*, 311-323.

[64] Siebert, *Underground Railroad*, appendix E, 431-434; Still (a negro), *The Underground Railroad*, etc.; 4 *Pa. Arch.*, VII, 610-614.

[65] The *Pennsylvanian*. *Cf. Pennsylvanian*, Nov. 16, 1850, where it was said, however, that scores of papers supporting the law could be found in the state.

Dislike of the law soon became intense hatred, for its effectiveness was almost instantly manifest. In all parts of Pennsylvania negroes were seized, and in many cases hurried back into slavery. During 1850, 1851, and 1852 it was enforced with vigor and success, and at Harrisburg, Pittsburg, and Philadelphia transpired such scenes as had not been witnessed for many years.[66] The fact that some of the negroes taken back to bondage had been living in Pennsylvania so long, that having married, raised children, and acquired property, they had come to regard themselves as free citizens of the state, and were so regarded by many of the white people, and also that there arose very strong suspicion that negroes undoubtedly free were being kidnapped, intensified the opposition, which at times became tremendous.[67] In 1853 more than sixty people from Pennsylvania went to Baltimore to give testimony for a negress who had been kidnapped from their neighborhood.[68]

But that even the strong protection of a Federal law could not make it safe to hunt for slaves in Pennsylvania was amply shown by the famous Christiana Riot in September, 1851. In that year Edward Gorsuch of Maryland, having procured the proper warrants, went to capture some of his slaves, who were known to be lurking near Christiana in Lancaster County. Accompanied by an officer and several friends he proceeded

[66] Cf. The Fugitive Slave Law and Its Victims, 11, 12, 14, 15, 16, 18, 20, 21, 22; for the years following, ibid., 25, 42, 44, 45, 65, 66, 91, 96, 109, 116-118, 131-133; Pennsylvanian, Oct. 2, 1850; (Harrisburg) Daily American, Jan. 25, 1851; (Harrisburg) Key Stone, Nov. 4, 1851.

[67] Cf. The Fugitive Slave Law and Its Victims, 14 (this case was dismissed), 95, 96. Also ibid., 15, 18, 21, 42, 44, 109, 131-133; Public Ledger, Feb. 7, 1851.

[68] The Fugitive Slave Law and Its Victims, 21.

to the house suspected; but finding it defended by armed negroes, and being fired upon, he came to a halt. Soon he was surrounded by a mob of nearly a hundred negroes armed with scythes, clubs, and corn-cutters. It was in vain that the officer showed the writs, and even that the attempt at capture was given over. An attack was made by the negroes, in which Gorsuch was shot down and beaten to death with clubs, while his son and his nephew escaped with the utmost difficulty.[69] A certain Castner Hanway was suspected of having incited the mob, and was indicted for treason against the United States. Great efforts were made to secure a conviction, but Hanway was acquitted after the jury had been out for twenty minutes.[70] Not a single person was punished.[71]

In the smaller towns and in the country the capture of a fugitive now became an extremely perilous undertaking. In some parts of the state bands of armed negroes prowled around in search of slave-hunters,[72] while elsewhere negroes could generally be found ready to rally in mobs and rescue runaways at the cost of any violence. In 1852 a policeman from Baltimore arrested an alleged fugitive at Columbia, whereupon he was immediately surrounded by a crowd of negroes. In the

[69] These facts were all proved. See charge of Judge Grier to the jury, 9 *Legal Intelligencer* 23; 2 Wallace Jr. 192-208.

[70] United States *v.* Hanway (1851, Third Circuit Court of the United States), 2 Wallace Jr. 139-208. For the Christiana Riot, *cf. Evening Bulletin*, Sept. 12, 13, 15, Nov. 24 (where it is called treason), 1851; (York) *People's Advocate*, Sept. 16, 1851; (Harrisburg) *Key Stone*, Sept. 16, 1851; *Pennsylvanian*, Feb. 29, 1852; Ampère, *Promenade en Amérique*, I, 408-410; Still, *Underground Railroad*, 348-368.

[71] Jenkins, *Pennsylvania Colonial and Federal*, II, 342, 343.

[72] *Cf.* 2 Wallace Jr. 165. For associations of men in Indiana County, and also in other parts of Pennsylvania, banded together to prevent recapture and to assist negroes, see *ibid.*, 213; *Pittsburg Journal*, July 17, 1855; J. H. W. Howard, *Bond and Free*, ch. XIX.

confusion he was bitten by the captive, whom he shot dead. It was only by travelling all night that he at last reached safety across the Maryland line.[73]

Meanwhile the legislative action of the state kept pace with the development of popular feeling. The conservative elements made a vain effort to stem the tide. At first they accomplished a little. In 1850 a bill to aid masters passed the House, but was overwhelmed by an avalanche of petitions in the Senate.[74] Two years later that part of the act of 1847 which forbade the lodging of fugitives in county jails was repealed in spite of an immense number of remonstrances.[75] After this it was not possible to get any further concessions made. In 1856 a petition came to the House asking that masters from other states be given the right to take their slaves through Pennsylvania as before the law of 1847, but the request was voted down by a decisive majority.[76] On the other hand the Legislature now began to receive petitions the fulfilment of which would have entailed direct defiance of the authority of the United States.

[73] (Harrisburg) *Whig State Journal*, May 6, 1852. As far back as 1834 several negroes of Philadelphia were sent to the penitentiary for trying to take a slave from the officers who had him in charge. *Niles's Register*, XLVI, 118, 174. *Cf.* also *Lewistown Republican*, June 15, 1842; 1 *American Law Journal* (new ser.), 10-14, 97-107 (1848); (Lancaster) *Daily Express*, Mar. 29, 1860.

[74] *J. of H.*, *1850, vol. I*, 495-502, 709, 732, 844, 845; *J. of S.*, *1850*, vol. I, 585, 608, 616, 636, 646, 657, 672, 679, 691, 707, 710, 720, 724, 768, 781, 794, 806, 816, 817, 833, 855, 858, 872, 909, 1081.

[75] *Laws of Assembly, 1852*, p. 295; *J. of H.*, *1851*, vol. I, 25, 28, 34, 47, 64, 66, 114, 142, 169, 209, 240, 272, 305, 319, 349, 374, 381, 415, 423, 441, 501, 573, 634; *J. of S.*, *1851*, vol. I, 14, 26, 59, 89, 98, 132, 141, 149, 156, 163, 172, 181, 191, 206, 211, 221, 252, 261, 268, 276, 288, 300, 314, 315, 324, 365, 372, 384, 396, 421, 430, 498, 574, 834; *J. of H.*, *1851*, vol. I, 661, 901; *J. of S.*, *1851*, vol. I, 15, 90, 283, 529, 588, 589, 601, 603, 928; *J. of H.*, *1852*, vol. I, 702, 721; *J. of S.*, *1852*, vol. I, 484, 719; 4 *Pa. Arch.*, VII, 491-496.

[76] *J. of H.*, *1856*, pp. 67, 68.

In 1859 a personal liberty bill was introduced into the
House,[77] and though this bill failed great pressure was
brought to have the state prevent the rendition of fugitives and even prohibit their return.[78] Finally in 1860
the provisions of the act of 1847 were incorporated into
the revised penal code in their most uncompromising
form.[79]

Thus during the fourteen years from 1847 to 1861
Pennsylvania was brought close to nullification of the
Federal laws. During those years no slave-holder had
the right of transit through the state with his slave
property. During five of those years the Federal authorities were forbidden to use the state jails. During
most of the time active and substantial encouragement
was given to runaway slaves; and such slaves came to
Pennsylvania in large numbers. For a few years the
Fugitive Slave Law of 1850 gave some relief to the

[77] *J. of H., 1859*, pp. 311, 398, 629, 940, 941. The details were not fully
worked out. It provided, however, that no state officer should assist in
recapturing a fugitive. What was desired may be learned from a petition
circulated by the Pennsylvania Anti-Slavery Society. " We the under-
signed, inhabitants of the State of Pennsylvania, respectfully ask that
you will pass a Law prohibiting the surrender of any human being claimed
as a Slave upon the soil of Pennsylvania." MS. Min. Exec. Com. Pa.
A-S. Soc., Nov. 3, 1858.

[78] *J. of H., 1859*, pp. 157, 386, 417, 468, 527, 642, 664; *J. of S., 1859*, pp.
106, 317, 432, 689; *J. of H., 1860*, pp. 123, 169, 179, 237, 280, 325,
338, 374, 375, 437, 438; *J. of S., 1860*, pp. 96, 121, 132, 157, 199, 222,
259, 260, 306, 627; *J. of H., 1861*, pp. 150, 246, 311; *J. of S., 1861*, pp. 113,
144, 224, 271. For the vigorous efforts made to obtain such a law, *cf.*
MS. Min. Exec. Com. Pa. A-S, Soc., Oct. 3, 1859; *Proceedings Pa. Yr.
M. Progressive Friends, 1859*, p. 29.

[79] " An Act To Consolidate, Revise, and Amend the Penal Laws of this
Commonwealth." *Laws of Assembly, 1860*, pp. 406, 407. " No judge . . .
nor any alderman or justice of the peace . . . shall have jurisdiction or
take cognizance of the case of any fugitive from labor, from any of the
United States or territories, under any act of Congress; nor . . . issue or
grant any certificate or warrant of removal of any such fugitive from labor
under any act of Congress; " . . .

South; but in Pennsylvania this law was obnoxious
from the first, its enforcement was attended with difficulty, and the net result was only to bring a greater
number of people into such violent hostility to it, that
they demanded that their officials refuse to obey it. It
can hardly be doubted that because of her proximity to
the South, because of the long, continuous, and powerful assistance which her people gave to fugitives, and
because of the decided stand taken by her Legislature,
Pennsylvania had much to do with bringing on the
crisis that was impending.

The truth of this appeared in 1860. When the great
conflict was looming up, there seems to have been an
uneasy feeling in the state. Many local newspapers
commented on the law of 1847 as one which had been
especially designed to defeat the laws of the United
States; and although particular efforts were made to
show that such was not the case, some admitted that
the charge was true.[80] On January 2, 1861, Governor
Packer urged the repeal of parts of the obnoxious
law.[81] He recommended that Pennsylvania assist in the
execution of the Fugitive Slave Law, that the act of
1826 be revived, and that masters from other states be
allowed to take their slaves through the state, and even

---

[80] *Inquirer*, Nov. 21, 1860; *Public Ledger*, Nov. 23, 1860; (Lancaster)
Daily Express, Nov. 26, 1860. " Virginia and the other Southern States
have made specific charges against the legislation of Pennsylvania upon
this subject, and some of their allegations are well founded." R. E.
Randall of Pennsylvania, *Speech on the Laws of the State relative to
Fugitive Slaves*, 4. Also speaking of sections 95 and 96 of the Revised
Penal Code (1860), he said they " are, in my judgment, a plain violation
of the Federal Constitution." *Ibid.*, 14, This whole speech is a very able
review of Pennsylvania's legislation on the fugitive slave question.

[81] " I earnestly recommend their unconditional repeal." 4 *Pa. Arch.*,
VIII, 295.

be permitted to reside therein for a limited period.[82] The powerful conservative influences in the state, which had hitherto been quiet, were now aroused. Meetings were held,[83] threats were made against anti-slavery workers,[84] and immense pro-Southern petitions were prepared.[85] Memorials poured into both houses of the Legislature asking that the unfriendly legislation be repealed, that Pennsylvania assist in carrying out the Fugitive Slave Law, that owners be allowed to take their slaves through the state, and that owners be paid by the state for slaves rescued from them.[86] Something was, indeed, attempted by the Legislature, but came to nothing.[87] Such efforts were now too late. The question was about to be settled by the Civil War.

The relations, then, between the white man and the negro in Pennsylvania afford a problem apparently complex. The majority of the white people of the state evidently disliked his presence there; they had little sympathy for him, they persecuted him, they did their best to relegate him to an inferior status, they seemed to wish most earnestly to have him stay out of the state; and yet during the whole time a majority of the white people refused to pass a law to keep him out, while on the contrary they helped him to come in, they

[82] *Ibid.*, VIII, 296.

[83] At a Union meeting which was held it was resolved " That every State is bound by the Constitution of the United States to aid in delivering up fugitive slaves to their owners, and all legislation which refuses such and throws obstacles in the way is unconstitutional, and should be repealed " . . . *Public Ledger*, Jan. 4, 1861.

[84] *Cf.* MS. Min. Exec. Com. Pa. A-S. Soc., June 14, 1860.

[85] One of them had 11,000 signatures, and had a total length of nearly five hundred feet. *Public Ledger*, Jan. 3, 1861.

[86] *J. of H., 1861*, pp. 46, 49, 69, 120, 121, 150, 165, 201, 364, 401, 467, 570; *J. of S., 1861*, pp. 53, 144, 270, 311, 312, 313. For counter-petitions, see above, p. 245, note 78.

[87] *J. of H., 1861*, pp. 73, 74; *J. of S., 1861*, pp. 134, 146.

hid him from his pursuers, they forfeited the good will
of Maryland and the states to the south, and at last
many of them practically nullified the law of the United
States, and others desired their state specifically to do
so. In all this, however, there was no real inconsistency.
In the first place the two courses of action were followed
by majorities not composed of the same people, but in
part of people violently antagonistic; in the second
place the two courses were in themselves not altogether contradictory. Pennsylvania was following two
courses not mutually irreconcilable. Far back in the
colony days she had lifted up her voice against slavery;
part of her people had voluntarily set free their slaves;
and the Assembly had followed with the first act of general abolition. Then her most ardent men and women
had set themselves to eradicate the last vestiges of the
evil in their own state, and to war against it in all states
where it still existed. As the years went on and slavery
in the Southern states grew in magnitude and became
a national problem, and as they saw it almost daily
bursting over their borders, their detestation of it became unquenchable. It mattered not that along with
this, but coming later in time, there had developed another feeling; that enthusiastic ideals in regard to negro
equality had been shattered; that such ideals had now
come to be unthinkable; that the negroes among them,
and the negroes who fled to them, were for the most
part persecuted, unassimilated, and undesired. They
had no love for the black man free, but they pitied him
as a slave. They came to detest the negro, but they
hated slavery more.[88]

[88] " Talk as we may in condemnation of the pride of race, we must still
admit that there are inherent differences in races that determine their

Nor must it be supposed that the most willing philanthropy toward fugitives, or the most lively hatred of slavery, brought much amelioration to the lot of the colored man in Pennsylvania. The runaway who was helped by some, was speedily forgotten by most, and soon regarded with the same aversion as others of his class. Therefore what was said above in regard to prejudice must be qualified only so far as the Friends and the anti-slavery workers are concerned. That the lot of the free negro in Pennsylvania was better than his lot would have been in most other states is doubtless true. That his condition in Pennsylvania had improved absolutely as time went by, and as he strove to improve himself, is also true. But that his condition had improved relatively, or as much as might have been expected, is emphatically not so. In 1861 it was true in Pennsylvania as elsewhere that for no one did a darker future seem in store, for no one did there seem less hope, than for the negro.[89]

---

condition much more than does the force of mere outward circumstances; nor can this difference be disregarded in practically dealing with men. True the inferiority of their race will not justify us in enslaving men . . . The views that we have thus expressed are not at all incompatible with the belief that slavery is a great ill . . . Nor are they inconsistent with a steady opposition to the slave power " . . . *North American*, Mar. 24, 1857.

[89] *Cf.* the words of Lincoln: " The Chief-Justice does not directly assert, but plainly assumes as a fact, that the public estimate of the black man is more favorable now than it was in the days of the Revolution. This assumption is a mistake. In some trifling particulars the condition of that race has been ameliorated; but as a whole, in this country, the change between then and now is decidedly the other way; and their ultimate destiny has never appeared so hopeless as in the last three or four years." Speech of June 26, 1857, quoted by Thorpe, *Constitutional History of the United States*, II, 548, 549.

CONCLUSIONS.

NEGROES began to be brought into Pennsylvania before the organization of the colony, but owing to eco-, nomic and industrial causes, and also to the effective opposition of many of the white people, the number imported was never large. Most of the first negroes seem to have been held for life, but otherwise their status in the beginning differed little from that of white servants. As time went on there arose differences and discriminations, the inevitable incidents of life service, which tended to make the status decidedly inferior. The process of differentiation between slavery and servitude was checked, however, in 1780 by the act for the gradual abolition of slavery. This act, which was the first of its kind passed anywhere in America, was the result primarily of economic causes, but directly of the splendid efforts of the Friends, and of the enthusiasm attending upon the Revolutionary War.

As the gap between freedom and slavery was broad the upward progress of the negro was gradual. As a rule he occupied some intermediate status of servitude before becoming free. Moreover even after freedom had been attained he was not generally upon a plane of equality with the white man. There was civil inequality until 1780, while politically the negro was inferior until 1870. Social equality was never claimed in colonial days, but thereafter when the question arose it was denied. Economic progress was slow and painful, although at first much assistance was given by white people.

That progress was not more rapid was owing to the growth of race prejudice. In colonial times slavery was exceedingly mild, and many white people took a kindly interest in their negroes. After 1800 there was a gradual but complete change. The influx of negroes from the South, the apparent deterioration in character, the immense increase in crime, and the rising pretensions of the negroes themselves, all caused a dislike which deepened into strong prejudice, and was manifested in attempts to exclude negroes from the state, in efforts to colonize them, in the desire to abridge their rights, in political and social discrimination, in petty persecution, and in fierce riots. This prejudice lasted throughout the period before 1861, so that in Pennsylvania there was none of the race equality which was assumed by Reconstruction statesmen in the solution of Southern problems after the Civil War.

Such progress as the negro made was due partly to his own efforts and partly to the continuous and powerful assistance of the Friends, the abolitionists, and the anti-slavery advocates. They helped and encouraged the negro, they protected him, and upheld his rights. To them largely was due the abolition of slavery, the suppression of the local slave-trade, and the management of the Underground Railroad. The methods of the abolitionists were earnest and quiet, but after 1830 their work was overshadowed by that of the more radical and violent anti-slavery agitators. The influence of all these men did much to arouse a general hatred of slavery, and to neutralize prejudice against the negro, so that after 1847 Pennsylvania entered upon a course which deeply offended the South, and endangered the continuance of the Union.

APPENDIX.

POPULATION OF PENNSYLVANIA.

Census.	Whites.	Free negroes.	Slaves.	Aggregate negroes.	Aggregate population.
1790	424,099	6,537	3,737	10,274	434,073
1800	586,095	14,564	1,706	16,270	602,365
1810	786,804	22,492	795	23,287	810,091
1820	1,017,094	32,153	211	32,364	1,047,507
1830	1,309,900	37,930	* 403	38,333	1,348,233
1840	1,676,115	47,854	64	47,918	1,724,033
1850	2,258,160	53,626	....	53,626	2,311,786
1860	2,849,259	56,949	....	56,949	2,906,215

* 386 according to another estimate. See above, p. 85, note 62.

POPULATION OF PHILADELPHIA.

1790	51,902	2,102	387	2,489	54,391
1800	74,129	6,795	85	6,880	81,009
1810	100,688	10,514	8	10,522	111,210
1820	123,746	11,884	7	11,891	135,637
1830	173,173	15,604	20	15,624	188,797
1840	238,204	19,831	2	19,833	258,037
1850	389,001	19,761	....	19,761	408,762
1860	543,344	22,185	....	22,185	565,529

BIBLIOGRAPHY.

ABBREVIATIONS.

A. P. S. ....American Philosophical Society, Phila.

Ct. H...........Court House.

Fr. Lib.........Friends' Library.

Fr. M. H........Friends' Meeting House.

H. S. P.........Historical Society of Pennsylvania, Philadelphia.

Hist. Soc. ......Historical Society.

L. C.............Library of Congress, Washington.

L. C. P........Library Company of Philadelphia.

Pea. ....Peabody Library, Baltimore.

P. L.............Pratt Library, Baltimore.

P. L. L. ....Philadelphia Law Library.

P. S. L..........Pennsylvania State Library, Harrisburg.

P. S. L., Div. Pub.
    Rec...........Pennsylvania State Library, Division of Public Records.

R. B............Ridgway Branch, Library Company of Philadelphia.

BIBLIOGRAPHY.

I.

MANUSCRIPTS.

Court Records.

Minutes, Dockets, Papers.

The court records are of primary importance, since in Pennsylvania the development of slavery and servitude depended less on statutory enactment than on usage as interpreted by the courts. This was preeminently so in the period prior to 1700. After that time the records are of less value, since negroes were then tried in special courts, of which only one docket remains. In many instances the volumes have been carelessly kept, and are now incomplete. A few have been copied.

County Courts.

Bucks County.

Minute Book, Common Pleas and Quarter Sessions, Bucks County. 1684-1730.—Ct. H., Doylestown, Pa. (Very important material for the history of servitude and slavery in Pennsylvania.)

Quarter Sessions Docket. 1715-1753.

Criminal Docket, Ct. Quarter Sessions. 1742-1810.

Chester County.

Minutes of the Chester County Courts. 1681-1697, 1697-1710. —Ct. H., West Chester, Pa. (Many references to negroes. Early prejudice against miscegenation.)

Quarter Sessions Dockets. 1723-1769.

Court Records of Penna. and Chester Co. 1681-1688. (Transcript.)—H. S. P.

Philadelphia County.

Philadelphia Court Records. 1685-1688. (Minutes of the Phila. Co. Ct.)—H. S. P.

Germantown Records of the Courts. 1691-1707.—H. S. P.
Dockets of the Court of Common Pleas, Phila. Co. 1706-1766. (Two actions against importers of Indian slaves.)—H. S. P.
Docket Phila. Ct. Quarter Sessions. 1773-1780.—City Hall, Phila.
Court Papers, Phila. Co. 1723-1744.—H. S. P.
Ancient Records of Philadelphia. (Collected by J. W. Wallace. Largely presentments of the grand jury. Interesting light on the conduct of negroes.)—H. S. P.
Three Lower Counties—Delaware.
Record of the Court at Upland in Penn. Nov. 14, 1676-June 2, 1681.—H. S. P.
New Castle Court Records: Liber A, 1676-1678; Liber B, 1678-1681. Coll. Genealogical Soc. of Pa. Transcribed. Also printed: *Records of the Court of New Castle on Delaware, 1676-1681* (Lancaster, 1904).—H. S. P.
New Castle Court Records. 1677-1682. (Logan Papers.)—H. S. P.
Ancient Records of Sussex County. 1681-1709. (This large folio is a storehouse of material for the early history of servitude in Pa. Some very important references to negroes occur).—H. S. P.

Supreme Court of Pennsylvania.
Miscellaneous Papers of the Supreme Court of Nisi Prius of the State of Pennsylvania. (844 vols. bound and indexed.)—Coll. Genealogical Soc. of Pa.—H. S. P.

High Court of Errors and Appeals.
Docket of the High Court of Errors and Appeals. April, 1790 to July, 1808. (Vol. 10 of Sup. Ct. Dockets. Contains references to the famous case testing the legality of slavery in Pennsylvania under the Constitition of 1790.)—Archives Sup. Ct., Phila. City Hall.

Special Courts.
Records of Special Courts for the Trial of Negroes, held at Chester, in Chester County. (The only docket of such courts known to exist.)—Ct. H., Media, Pa.

Wills and Deeds.

Philadelphia Deeds: Deed Book E. 1, vol. V. (Not arranged chronologically. Negroes sold "forever"—slaves.)—Office Recorder of Deeds, City Hall, Phila.

Wills and Inventories of Estates.—Office Register of Wills, Ct. H., West Chester, Pa.

Philadelphia Wills, Book A, 1683-1699. (Many hints as to the legal status of negroes.)—Office Register of Wills, City Hall, Phila.

Will of William Penn. Newcastle on Delaware, 30th 8br, 1701. (Freedom for his negroes.)—H. S. P.

Board of Trade Records.

Board of Trade Journals. 1675-1782. 90 vols. Transcribed 1898. (Some few references to negroes in Pa.—The Journals and Papers of the Board of Trade were transcribed from the original MS. vols. in the Public Record Office, England, for the H. S. P.)—H. S. P.

Board of Trade Papers, Plantations General. 1689-1780. Vols. 2-31. Tr. 1904. (These and the following contain valuable information about negroes. Numbers, etc.)—H. S. P.

Board of Trade Papers, Proprieties. 1697-1776. Vols. 2-24. Tr. 1901-1902.—H. S. P.

Letters, Diaries, Cash Books, and Ledgers.

In separate groups may be arranged sources such as letter-books, diaries, cash books, ledgers, etc., of small individual importance, and seldom containing any fundamental information, yet affording an almost infinite number of notices concerning matters legal, social, and economic, which have made up no small part of this book. They constitute a mine of material which it is nearly impossible to exhaust. Perhaps no state south of New England has a richer store of such MSS.

Letters.

Very important are the various collections of Penn Papers. William Penn had negro slaves, as did some of the Penns after him. Their letters, papers, accounts, etc., contain many notices interesting and pertinent as to the management of slaves, the cost of their maintenance, treatment, etc.

Letters and Papers of (William) Penn. 1666-about 1857.
(Not chron. Coll. by F. J. Dreer.)—H. S. P.

Penn Papers. Accounts. (Unbound.)—H. S. P.

Penn MSS. Domestic Letters. William Penn 1681-1709;
Hannah Penn, 1716-1718.—H. S. P.

Penn MSS. Forbes Coll. I. 1652-1722; II. 1695-1706.—H.
S. P.

Penn MSS. Miscellaneous MSS. of Wm. Penn. Ford *v.*
Penn. Beranger *v.* Penn. 1674-1716.—H. S. P.

Penn MSS. Official Correspondence. 1683-1727.—H. S. P.

Penn MSS. Papers Relating to the Three Lower Counties.
1629-1774.—H. S. P.

Penn *v.* Baltimore. Depositions. Phila., 1740.—H. S. P.

Penn-Physick MSS. Land Grants and Surveys. IV. 1676-
1801.—H. S. P.

Early Quakers and Penn Family. Etting Papers. 1661-
1829.—H. S. P.

Pennsylvania Miscellaneous Papers. Penn and Baltimore
Family. 1653-1724.—H. S. P.

Logan Papers. VIII. Dickinson Family. 1702-1793. (Jonathan Dickinson was one of the most famous of the early merchants of Phila.)—H. S. P.

Selections from the Correspondence of the Honourable
James Logan. 1699-1712. (Compiled by D. Logan.)—A. P. S.

Isaac Norris (1. I. N., mayor of Phila. and provincial coun-
cillor, 1671-1735. 2. His son, I. N., speaker of Assembly,
1701-1766. Great merchants of Phila. Imported slaves). Letter Books. 1699-1702, 1702-1704, 1704-1706, 1706-1709, 1709-
1716, 1716-1730, 1719-1756, 1756-1766.—H. S. P.

Isaac Norris. Letter Book. 1717-1753.—H. S. P.

Isaac Norris, Extracts from the Letter Books of, 1699-1734.—
H. S. P.

Pemberton Papers. I. Etting Papers. 1672-1760.—H. S. P.

Shippen Family, Papers of the, 1701-1755.—H. S. P.

Smith MSS. 1678-1879.—R. B.

Streeper Papers. Bucks County. 1682-1772.—H. S. P.

Correspondence of Prominent Men west of the Alleghanies
during the years 1769, 1770 and 1771. (Letter book. Request
for negroes to be sent from Pa. to the West.)—P. S. L.

Diaries.

Diary of James Allen of Philadelphia. 1770-1778. (Important for social conditions during period of disturbance. Describes disorders at length, but mentions no trouble due to negroes.)—H. S. P.

Diary of Richard Barnard of East Marlborough Township, Chester Co., Pa. 1774-1792.—A. C. Myers, Moylan, Pa., (Extracts by).

Journals of Joshua Brown of Little Britain, Lancaster Co., Pa. 1756-1790.—Fr. Lib., 142 N. 16th St., Phila.

Christopher Marshall's Remembrancer. Jan. 2, 1774-Sept. 24, 1781. (Numerous references to negroes.)—H. S. P.

An Account of Negroes Set Free. Kept by James Moon of Woodbourne, etc. 1776-1785. (Perhaps the most detailed of all existing accounts of the efforts made by Friends' Visiting Committees to persuade owners to set their negroes free.)— S. C. Moon, Fallsington, Pa. Copy owned by President I. Sharpless, Haverford, Pa.

Diary of Joel Swayne. 1823-1833. (East Marlborough Township, Chester Co., Pa. References to kidnapping, fugitives, etc.)—W. M. Swayne, Kennett Square, Pa.

Ledgers, Account Books, Cash Books.

Ledger and Letter Book of Peter Baynton. 1721-1726.— H. S. P.

Account Book, Samuel Carpenter's Estate, Philadelphia. 1737-1742. (Numerous references to care and maintenance of negroes, cost of clothing, etc.)—Orphans' Ct., Phila.

Account Book and Ledgers of Benjamin Franklin. 1730-about 1742.—A. P. S.

Richard Hayes's Ledger. 1708-1740.—H. S. P.

James Logan's Account Book. 1712-1719.—H. S. P.

Isaac Norris. Account Books. 1709-1724, 1724-1764.—H. S. P.

William Penn with Samuel Jennings R. G. 1690-1693. (Personal account book of W. P.)—P. S. L., Div. Pub. Rec.

William Penn Proprietor and Governour of the Province of Pensilvania etc. his Cash Book Commencing the 7th of the 10th mōᵗʰ Anno Domini 1699. (Hired negroes, lent them money, etc.)—A. P. S.

William Penn's Cash Book. 1710-1726.—H. S. P.
Philadelphia Account Books. 1694-1698, 1722-1729.—H. S. P.
John Ross. Day Book. 1758-1783.—H. S. P.
John Stamper's Letter Book. 1751-1772.—H. S. P.
William Trent's Ledger. 1703-1708. (Merchant of Phila. Imported negroes.)—Mercantile Lib., Phila.
John Wilson's Cash Books. 1768, 1770, 1773, 1774, 1775, 1776, 1777.—H. S. P.

Assessment Books and Tax Lists.

Primary source for the numbers and distribution of negroes.
Bucks Co. Assessment Books. 1779, 1781, 1782.—P. S. L.
Chester Co., Assessment List of, 1764-1765. (Supposed to be the earliest remaining.)—G. Cope, West Chester, Pa.
Chester Co. Assessment Books. 1765, 1766, 1767, 1768, 1769, 1771, 1774, 1779, 1780, 1781.—P. S. L.
Returns of Property, Chester Co. 1781.—P. S. L.
Northampton Co. Provincial Tax Assessments. 1767, 1768. —H. S. P.
Philadelphia Co. Assessment Book. 1769.—P. S. L.

Church Records.

These are of much value as showing the kind of religious work done among negroes.
Christ Church, Phila., Records of. I-IV. Baptisms, 1709-1900. V-VII. Marriages, 1709-1900. Mr. Cummin's Private Register, 1726-1741. (Show excellent work done by this church for negroes.) Tr. for Gen. Soc. of Pa.—H. S. P.
First Presbyterian Church, Phila., Records of. Baptisms, 1701-1856. Marriages, 1760-1855. Tr. for Gen. Soc. of Pa.— H. S. P.
First Reformed Church of Phila., Records of. Baptisms, 1748-1860. Burials, 1748-1809. Marriages, 1748-1860. Tr. for Gen. Soc. of Pa.—H. S. P.
St. Michael's and Zion Church, Phila., Records of. Baptisms, 1745-1771. Burials, 1745-1771. Marriages, 1745-1764. Tr. for Gen. Soc. of Pa.—H. S. P.
Book of Record of Merion Meeting Grave-Yard.—Friends' Meeting House, 15th and Race Streets, Phila.
Record of Sandy Bank Cemetery, Delaware Co., Pa.—H. S. P.

Records of Friends' Meetings.

These records are of preeminent importance for the history of the negro in Pennsylvania. Careful, reliable, and sincere, they reveal as do no other sources the cause of the early overthrow of slavery there, and the first efforts to elevate the negro race.

Monthly Meetings.

Minutes of Abington M. M. 1682-1746. Tr. for Gen. Soc. of Pa.—H. S. P.

Minutes of Abington M. M. 1746-1774. Abstract by G. Cope for Gen. Soc. of Pa.—H. S. P.

Buckingham M. M., Extracts from Minutes of. 1720-1803. Tr. for Gen. Soc. of Pa.—H. S. P.

Chester M. M. Minutes. 1708-1721, 1745-1778.—Orthodox Fr. M. House, Media, Pa.

Chester M. M. Acknowledgments. 1700-1733. Same place.

Chester M. M. Certificates, Testimonies and Acknowledgments. 1733-1774.—Same place.

Chester M. M. Miscellaneous Papers.—Same place.

Darby M. M. Minutes. 1684-1780.—Fr. M. H., Darby, Pa.

Exeter M. M. Minutes, Book B. 1765-1785.—Fr. M. H., 15th and Race Streets, Phila.

Gwynedd M. M. Minutes. 1714-1801. (Many manumissions noted.) Abstract for Gen. Soc. of Pa.—H. S. P.

Middletown M. M. Minutes. 1683-1809. Tr. for Gen. Soc. of Pa.—H. S. P.

Middletown M. M., Papers of. 1759-1786.—Fr. M. H., 15th and Race Streets, Phila.

Radnor M. M. Minutes. 1763-1772, 1772-1782.—Same place.

Sadsbury M. M. Minutes. 1737-1783.—Same place.

Warrington M. M. Minutes. 1747-1856. Abstract for Gen. Soc. of Pa.—H. S. P.

Quarterly Meetings.

Minutes of Women's Quarterly Meetings in Bucks County. 1685-1805.—Fr. M. H., 15th and Race Streets, Phila.

Chester Quarterly M. Minutes. 1683-1767, 1768-1800.—Orthodox Fr. M. H., Media, Pa.

Quarterly Meeting Book for Women Friends in Chester County. 1715-1803.—Same place.

(Providence Q. ᴵM. Minutes. 1687-1709. Binder's title =)
Chester Q. M. Minutes.—Same place.
Warrington Q. M. Minutes. 1787-1801. Tr. for Gen. Soc.
of Pa.—H. S. P.

Yearly Meeting.

Minutes of the Yearly Meeting for Pa., N. J., and Parts
Adjacent. 1682-1746, 1747-1779. (Invaluable. Decisions of
the Friends as to slavery and the slave-trade.)—Fr. M. H., 4th
and Arch Streets, Phila.
Yearly Meeting Advices. 1682-1777.—Orth. Fr. M. H.,
Media, Pa.

Records of the Abolition and Anti-Slavery Societies.

Supplementary to the Friends' records, but of wider interest,
and forming a class by themselves are the records of the
Pennsylvania Society for the Abolition of Slavery, etc. They
are of fundamental importance for the beginnings of abolitionism in Pennsylvania and the United States, and are besides a
vast storehouse of information of every kind about slavery
and the negro. After 1831 they are supplemented by the records of the anti-slavery societies.

Pennsylvania Society for the
Abolition of Slavery, etc.

Alphabetical List of the Residing Members in Pennsylvania
of the P. S. A. S., etc. 1784-1819.—H. S. P.
Constitution of the P. S. A. S., etc., with a List of the Members' Autographs.—Fr. M. H., 15th and Race Streets.
Constitution and Minutes of the P. S. A. S., etc. 1787-1847.
3 vols.—H. S. P.
Records of the Pennsylvania Society for Promoting the Abolition of Slavery, for the Relief of Free Negroes Unlawfully
Held in Bondage, and for Improving the Condition of the African Race. 1748-1868. 11 vols. (This was the official title.
These volumes are a mine of information about slaves, man-
umission, freedmen, kidnapping, runaways, etc.)—H. S. P.
Minutes of the Acting Committee of the P. S. A. S. 1784-
1842, 4 vols.—H. S. P.
Minutes of. 1842-1865.—Fr. M. H., 15th and Race Streets.

Minutes of the Committee on the African Slave Trade. 1805-1807.—H. S. P.

Petition to the Assembly of Pa. (Petition printed. 1688 signatures.)—H. S. P.

Minutes of the Board of Education. 1819-1839, 1840-1865. (Illustrates the Society's active work for the education of the negro.)—H. S. P.

Entrance Book for Girls' School. 1827-1838. (Information as to pupils in the Society's school.)—H. S. P.

Roll Book of Scholars Attending at Clarkson Hall High School, commencing June 3, 1834.—H. S. P.

Minutes of the Committee for Improving the Condition of Free Blacks. 1790-1803.—H. S. P.

Letter Book. 1794-1809.—H. S. P.

Census of Colored Population of Phila. No. 1. 1837. (These and the following were taken by agents of the Society.)—H. S. P.

Census of the Condition of the People of Colour in the City and District of Philadelphia. 1847. (Minute statistics in long tables.)—H. S. P.

Education and Employment Statistics of the Colored People of Philadelphia. (Prepared by Nathan Kite.)—H. S. P.

Education and Employment Statistics of the Colored People of Philadelphia. (Taken by B. C. Bacon. 1856.)—H. S. P. (The foregoing censuses contain the most accurate and exhaustive information in existence as to the social and economic condition of the negroes of Phila. 1837-1857.)

Books of Indentures of Negro Apprentices. (Bound out under the auspices of the P. S. A. S.)—H. S. P.

Records of Manumissions. Books A, B, C, D, E, F, G. 1794-1851. (Contain thousands of records of manumissions in which the Society was interested.)—H. S. P.

Copies of Nineteen Laws of Pa. relating to Negroes. 1700-1793. (Procured for the Society 1797.)—H. S. P.

W[illiam] J. B[uck], History of the Pennsylvania Abolition Society. 1773-1841. 2 vols.—H. S. P.

Anti-Slavery Societies.

Minute Book of the Junior Anti-Slavery Society. 1836-1846.—H. S. P.

Constitution of the Philadelphia Anti-Slavery Society. (Book contains names of members.)—H. S. P.

Minutes of the Executive Committee of the Pennsylvania Anti-Slavery Society. Book 4. 1856-1870.—H. S. P.

American Convention for promoting the Abolition of Slavery, etc., Minutes of. 1794-1804, 1805-1809.—H. S. P.

Id., Minutes of the Acting Committee of. 1827-1837.—H. S. P.

Miscellaneous.

Buck, W. J., History of Bucks County. (Author's MS. and scrap-book.)—A. C. Myers, Moylan, Pa.

Book of Record of Indentures of Apprentices, Servants, Redemptioners bound in the Office of the Mayor. Philadelphia, October, 1771-October, 1773. (Very important. Early records of negro apprentices.)—A. P. S.

Indentures, manumission papers, etc.—Miss M. B. Clark, Lancaster, Pa.

Inventories of estates. (Frequently contain values of negroes.)—H. S. P. and other places.

Miscellaneous Collection, Box 10, Negroes. (Of great value. Indentures, manumission papers, etc., etc.)—H. S. P.

Miscellaneous MSS. 1744-1859. Northern Interior and Western Counties.—H. S. P.

Miscellaneous MSS. 1738-1806. York and Cumberland Counties.—H. S. P.

Miscellaneous Papers. 108 vols. 1754-1787. (Unclassified. Arranged chronologically. Largely communications to the Supreme Executive Council, papers regarding military matters, petitions, etc., etc.)—P. S. L., Div. Pub. Rec.

Miscellaneous Papers. 1684-1847. Chester Co.—H. S. P.

Miscellaneous Papers. 1724-1772. Lancaster Co.—H. S. P.

Miscellaneous Papers. 1685-1805. Three Lower Counties, Delaware.—H. S. P.

List of the Poor, Chester Co., Pa. 1800.—Poor House, Embreeville, Pa.

Returns of the Directors of the Poor to the Judges of the Court of General Quarter Sessions for the County of Chester. (Beginning 1801.)—G. Cope, West Chester, Pa.

Provincial Papers. 32 vols. 1664-1776. (Much of this material already printed in *Col. Rec.* and I *Pa. Arch.*)—P. S. L., Div. Pub. Rec.

Records and evidence in runaway slave cases. 1821-1838. (Chester Co. Bundles of unbound MSS.)—G. Cope, West Chester.

Evidence in cases of runaway slaves given before Isaac Darlington. 1828-1837. (Prest. Judge of the Judicial District comprising Delaware and Chester counties.)—G. Cope.

Register of slaves in Chester County, 1780. (Made in accordance with the Act of 1780 for the gradual abolition of slavery. Probably the only such register extant.)—Library West Chester State Normal School, Pa.

Watson's Annals of Philadelphia, with additions. (Author's MS. and notes. 1829. Contains many things not in the printed *Annals,* especially drawings by Watson.)—H. S. P.

II.

NEWSPAPERS.

Effort has been made to use newspapers for the entire period covered by' this work after 1719, when the publication of the *American Weekly Mercury* began. For years of special significance, notably 1837-1838, every accessible paper has been consulted. Much material of this kind has been used, though chiefly for illustrative purposes. No single statement of importance rests upon any newspaper notice, and no conclusions are based on this source alone. (N. B.—The enclosed dates in this section indicate the years for which the paper was examined; w. = weekly; s-w. = semi-weekly; tri-w. = tri-weekly; d. = daily.)

The Adams Sentinel and General Advertiser, w. Gettysburg, Pa. (Jan. 4-Sept. 27, 1841.)—York Co. Hist. Soc.

Allegheny Democrat, and Farmers' and Mechanics' Advertiser. w. Pittsburg, Pa. (1826. Some numbers missing.)—P. S. L.

American Daily Advertiser, Dunlap and Claypoole's. d. Phila. (1793-1795, and some numbers.)—L. C.

American Daily Advertiser, Claypoole's. d. (1796-1800, and some numbers.)—L. C.

American Herald. w. Greensburg, Pa. (1859.)—P. S. L.

The American Sentinel and Mercantile Advertiser. d. Phila. (1835, 1837, 1838, and some numbers.)—R. B.

American Volunteer. w. Carlisle, Pa. (Jan. 3-June 13, 1839, and some numbers.)—P. S. L.

American Weekly Mercury. w. Phila. (1719-1741.) The first newspaper published in Pa. The only existing file is in the Ridgway Branch of the Library Company of Phila.

The Anti-Masonic Herald, and Lancaster Weekly Courier. w. Lancaster. (Jan. 1-Dec. 10, 1830.)—P. S. L.

Aurora, General Advertiser. d. Phila. (1806, 1808, 1814, 1818, 1821, and some numbers.)—R. B.

Bedford Gazette. w. Bedford, Pa. (1837-1838.)—P. S. L.

The Bradford Reporter. w. Towanda, Bradford Co., Pa. (1848.)—P. S. L.

The Butler Repository. w. Butler, Pa. (June 4-Dec. 31, 1836.)—P. S. L.

The Chronicle. w. Harrisburg, Pa. (1831.)—P. S. L.

The Chronicle, and Harrisburg Advertiser. w. (1819.)—P. S. L.

Chronicle of the Times. w. Reading, Pa. (June 4-Dec. 31, 1833.)—P. S. L.

The Columbia Spy, and Lancaster and York County Record. w. Columbia, Pa. (1834.)—York Co. Hist. Soc.

The Constitutional Democrat. w. Lancaster, Pa. (1807. Some numbers missing.)—P. S. L.

Crawford Democrat and Meadville Courier. w. Meadville, Pa. (Jan. 4-Dec. 22, 1840, and some numbers.)—P. S. L.

The Daily American. d. Harrisburg. (Jan. 1-May 28, 1851. Some numbers missing.)—P. S. L.

Daily Evening Express. d. Lancaster, Pa. (1860.)—P. S. L.

Daily Patriot and Union. d. Harrisburg. (Sept. 1-Dec. 31, 1859.)—P. S. L.

Dauphin Guardian. w. Harrisburg. (1808, 1811.)—P. S. L.

The Democratic Press. d. Phila. (1819, and some numbers.)—R. B.

Democratic Press. w. Reading, Pa. (1837-1838.)—P. S. L.

Evening Bulletin. d. Phila. (1851-1856, and some numbers.)—R. B.

The Farmer's Instructor, and Harrisburg Courant. w. Harrisburg. (Jan. 8-Dec. 31, 1800.)—P. S. L.

The Federal Gazette, and Philadelphia Evening Post. d. Phila. (Aug. 27-Dec. 28, 1789.)—P. S. L.

Franklin Gazette. d. Phila. (Aug. 23-Dec. 31, 1819.)—P. S. L.
Franklin Repository. w. Chambersburg, Pa. (Mar. 19-Dec. 24, 1839.)—P. S. L.
General Advertiser. d. Phila. (1792-1794, some numbers.)— R. B.
Greensburgh Gazette. w. Greensburg, Pa. (1825.)—P. S. L.
Harrisburg Argus. w. Harrisburg. (1828.)—P. S. L.
Harrisburg Semi-Weekly Telegraph. s-w. (1856.)—P. S. L.
Harrisburger Morgenröthe und Dauphin und Cumberland Counties Anzeiger. w. (1838.)—P. S. L.
Huntingdon Journal and American. w. Huntingdon, Pa. (1860.)—P. S. L.
The Independent Gazeteer, and Agricultural Repository. s-w. Phila. (1792, 1793, and some numbers.)—R. B.
The Independent Republican, and York Recorder. w. York. (Mar. 27-Dec. 25, 1821.)—York Co. Hist. Soc.
The Inland Daily. d. Lancaster. (July-Dec. 1854.)—P. S. L.
The Intelligencer and Weekly Advertiser. w. Lancaster. (July 31-Dec. 25, 1799.)—P. S. L.
The Key Stone. w. Harrisburg. (June-Dec. 1851.)—P. S. L.
Lancaster Intelligencer, and Weekly Advertiser. w. Lancaster. (June 20-Dec. 26, 1818.)—P. S. L.
Lancaster Journal. tri-w. Lancaster. (Aug. 28-Dec. 29, 1815.) —P. S. L.
Lebanon Advertiser. w. Lebanon, Pa. (Jan.-June, 1857. Some numbers missing.)—P. S. L.
The Lewistown Republican, and Mifflin County Working-Men's Advocate. w. Lewistown, Pa. (Feb. 19, 1840-Aug. 31, 1842. Many numbers missing.)—P. S. L.
The Luzerne Union. w. Wilkesbarre, Pa. (Jan. 19-Dec. 28, 1853.)—P. S. L.
The Marietta Advocate and Farmers' and Mechanics' Intelligencer. w. Marietta, Pa. (1834. Some numbers missing.)— P. S. L.
The Mifflin Eagle, and Lewistown Intelligencer. w. Lewistown, Pa. (Jan. 6-Dec. 15, 1831.)—P. S. L.
Morning Herald. d. Harrisburg. (Jan.-June, 1854.)—P. S. L.
National Enquirer, and Constitutional Advocate of Universal Liberty. s-m. and w. Phila. (Ed. and pub. by Benjamin Lundy. Aug. 3, 1836, when it began,—Mar. 8, 1838.)—R. B.

268   BIBLIOGRAPHY

The National Gazette and Literary Register. d. Phila. (1821, 1837, 1838, and some numbers.)—R. B.

Norristown Herald, and Weekly Advertiser. w. Norristown, Pa. (1824.)—P. S. L.

North American and United States Gazette. d. Phila. (Jan.-June, 1857.)—L. C. P.

The Pennsylvania Chronicle and Universal Advertiser. w. Phila. (1767-1772. Some numbers.)—R. B.

The Pennsylvania Freeman. New Series. w. Phila. (Pub. by the Pa. Anti-Slavery Soc. 1844-1853.)—R. B.

Pennsylvania Gazette. w. (1735-1804.)—L. C. and R. B.

The Pennsylvania Herald, and York General Advertiser. w. (1797.)—York Co. Hist. Soc.

Pennsylvania Inquirer. d. Phila. (1830-1838, and some numbers.)—R. B.

Pennsylvania Intelligencer. s-w. and w. Harrisburg. (Jan. 5-Nov. 6, 1827. Some numbers missing.)—P. S. L.

The Pennsylvania Journal and the Weekly Advertiser. w. Phila. (1791, 1792, and some numbers.)—R. B.

The Pennsylvania Packet or the General Advertiser. w. and s-w. Phila. (1778-1790.)—L. C. and R. B.

Pennsylvania Reporter, and Democratic State Journal. w. Harrisburg. (Sept.-Dec., 1838.)—P. S. L.

Pennsylvania Telegraph, w. Harrisburg. (July 7, 1841-June 29, 1842.)—P. S. L.

The Pennsylvanian. d. Phila. (1837-1847, and some numbers.)—R. B.

People's Advocate. w. York, Pa. (Jan. 8-Dec. 31, 1850.)—York Co. Hist. Soc.

The Philadelphia Gazette and Universal Daily Advertiser. d. Philadelphia. (1794-1795, some numbers.)—R. B.

The Philadelphia Gazette and Daily Advertiser. d. Phila. (1820-1840.)—R. B.

The Philadelphian. w. Phila. (Jan. 1, 1835-Dec. 31, 1835.)—P. S. L.

Philadelphische Correspondenz. w. Phila. (1793.)—P. S. L.

Philadelphische Staatsbote. w. Phila. (1763-1769.)—R. B.

Porcupine's Gazette. d. Phila. (1799, and some numbers.)—R. B.

Poulson's American Daily Advertiser. d. Phila. (1814, 1815, 1837, 1838.)—R. B. and L. C. P.

The Press. d Phila. (1857, 1858, 1859, and some numbers.) —L. C. P.

Public Ledger. d. Phila. (1850, 1851, 1857, 1859, 1860.)—L. C. P.

Record of the Times, and Wilkes-Barre Advocate. w. Wilkesbarre. (1855.)—P. S. L.

Republican Farmer and Democratic Journal. w. Wilkesbarre. (Jan.-Aug., 1838.)—P. S. L.

The Somerset Whig. w. Somerset, Pa. (1818.)—P. S. L.

Spirit of the Times and Daily Keystone. d. Phila. (1848.)— R. B.

Star and Republican Banner. w. Gettysburg, Pa. (Mar. 31-Dec. 21, 1840.)—York Co. Hist. Soc.

The Times. w. Lancaster. (1809. Some numbers missing.)— P. S. L.

The Union Times and Republican Herald. w. New Berlin, Union Co., Pa. (Jan. 3-Dec. 19, 1834.)—P. S. L.

United States Gazette. d. Phila. (1837-1840, and some numbers.)—R. B.

The Upland Union, Delaware County Democrat and People's Advocate. w. Chester, Pa. (May 29, 1838-Dec. 31, 1839.)—P. S. L.

Westmoreland Intelligencer. w. Greensburg, Pa. (Feb. 8, 1833-Jan. 31, 1834.)—P. S. L.

The Whig. w. Chambersburg, Pa. (Jan. 8-Dec. 30, 1836. Some numbers missing.)—P. S. L.

Whig State Journal. w. Harrisburg. (Jan. 29-Dec. 30, 1852.)— P. S. L.

York Gazette. w. (Mar. 7-Dec. 26, 1828. German.)—York Co. Hist. Soc.

York Recorder. w. (1812.)—Same place.

York Republican, and Anti-Masonic Expositor. w. (Mar. 16-Dec. 28, 1830.)—Same place.

III.

BOOKS AND PAMPHLETS.

This list is designed to include only the sources. On account of its length, however, it was necessary to omit certain classes of works. Most of the early travellers came to Philadelphia, and they frequently allude to the negroes there. They furnish much curious information, but their books are sufficiently well known to be omitted here. The county histories as a rule are poor, but they contain a great deal of source material not to be had elsewhere, some of which has been used. These histories also are well known. Many other books, such as family records, genealogical collections, etc., afforded hints, but are not listed, because the help given was small in amount. In general books with descriptive titles are not described. This is particularly the case with the abolitionist and anti-slavery literature cited.

(Abolition of Slavery, Bill for), *No. 399. House of Representatives. Read Feb. 14, 1826.* These bills as a rule are merely mentioned in the House and Senate Journals.—Fr. Lib., 142 N. 16th Street, Phila.

Abolition Exposed Corrected. By a Physician, Formerly Resident of the South, etc. Phila., 1838.—L. C. P.

Achenwall's in Göttingen über Nordamerika und über dasige Grosbritannische Colonien aus mündlichen Nachrichten des Herrn Dr. Franklins . . . Anmerkungen. Frankfort and Leipzig, 1769. Some excellent information. Apparently trustworthy.—R. B.

Acrelius, Israel, *Description of . . . New Sweden*, etc. Stockholm, 1759. Tr. by W. M. Reynolds, Phila., 1874.—In *Mem. Hist. Soc. Pa.*, XI.

An Address from the Pa. Soc. Abol. Slavery, etc. . . . On the Origin, Purposes and Utility of Their Institution. Phila., 1819. —H. S. P.

Address of the Eastern Executive Committee of the State Anti-Slavery Society, to the Citizens of Pennsylvania. Phila., 1838.—H. S. P.

Address of the Members of the Philadelphia Anti-Slavery Society to Their Fellow Citizens. Published by the Board of Managers. Phila., 1835.—H. S. P.

Address of the State Anti-Slavery Society, To the Ministers of the Gospel in the State of Pennsylvania. Phila., 1838.—H. S. P.

An Address to a Portion of our Southern Brethren in the United States, on the Subject of Slavery, etc. Phila., 1839.— Fr. Lib., Park Place, Baltimore.

Address to Abolitionists. Phila., 1838.—In behalf of the Re-
quited Labor Convention.—H. S. P.

*An Address to Christians of All Denominations, on the In-
consistency of Admitting Slave-Holders to Communion and
Church Membership.* Phila., 1831. [Evan Lewis.] H. S. P.

*An Address to Friends and Friendly People ; being an Exhor-
tation to Faithfulness in the Maintenance of our Christian Testimony against Slavery.* Phila., 1848.—F. Lib., Balto.

Address to the Citizens of Pennsylvania. Phila., 1837.—By
convention held at Harrisburg to form a state anti-slavery society.—H. S. P.

*An Address to the Inhabitants of the British Settlements in
America upon Slave-Keeping,* etc. 2d ed., Phila., 1773.—R. B.

*An Address to the . . . Meetings . . . by the Committee . . .
Subject of Slavery.* Phila., 1839.—Fr. Lib., Balto.

*Address to the People of Colour at the Exhibition of the
Mary-Street Public School,* etc. Phila., 1825.—Fr. Lib., 142 N.
Sixteenth Street, Phila.

*Address to the Senators and Representatives of the Free
States, in the Congress of the United States.* Phila., 1838.—
By the A-sl. Conv. of American Women at Phila.—H. S. P.

*Addresse an das Volk über Sclaverei. Eine Vertheidigung
der Grundsätze und Maszregeln der Abolitionisten.* Heraus-
gegeben von der östlichen Abtheilung der pennsylvanischen
Anti-Sclaverei-Gesellschaft.—H. S. P.

*Addresses Delivered in the . . . House of Representatives,
Harrisburg.* Pub. by order of the Pa. Colonization Soc. Phila.,
1852.—H. S. P.

*The African Observer. A Monthly Journal Containing Es-
says and Documents Illustrative of the General Character, and
Moral and Political Effects, of Negro Slavery.* (Vol. I. 4 mo.,
1827, to 3 mo., 1828.) Phila., 1828.—H. S. P.

The African Repository and Colonial Journal. m. Washington, 1826-1842.—Pub. by the Amer. Col. Soc.—R. B.

The African's Right to Citizenship. Phila., 1865.—H. S. P.

The American Free Produce Journal. Circular. Phila., Oct
1, 1842.—H. S. P.

The Anti-Slavery Alphabet. Phila., 1847.—H. S. P.

(Anti-Slavery Tracts. Phila., no date.)

   1. *Extracts from the American Slave Code.*

2. *Declaration of Sentiments of the American Anti-Slavery Society.*
3. *The No-Voting Theory.*
4. *The Political Economy of Slavery.*
5. *The Superiority of Moral over Political Power. By Adin Ballou.*
6. *Immediate Emancipation Safe and Profitable.*
10. *The American Slave Trade.*—H. S. P.

Appeal of Forty Thousand Citizens, Threatened with Disfranchisement, to the People of Pennsylvania. Phila., 1838.— Memorial by negroes against the constitutional amendment of 1838.—H. S. P.

The Appeal of the Religious Society of Friends . . . on Behalf of the Coloured Races. Phila., 1858.—Deprecates existing prejudice.—R. B.

The Arrest, Trial, and Release of Daniel Webster, a Fugitive Slave. Correspondence of the Anti-Slavery Standard. Phila., 1859.—Condemning Fugitive Slave Law.—L. C. P.

The Articles Settlement and Offices of the Free Society of Traders in Pennsylvania, Agreed upon by divers Merchants and Others for the better Improvement and Government of Trade in That Province. London, 1682.—Company to hold negroes as servants.—H. S. P.

Atlee, Edwin P., *An Address to the Citizens of Philadelphia on the Subject of Slavery.* Phila., 1833.—H. S. P.

Benezet, Anthony. (Probably the most influential of the early abolitionist writers. His books are earnest and impassioned, but apparently accurate.)

A Short Account of that Part of Africa Inhabited by the Negroes, etc. Phila., 1762.—H. S. P.

A Caution and Warning to Great Britain and Her Colonies in a Short Representation of the Calamitous State of the Enslaved Negroes, etc. Phila., 1766.—H. S. P.

Some Historical Account of Guinea, etc. Phila., 1771.— H. S. P.

A Collection of Religious Tracts, etc. (Benezet Tracts.) Phila., 1773.—H. S. P.

Notes on the Slave Trade. 1780.—H.S. P.

Short Observations on Slavery, etc. Phila., 1783.—H. S. P.

Missive van Cornelis Bom, Geschreven uit de Stadt Philadel-

phia, In de Provintie van Pennsylvania, Leggende op d'Oost-zyde van de Zuyd Revier van Nieuw Nederland, Verhalende de groote Voortgank van de selve Provintie, etc. Rotterdam, 1685.—Early notice of negroes in Pa.—H. S. P.

Bradford, Sarah H., *Scenes in the Life of Harriet Tubman.* Auburn, 1869.—Fugitive slave.—R. B.

Branagan, Thomas, *Serious Remonstrances . . . Consisting of Speculations and Animadversions, on the Recent Revival of the Slave Trade,* etc. Phila., 1805.—Contains strong indictment of criminality of negroes in Pa. by opponent of slavery.—R. B.

Brief Considerations on Slavery, and the Expediency of Its Abolition. With Some Hints on the Means whereby it may be gradually effected. Burlington, 1773.—Contains " An Account Stated on the Manumission of Slaves "—a plan for making manumission easier.—H. S. P.

A Brief Narrative of the Struggle for the Rights of the Colored People of Philadelphia in the City Railway Cars, etc. Phila., 1867.—Shows prejudice against negroes.—H. S. P.

A Brief Sketch of the Schools for Black People and Their Descendants Established by the Religious Society of Friends in 1770. Phila., 1867.—H. S. P.

A Brief State of the Province of Pennsylvania . . . In a Letter from a Gentleman who has resided many Years in Pennsylvania to his Friend in London. London, 1755.—R. B.

A Brief Statement of the Rise and Progress of the Testimony of the Religious Society of Friends, against Slavery and the Slave Trade. Phila., 1843.—Pub. by the Phila. Yr. Meeting. Based upon the Friends' Records. Contains much that cannot easily be seen in the original.—R. B.

Brissot de Warville, J. P., *Mémoire sur les Noirs de l'Amérique Septentrionale.* Paris, 1789.—R. B.

Brissot de Warville, J. P., *Nouveau Voyage dans Les Etats-Unis de L' Amérique Septentrionale, fait en 1798,* etc. 3 vols. Paris, 1791.—Brissot a French republican, enthusiastic for the free government of America. Accurate for what he saw. Judgments warped by idealism.—R. B.

Brown, David Paul, *Eulogium upon William Rawle, LL. D. Delivered on the 31st of December, 1836.* Phila., 1837.—Rawle was a prominent abolitionist, and at one time president of the Pa. Soc. Abol. Sl.—H. S. P.

Brown, David Paul, *Letter of, to the Incorporated "Pennsylvania Society for Promoting the Abolition of Slavery,"* etc. Phila., 1860.—On fugitive slave trials.—P. L. L.

Burden, Dr. J. R., of Philadelphia Co., *Remarks of, in the Senate of Pennsylvania, on the Abolition Question, February, 1838.* etc. Phila., 1838.—Notices harm caused by anti-slavery extravagances.—P. L. L.

Carey, Matthew, *Letters on the Colonization Society; and of its Probable Results,* etc. 4th ed., Phila., 1832.—R. B.

Carey, Matthew, *A Short Account of the Malignant Fever Lately Prevalent in Philadelphia,* etc. 4th ed., Phila., 1794.—R. B.

Case of the Slave Isaac Brown, An Outrage Exposed.—Tract.—Fr. Hist. Lib., Swarthmore, Pa.

[Catto, Rev. William T., pastor], *A Semi-Centenary Discourse, Delivered in the First African Presbyterian Church, Philadelphia, 1857: with a History of the Church from Its First Organization: etc. Also, an Appendix, Containing Sketches of All the Colored Churches in Philadelphia.* Phila., 1857.—The beginnings of negro church organization.—H. S. P.

Centennial Anniversary of the Pa. Soc. Ab. Sl., etc. Phila., 1875.—Fr. Lib., Park Place, Baltimore.

Child, Lydia Maria, *Isaac T. Hopper: A True Life.* Boston, Cleveland, London, 1853.—Hopper was a Friend with strong anti-slavery sympathies.—H. S. P.

Circular. To the members and friends of the "Pennsylvania Society for promoting the abolition of Slavery." Phila., 1837.—H. S. P.

To the Clergy of Pennsylvania.—No date. Broadside circulated by the Col. Soc. of Pa.—In Miscellaneous Coll., Box 10, Negroes.—H. S. P.

Collections of the Historical Society of Pennsylvania. Phila. 1853.

The Colonization Herald and General Register. m. Mar. 1848-Dec. 1856.—Conducted by the Pa. Col. Soc. Phila.—R. B.

[Colton, Calvin], *Abolition A Sedition. By a Northern Man.* Phila., 1839.—H. S. P.

Condie, Thomas, and Folwell, Richard, *History of the Pestilence, Commonly Called Yellow Fever, which Almost Desolated Philadelphia, in . . . 1798.* Phila.—R. B.

On the Condition of the Free People of Color in the United States. New York. 1839.—*Anti-Slavery Examiner* No. 13. Discrimination against negroes.—R. B.

Constitution, By-Laws, and List of Officers of the Young Men's Anti-Slavery Society of the City and County of Philadelphia. Instituted April, 1835. Phila., 1835.—Inserted in MS. Rec. Pa. Soc. Abol. Sl., X, 237.—H. S. P.

Constitution of the American Society of Free Persons of Colour, etc. Phila., 1831.—Beginnings of negro organization.— R. B.

The Constitution of the Pennsylvania Society for Promoting the Abolition of Slavery, etc. Phila., 1788.—The most important abol. soc. in the U. S.—H. S. P.

Constitution of the Philadelphia Anti-Slavery Society. Instituted . . . 1834.—The beginnings of anti-sl. in Pa.—H. S. P.

Cranz, David, *The Ancient and Modern History of the Brethren . . . Unitas Fratrum.* Tr. by Benjamin Latrobe. London, 1780.—Moravians and negroes.—R. B.

Crawford, Charles, *Observations upon Negro-Slavery,* etc. Phila., 1784.—Early abol. tract. Contains terrible picture showing negroes crowded between decks of slave-ship.—H. S. P.

Crèvecœur, J. Hector St. John, *A Farmer in Pennsylvania: Letters from an American Farmer; Describing Certain Provincial Situations, Manners, and Customs, not Generally Known,* etc. London, 1783.—Mildness of slavery in Pa.—P. L.

Darlington, William, *Memorials of John Bartram and Humphrey Marshall,* etc. Phila., 1849.—Early abols.—R. B.

Davies, Benjamin, *Some Account of the City of Philadelphia,* etc. Phila., 1794.—R. B. (Loganian.)

Desilver's *Philadelphia Directory and Stranger's Guide,* for 1828, etc. Phila., 1828.—H. S. P.

Delany, Martin R., *The Condition, Elevation, Emigration, and Destiny of the Colored People of the United States, Politically Considered.* Phila., 1852.—Careful statement.—H. S. P.

Denny, John F., *An Essay on the Political Grade of the Free Coloured Population under the Constitution of the United States, and the Constitution of Pennsylvania.* Chambersburg, Pa., 1836.—Excellent and learned argument by one who denies the right of the negro to full citizenship.—H. S. ?.

Douglass, William, *A Summary, Historical and Political, . . .*

of the British Settlements in North-America, etc. 2 vols., Boston, 1749.—R. B.

The Duty of Pennsylvania Concerning Slavery. Phila., 1840. —Pub. at the Anti-Slavery Office. Advocates decisive measures.—H. S. P.

Ebeling, Christoph Daniel, *Erdbeschreibung und Geschichte von Amerika,* etc. Hamburg, 1797.—In A. F. Büsching's *Erdbeschreibung,* etc. Not a source, but based upon sources some of which are apparently inaccessible now. A wonderful book for its time. Contains full bibliographies.—R. B.

An Epistle from the Yearly Meeting of Friends, Held in Philadelphia . . . 1832 . . . to the People of Colour Residing in Pennsylvania, etc. Phila., 1832.—Good advice to free negroes.— Fr. Hist. Lib., Swarthmore, Pa.

An Epistle of Caution and Advice, Concerning the Buying and Keeping of Slaves. Phila., 1754.—Early Quaker abolitionism.—H. S. P.

Falkner, Daniel ("Bürgern und Pilgrim allda"), *Curieuse Nachricht von Pennsylvania in Norden-America,* etc. Frankfort and Leipzig, 1702. Ed. by J. Sachse, Phila., 1905.—Early economic information about Pa.—R. B.

Fox, The Hon. John, Opinion of, . . . against the Exercise of Negro Suffrage in Pennsylvania, etc. Harrisburg, 1838.—A document that was effectively circulated in Pa.—H. S. P.

To the Free Africans and other free People of Color in the United States. Phila., 1796.—Broadside. Good advice.—H. S. P.

To the Free People of Colour in the United States. Phila., 1829.—Pub. by the Amer. Convention Abol. Sl. Good advice.— H. S. P.

Free Remarks on the Spirit of the Federal Constitution, the Practice of the Federal Government, and the Obligations of the Union Respecting the Exclusion of Slavery from the Territories and New States, etc. *By a Philadelphian.* Phila., 1819.—Urges exclusion.—H. S. P.

The Friend. A Religious and Literary Journal. 1828- present time. Phila.—Contains many historical and biographical pieces of value.—77 vols. in R. B.

The Friends' Library: Comprising Journals, Doctrinal Treatises, and Other Writings of Members of the Religious Society of Friends. Ed. by W. and T. Evans. 14 vols. Phila., 1837-1850.—Reprints many diaries.—H. S. P.

The Fugitive Slave Law and Its Victims. New York, 1861.—No. 15 of Anti-Slavery Tracts. New Series. Pub. by Amer. Anti-Sl. Soc. Contains long list of negroes reclaimed and kidnapped. Probably exaggerated.—H. S. P.

Furness, W. H., *An Address Delivered before a Meeting of the Members and Friends of the Pennsylvania Anti-Slavery Society during the Annual Fair, Dec. 19, 1849.* Phila., 1850.—Progress of anti-slavery.—H. S. P.

Furness, W. H., *The Blessings of Abolition. A Discourse Delivered in the First Congregational Unitarian Church, Sunday, July 1, 1860.* Phila., 1860.—H. S. P.

Furness, W. H., *Christian Duty. Three Discourses Delivered in the First Congregational Unitarian Church of Philadelphia.* Phila., 1854.—L. C. P.

Furness, W. H., *Two Discourses Occasioned by the Approaching Anniversary of the Declaration of Independence,* etc., Phila., 1843.—Contrasts the spirit of freedom with the existence of slavery.—H. S. P.

Garrison, William Lloyd, *An Address Delivered before the Free People of Color, in Philadelphia, New York,* etc. Boston. 1831.—Over-zealous advice.—R. B.

Garrison, William Lloyd, *Thoughts on African Colonization: or an Impartial Exhibition of the Doctrines, Principles and Purposes of the American Colonization Society,* etc. Boston, 1832.—Bitterly denounces colonization.—H. S. P.

Hanway, Castner, A History of the Trial of . . . for Treason at Philadelphia . . . 1851, etc. Phila., 1852.—Notices famous legal questions which arose under the law of 1847 relative to kidnapping and fugitive slaves.—L. C. P.

Hazard, Samuel, *Annals of Pennsylvania . . . 1609-1682.* Phila., 1850.—Contains many indispensable documents. Hazard was probably the ablest of the early archivists of Pa.

Hazard's Register of Pennsylvania. Ed. by Samuel Hazard. 16 vols. Phila., 1828-1835.—The *Niles's Register* of Pa. One feels a distinct loss when the *Register* comes to an end.

Heckewelder, John, *A Narrative of the Mission of the United Brethren among the Delaware and Mohegan Indians, from Its Commencement, in the Year 1740, to the Close of the Year 1808.*

etc. Phila., 1820.—Notices Whitefield's proposed school for negroes.—Pea.

[Richard Hildreth], *The Slave; or Memoirs of Archy Moore,* 6th ed. 2 vols. in one. Boston, 1846.— Declared that he passed through Pa. as a fugitive.—H. S. P.

History of Pennsylvania Hall, Which Was Destroyed by a Mob, etc. Phila., 1838.—Gives the anti-sl. side.—R. B.

History of the Associations of Friends for the Free Instruction of Adult Colored Persons in Philadelphia. Phila., 1890.—From the sources. Pub. by direction of the Association. —H. S. P.

Hooker, Herman (publisher), *Colonization and Abolition Contrasted.* Phila., (no date.)—R. B.

A Humble Attempt at scurrility, etc. By Jack Retorts Student in Scurrility. Quilsylvania. Printed 1765.—Accuses Benjamin Franklin of having a negro mistress.—R. B.

Hunt, Benjamin, Diary of, 1799-1812.—Reprinted from the *Daily Local News* for the Chester Co. Hist. Soc., 1898. In *Bulletins of the Chester Co. Hist. Soc.,* 1898. Local notices of negroes.—H. S. P.

An Impartial Appeal to the Reason, Interest and Patriotism, of the People of Illinois, on the Injurious Effects of Slave Labour. 1824.—Abolitionist propaganda.—H. S. P.

An Inquiry into the Condition and Prospects of the African Race in the United States, etc. . . . by an American. Phila., 1839.—R. B.

Jackson, William, of Chester Co., Pennsylvania, *Views of Slavery in Its Effects on the Wealth, Population, and Character of Nations.* Phila., 1838.—Denies right of Congress to abolish slavery in the D. C.—H. S. P.

Jay, William, *An Inquiry into the Character and Tendency of the American Colonization, and American Anti-Slavery Societies.* 2d ed. New York, 1835.—H. S. P.

Jones, Absalom, Rector, *A Thanksgiving Sermon, Preached by, Jan. 1, 1808, in . . . the African Episcopal Church, Philadelphia.* Phila., 1808.—A noted negro preacher of Phila.—R. B.

J[ones], A., and A[llen], R., *A Narrative of the Proceedings of the Black People, during the Late Awful Calamity in Philadelphia, in the Year 1793: and a Refutation of some Censures*

Thrown upon them in some late Publications. Phila., 1794.—
Defends conduct of negroes during pestilence.—S. H. P.

Journals, Legislative.—Pennsylvania.
*Votes and Proceedings of the House of Representatives of
the Province of Pennsylvania, 1682-1776.* Phila., 1752-1776.—
R. B.
*Journals of the House of Representatives of the Common-
wealth of Pennsylvania. 1776-1781.* Phila., 1782.—R. B.
Minutes of the . . . General Assembly, etc. 1781-1790. Phila.—
Apparently only existing copy in the H. S. P.
*Journals of the House of Representatives of Pennsylvania.
1790-1861.* Phila., Lancaster, Harrisburg.—L. C. P.
Journals of the Senate of Pennsylvania. 1790-1861. Phila.,
Lancaster, Harrisburg.—L. C. P.

These volumes are a store-house of information. Prior to
1800 they contain comparatively little about negroes
or slavery, but after that time, as the black population
increased, and as abolitionism and anti-slavery became
strong forces, much more attention was given to negroes, until in the later years no small part of the proceedings was taken up in discussing them. The
Journals never give debates in full, but they furnish a
summary of all business, the history of all bills, and
note all petitions received. Accordingly from the apparently meagre record it was possible to study the
growth of race prejudice, the ebb and flow of abolitionism, and the attempts to pass discriminatory laws. In
the later years additional light is thrown upon the subject by the extra volumes, which frequently print
committee reports in full. After the laws, and the court
decisions, the legislative journals proved to be the most
important source used in the preparation of this work.

Keimer, S., *Ways and Means for the Inhabitants of Delaware
to become Rich,* etc. Phila., 1725.—Suggests negroes for agricultural work.—R. B. (Loganian.)
Kenworthy, Jesse, *Thoughts on Slavery.* Washington, Pa.
1851.—Fr. Lib., Park Place, Balto.
Langston, J. M., *The Great Oration . . . upon the Life and Ser-*

vices of the Rt. Rev. Richard Allen, Founder and First Bishop of the African Methodist Episcopal Church. Phila., 1877.— Beginnings of negro church organization in Pa.—H. S. P.

Laws of Pennsylvania.

Laws of the Province of Pennsylvania, . . . 1682-1700, preceded by the Duke of York's Laws . . . 1676-1682, etc. Harrisburg, 1879.—Pub. under direction of J. B. Linn. Contains "laws" in effect before Penn's coming. Moreover, until the first volume of the *Statutes at Large* is allowed to appear, it affords the only printed collection of the laws of Pa. from 1682 to 1700.

Laws of the Commonwealth of Pennsylvania. 1700-1801. Re-published under the Authority of the Legislature by Alexander James Dallas. 4 vols. Phila., 1797-1801.—P. L. L.

The Statutes at Large of Pennsylvania from 1682 to 1801, compiled by James T. Mitchell and Henry Flanders, Commissioners. 11 vols. (vols. II-XII, 1700-1787, published), 1896-1906.—By far the best edition of the laws of Pa. for the period covered. Full historical appendices. Subsequent history of every statute appended to the text of the statute. The volumes are admirably indexed.

Acts of the General Assembly of the Commonwealth of Pennsylvania, etc., 1801-1826. Lancaster, Octoraro, Phila., Harrisburg, 1802-1826.—L. C. P.

Laws of the General Assembly of . . . Pennsylvania, 1826-1861. Harr., 1827-1861.—L. C. P.

Laws of the Emlen Institution. Germantown, Pa., 1843.— Established for negroes.—H. S. P.

Lay, Benjamin, *All Slave-Keepers That Keep the Innocent in Bondage, Apostates, etc.* Phila., pr. for the Author, 1737.— A fierce, uncompromising abolitionist. His views to be taken with caution.—H. S. P.

Legislative Documents. (Pa.) 1854-1860.—Reports, etc.—L. C. P.

Lewis, Evan, *Address to the Coloured People of Philadelphia. Delivered at Bethel Church . . . 1833.* Phila., 1833.— H. S. P.

Liberty-Catalogue of A. S. Works . . . 1839.—Contains extracts from anti-sl. writers. Illustrated.—H. S. P.

The Little Western against the Great Eastern . . . Being a Review by a Plebeian of the Western Hemisphere of Abolitionism as Exposed by Doctor Sleigh. Phila., 1838.—Abolitionist controversy.—H. S. P.

Lloyd, Elizabeth, Jr., *An Appeal for the Bondwoman, To Her Own Sex.* Phila., 1846.—Anti-sl. poem.—H. S. P.

McLanahan, J. X., of Pennsylvania, Speech of, on the Slave Question. Delivered in the House of Representatives, Feb. 19, 1850. Washington, 1850.—P. L. L.

Mease, James, *The Picture of Philadelphia,* etc. Phila., 1811. —Notices negroes.—R. B.

Memoirs of the Historical Society of Pennsylvania. 14 vols. Phila., 1826-1895.—Contains journals, letters, and excellent monographs.

Memorial of the Free Citizens of Color in Pittsburg and Its Vicinity, Relative to the Right of Suffrage. Read in Convention July 8, 1837. Harrisburg, 1837.—Negroes asked to be allowed to vote. Aroused heated controversy.—H. S. P.

Memorial of Thirty Thousand Disfranchised Citizens of Philadelphia, to the Honorable Senate and House of Representatives. Phila., 1855.—Ask recognition of their rights.—H. S. P.

[*Memorial to the House and Senate of Pa. by colored people of Phila. and vicinity, protesting against repeal of act of 1826. About 1844.*]—TW* 99, vol. 27.—H. S. P.

Mr. Miner of Pennsylvania, Speech of, Delivered in the House of Representatives . . . 1829, on the Subject of Slavery and the Slave Trade in the District of Columbia, etc. Washington, 1829.—Attitude of Pa.—H. S. P.

Minutes and Proceedings of the First Annual Convention of the People of Colour . . . Philadelphia . . . 1831. Phila., 1831. —R. B.

Minutes and Proceedings of the Second Annual Convention, for the Improvement of the Free People of Color in These United States, etc. Phila., 1832.—This and the preceding illustrate negro organization.—H. S. P.

Minutes of the Common Council of the City of Philadelphia. 1704-1776. Printed by order of the Select and Common Councils of the City of Philadelphia., Phila., 1847.—Turbulence and disorder of negroes in early times.—R. B.

Minutes of the Proceedings of Conventions of Delegates from the Abolition Societies Established in Different Parts of the United States. 1794-1803. Phila., 1794-1803.

Minutes of the Proceedings of American Conventions for promoting the Abolition of Slavery and Improving the Condition of the African Race. 1804-1817. Phila., 1804-1817.

Minutes of American Conventions for promoting the Abolition of Slavery, and Improving the Condition of the African Race. 1818-1837. Phila., etc., 1818-1839.
These minutes are a storehouse of information about free negroes, slavery, and abolition. A great deal of the matter is contained in the MS. Rec. of the Pa. Soc. Abol. Sl.—H. S. P.

Minutes of the Proceedings of the Committee Appointed . . . 1793 . . . to Alleviate . . . the Malignant Fever, etc. Phila., 1794. —R. B.

Minutes of the Provincial Council of Pennsylvania, from the Organization to the Termination of the Proprietary Government. Pub. by the State. 10 vols. Harrisburg, 1851-1852.—"*Colonial Records.*" Executive documents for the period covered, 1682-1776.

Minutes of the Supreme Executive Council of Pennsylvania, from Its Organization to the Termination of the Revolution. Pub. by the State. 5 vols. Harrisburg, 1852-1853.—"*Colonial Records.*" Executive documents. 1776-1789.—N. B. The paging of the 1838 edition is different from that in the edition cited.

Minutes of the State Convention of the Coloured Citizens of Pennsylvania, Convened at Harrisburg, etc. Phila., 1849.— For negro organization.—H. S. P.

A Mite cast into the Treasury: or, Observations on Slave-Keeping, etc. Phila., 1792.—Early abol. tract.—R. B.

Mittelberger, Gottlieb, *Journey to Pennsylvania in the Year 1750,* etc. Stuttgart, 1756. Tr. by Carl T. Eben, 1898.—Careful account by a German traveller.

More, Doctor Nicholas, *A letter from, with Passages out of several Letters from Persons of Good Credit, Relating to the State and Improvement of the Province of Pennsilvania. Published to prevent false Reports. Printed in the Year 1687.*— Original in John Carter Brown Library, Providence. Reprinted also in *Pa. Mag.,* IV, 445.—P. S. L.

Morse, Jedediah, *The American Gazeteer,* etc. Boston, 1797. —H. S. P.

Morse, Jedediah, *The American Geography or a View of the Present Situation of the United States of America,* etc. New ed., London, 1794.—Negroes and negro church in Phila.— H. S. P.

Narrative of Facts in the Case of Passmore Williamson. Phila., 1855.—Famous fugitive slave case.—H. S. P.

Needlès, Edward, *Ten Years' Progress: or a Comparison of the State and Condition of the Colored People in the City and County of Philadelphia from 1837 to 1847.* Phila., 1849.— Based on the best statistics available.—H. S. P.

Nîles, Nathaniel, and Russ, John D., *Medical Statistics; or a Comparative View of the Mortality in New York, Philadelphia, Baltimore, and Boston for a Series of Years,* etc. New York, 1827.—Comparative mortality of negroes and white people.— R. B.

Nourse, Rev. James, *Views on Colonization.* Phila., 1837.— L. C. P.

Objects and Regulations of the Institute for Colored Youth, etc. Phila., 1860.—R. B.

Observations on the Inslaving, importing and purchasing of Negroes, etc. 2d ed. Pr. by Christopher Sower, Germantown, 1760.—L. C.

O'Callaghan, E. B. (ed.), *Documents relative to the Colonial History of the State of New York,* etc. Albany, 1855.—Superb collection. Contains references to negroes in Pa.

O'Callaghan, E. B. (ed.), *Voyages of the Slavers St. John and Arms of Amsterdam, 1659, 1663; together with Additional Papers Illustrative of the Slave Trade under the Dutch.* Albany, 1867.—Documents illustrative of legal slavery among the Dutch. —H. S. P.

Ogden, John C., *An Excursion into Bethlehem and Nazareth in Pennsylvania, in the Year 1799,* etc. Phila., 1805.—Work of Moravians for negroes.—R. B.

Parrish, Isaac, *Brief Memoirs of Thomas Shipley and Edwin P. Atlee, Read before the Pennsylvania Society for Promoting the Abolition of Slavery,* etc. Phila., 1838.—Active abolitionists. —H. S. P.

Parrish, John, *Remarks on the Slavery of the Black People;*

Addressed to the Citizens of the United States, etc. Phila., 1806.—Abol. tract.—R. B.

Parsons, J. C. (ed.), *Extracts from the Diary of Jacob Hiltzheimer, of Philadelphia, 1765-1798.* Phila., 1893.—Refers to abolition law of 1788.—H. S. P.

Passmore Williamson v. John K. Kane. Argument for the Defendant. Legal discussion of some laws of Pa. in connection with the Federal Fugitive Slave Law.—H. S. P.

Patton, Rev. William W., *Thoughts for Christians Suggested by the Case of Passmore Williamson,* etc. Hartford, 1855.—H: S. P.

Pennsylvania and the Fugitive Slave Law, etc. Correspondence between the Hon. John Letcher, Gov. of Va., and Lewis D. Vail, Esq., of Phila., etc. Phila., [1860.]—H. S. P.

Pennsylvania Archives. Selected and Arranged from Original Documents in the Office of the Secretary of the Commonwealth, etc. Ed. by Samuel Hazard. First Series. 12 vols. Phila., 1852-1856.—Misc. colonial docs.

Pa. Arch. Second Series. Ed. by J. B. Linn and W. H. Egle. 19 vols. Harr., 1878-1896.—Misc. papers—war, navy, colonial.

Pa. Arch. Third Series. Ed. by W. H. Egle. 30 vols. Harrisburg, 1894-1899.—Misc. papers,—Board of Property,—tax-lists, etc.

Pa. Arch. Fourth Series. Ed. by George E. Reed, 12 vols. Harrisburg, 1900-1902.—Messages of the governors, etc.

Pa. Arch. Fifth Series. Ed. by Thomas L. Montgomery. 8 vols. Harrisburg, 1906.—Muster-rolls.

Pa. Arch. Sixth Series. Ed. by Thomas L. Montgomery. 15 vols. Harrisburg, 1906-1907.—Muster-rolls, forfeited estates, etc.

The *Pa. Arch.* contain an immense amount of information bearing upon the history of Pa. The different series are of very unequal merit, both in choice of material and in the manner of handling it. Perhaps the most valuable is the first series, which was prepared by Hazard.

The Pennsylvania Magazine of History and Biography. Phila., 1877-1911.—Indispensable to any student of Pa. history. Contains numerous monographs, reprints, statistical tables, etc. Also prints very many letters, statements, inventories, etc., etc., of the character of rare original material.

Pennsylvania Society for Promoting the Abolition of Slavery, etc., Five Years' Abstract of Transactions of the. Phila., 1853. —H. S. P.

Personal Slavery Established, by the Suffrages of Custom and Right Reason, etc. Phila., 1773.—Defends slavery.—R. B.

Peterson, Henry, *Address on American Slavery, Delivered before the Semi-Annual Meeting of the Junior Anti-Slavery Society of Philadelphia, July 4th, 1838.* Phila., 1838.—H. S. P.

Philadelphia Anti-Slavery Society, First Annual Report of the Board of Managers of the, Read and Accepted at the Annual Meeting of the Society, July 4th, 1835. Phila., 1835.—H. S. P.

Pickard, Kate E. R., *The Kidnapped and the Ransomed. Being the Personal Recollections of Peter Still and His Wife "Vina,"* etc. Syracuse, 1856.— Peter Still became prominent among the negroes of Phila.—R. B.

A Poetical Epistle to the Enslaved Africans, in the Character of an Ancient Negro, Born a Slave in Pennsylvania, etc. Phila., 1790.—The footnotes contain matter of some slight value.— H. S. P.

The Present State and Condition of the Free People of Color, of the City of Philadelphia, etc. Phila., 1838.—Based on information and statistics collected by agents of the Pa. Soc. Abol. Sl. Contains more information of value on social and economic status of the negro in Phila. than any other contemporary writing.—H. S. P.

Proceedings and Debates of the Convention of the Commonwealth of Pennsylvania, to Propose Amendments to the Constitution, Commenced and Held at Harrisburg, on the Second Day of May, 1838. Reported by John Agg, etc. 14 vols. Harrisburg, 1837-1839.—Indispensable for study of the question of negro suffrage.—R. B.

Proceedings of the Pennsylvania Convention Assembled to Organize a State Anti-Slavery Society, at Harrisburg, . . . 1837. Phila., 1837.—The beginnings of the anti-sl. movement in Pa.— H. S. P.

Proceedings of the Pennsylvania Yearly Meetings of Progressive Friends, From the Organization 1853 to 1869. Nos. I to XVII. New York, 1853-1869.—The anti-sl. Friends.—The only copies of the above, apparently, are in the Lib. of the University of Pa., Phila. Some later numbers in possession of the author.

Proceedings of the State Convention of the Colored Freemen of Pennsylvania Held in Pittsburg for the Purpose of Considering Their Condition and the Means of Its Improvement. Pittsburg, 1841.—Reveals growing consciousness of solidarity among negroes.—H. S. P.

Proceedings of the Third Anti-Slavery Convention of American Women Held in Philadelphia, 1839. Phila., 1839.—Illustrates important part taken by women in this movement.—H. S. P.

Randall, Robert E., of Philadelphia, Speech of, on the Laws of the State Relative to Fugitive Slaves, Delivered in the House of Representatives of Pennsylvania, January 16, 1861. Hamilton, Printer.—Asserts Pa's. legislation on fugitive slave question to be unwise and unjust to the South.—P. L. L.

Reflections on Slavery; with Recent Evidence of its Inhumanity, etc. By Humanitas. Phila., 1803.—R. B.

Register of the Trades of the Colored People in the City of Philadelphia and Districts. Phila., 1838.—Valuable. Compiled by the Pa. Soc. Abol. Sl.—H. S. P.

Reise von Hamburg nach Philadelphia. Hannover, 1800.—Notices slave-trade at Phila.—H. S. P.

Remarks on Hayti as a Place of Settlement for Afric-Americans; and on the Mulatto as a Race for the Tropics. Phila., 1860.—H. S. P.

Remarks on the African Slave Trade.—Contains picture of " Plan of an African Ship's lower Deck, with Negroes, in the proportion of not one to a Ton." Extracted from the *American Museum,* for May, 1789, and published by order of the Pennsylvania Society for promoting the Abolition of Slavery, etc.—H. S. P.

Remarks on the Life and Character of James Forten. Phila., 1842.—Delivered at Bethel Church by Robert Purvis. Eulogy of one of Pa's. best negroes.—H. S. P.

Remarks on the Quaker Unmasked; or Plain Truth found to be Plain Falshood: Humbly address'd to the Candid. Phila., [1764.]—Controversial pamphlet favorable to Quakers, adverse to Presbyterians.—H. S. P.

Remonstrance of the Religious Society of Friends against

Prohibiting the Immigration of Colored People.—The full text of one of the numberless petitions in behalf of the negro sent to the Legislature by Friends.—(Uncatalogued.) Fr. Lib., 142 N. 16th Street, Phila.

Report. Board of Managers of the American Moral Reform Society. 1837.—H. S. P.

Report of the Committee Appointed for the Purpose of Securing to Colored People in Philadelphia the Right to the Use of the Street-Cars. Phila.—Shows strong prejudice against negroes in Phila.—H. S. P.

Report of the Committee Appointed in the Senate of Pennsylvania to Investigate the Cause of an Increased Number of Slaves, etc. Harrisburg, 1833.—Explains apparent increase in number of slaves between 1820 and 1830.—H. S. P.

Report of the Committee on the Comparative Health, Mortality, Length of Sentences, etc., of White and Colored Convicts. Phila., 1849.—R. B.

Report of the Committee on the Judiciary Relative to the Abolition of Slavery in the District of Columbia, and in Relation to the Colored Population of This Country. Harrisburg, 1839.—Pa's. official attitude on slavery and abolitionism.—H. S. P.

Report of the House of Refuge of Philadelphia, etc., Twenty-First Annual. Phila., 1849.—R. B.

Reports. Board of Managers of the Association of Friends for the Free Instruction of Adult Colored Persons. Phila.— Work of Friends for education of the negro.—H. S. P.

Annual Reports of the American Free Produce Association. Phila.—Boycotting of slave-products.—H. S. P.

Annual Reports of the Association of Friends for Promoting the Abolition of Slavery and Improving the Condition of the Free People of Color. Phila.—Some, R. B.

Annual Reports of the Board of Managers of the Association of Friends for the Free Instruction of Adult Colored Persons. Phila., 1831-1860.—R. B.

Annual Reports of the Home for Destitute Colored Children. Phila., 1856-1860.—R. B.

Annual Reports of the Philadelphia Female Anti-Slavery Society. Phila.—Zealous work of women.—L. C. P.

288   BIBLIOGRAPHY

Reports (Court).

The reports, mostly of the Supreme Court of the state, are indispensable for a knowledge of the status of the negro, whether free or slave. They give luminous interpretations of the laws, frequently discuss the history of the events which led to their passage, and sometimes disclose the sentiment of the people of Pennsylvania. Some of the decisions of the Supreme Court of the United States, and of the lower Federal courts, have to do with the fugitive slave question. At times decisions in the courts of other states throw light upon similar questions in Pennsylvania.

Pennsylvania.

Dallas, A. J., *Reports of Cases ... in the Courts of Pennsylvania before and since the Revolution.* 4 vols. Phila., 1790-1807. (1754-1806.)

Addison, Alexander, *Reports of Cases in the County Courts of the Fifth Circuit, and in the High Court of Errors and Appeals ... of Pennsylvania,* etc. Washington, 1800. (1791-1799.)

Yeates, Hon. Jasper, *Reports of Cases Adjudged in the Supreme Court of Pennsylvania: with some Select Cases at Nisi Prius, and in the Circuit Courts.* 4 vols. Phila., 1817-1818. (1791-1808.)

Binney, Horace, *Reports of Cases Adjudged in the Supreme Court of Pennsylvania.* 6 vols. Phila., 1878-1879. (1799-1814.)

Browne, Peter A., *Reports of Cases Adjudged in the District Court of the City and County of Philadelphia,* etc. Phila., 1813. (1806-1811.)

Ashmead, John W., *Reports of Cases Adjudged in the Courts of Common Pleas, Quarter Sessions, Oyer and Terminer, and Orphans' Court of the First Judicial District of Pennsylvania.* 2 vols. Phila., 1831, 1841. (1808-1841.)

Brightly, Frederick, *Reports of Cases ... in the Court of Nisi Prius at Philadelphia and also in the Supreme Court,* etc. Phila., 1851. (1809-1851.)

Reports of Cases Adjudged in the Court of Common Pleas of the First Judicial District of Pennsylvania. Phila., 1811.

Sergeant, Thomas, and Rawle, William, Jr., *Reports of Cases Adjudged in the Supreme Court of Pennsylvania.* 17 vols. Phila., 1818-1829. (1814-1828.)

Grant, Benjamin, *Reports of Cases Argued and Adjudged in the Supreme Court of Pennsylvania.* I-III. Phila., 1859-1864. (1814-1863.)

Rawle, William, Jr., *Reports of Cases . . . Supreme Court of Pennsylvania.* 5 vols. Phila., 1869. (1828-1835).

Penrose, Charles, and Watts, Frederick, *Reports of Cases . . . Supreme Court of Pennsylvania.* 2d ed. 3 vols. Phila., 1843. (1829-1832.)

Watts, Frederick, *Reports of Cases . . . Supreme Court of Pennsylvania.* Phila., 1834-1841. (1832-1840.)

Wharton, Thomas L., *Reports of Cases . . .Supreme Court of Pennsylvania in the Eastern District.* Phila., 1884. (1835-1841.)

Watts, Frederick, and Sergeant, Henry J., *Reports of Cases . . . Supreme Court of Pennsylvania.* 9 vols. Phila., 1824-1846. (1841-1844.)

Parsons, A. V., *Select Cases in Equity . . . Court of Common Pleas . . . First Judicial District of Pennsylvania.* 2d ed. 2 vols. Phila., 1888. (1841-1851.)

Pennsylvania Law Journal Reports, Containing Cases Decided by the Federal and State Courts of Pennsylvania.. Rep. by J. A. Clark. I-IV. Phila., 1872-1873. (1842-1852.)

Vaux, Richard, Recorder of the City of Philadelphia, Reports of Some of the Cases on Primary Hearing before, etc. Phila., 1846.

Pennsylvania State Reports Containing Cases . . . Supreme Court.

Barr, Robert M. 10 vols. (1845-1849.)

Jones, J. Pringle. 2 vols. (1849.)

Harris, George W. 12 vols. (1849-1855.)

Casey, Joseph. 12 vols. (1855-1860.)

Wright, Robert E. (1860-   .) Phila., 1846-1861.

Wallace, Henry E., *Philadelphia Reports (Legal Intelligencer Condensed).* I-IV. Phila., 1871. (1850-1861.)

Pearson, William, *Decisions of the Hon. John J. Pearson, Judge of the Twelfth Judicial District.* 2 vols. Phila., 1879-1880. (1850-1880.)

Massachusetts.

Tyng, D. A., *Reports of Cases . . . in the Supreme Judicial Court of the Commonwealth of Massachusetts*. IV. Newburyport, 1809. (1808.)

Federal.

Washington, Bushrod, *Reports of Cases . . . Circuit Court of the United States . . . Third Circuit*, etc. Phila., 1829. (1820-1827.)

Wallace, John W., *Cases in the Circuit Court of the United States for the Third District*. I-III. Phila., 1849-1871. (1842-1862.)

Peters, Richard, *Reports of Cases . . . Supreme Court of the United States*. XVI. Boston, 1842.

Review of the Report of the Committee on Police to the Councils of Philadelphia in Relation to the Destruction of Pennsylvania Hall . . . by Charles Hammand, Esq., ed. of the *Cincinnati Daily Gazette*. Phila., 1838.—Fury awakened by anti-slavery agitation.—H. S. P.

A Review of the Trial, Conviction and Sentence, of George F. Alberti, for Kidnapping.—H. S. P.

Ruffner, W. H., *Africa's Redemption. A Discourse . . . Preached . . . in the Seventh Presbyterian Church, Philadelphia.* Phila., 1852.—The pulpit and slavery.—H. S. P.

[Rush, Benjamin], *An Address to the Inhabitants of the British Settlements in America upon Slave-Keeping, etc., by a Pennsylvanian.* 2d ed. Phila., 1773.—Early abolition sentiment.—H. S. P.

[Rush, Benjamin], *A Vindication of the Address,* etc. Phila., 1773.—H. S. P.

[Rush, Benjamin], *Considerations Upon the Present Test-Law of Pennsylvania: Addressed to the Legislature and Freemen of the State.* 2d ed. Phila., 1785.—Notices semi-citizenship of free negroes.—R. B.

Rush, Benjamin, *An Account of the Manners of the German Inhabitants of Pennsylvania,* etc. 1789. Notes added by I. D. Rupp. Phila., 1875.—L. C. P.

Extract of a Letter from Dr. Benjamin Rush of Philadelphia to Granville Sharp. London, 1792.—Origin of negro church in Phila.—H. S. P.

Rush, Benjamin, *An Account of the Bilious remitting Yellow Fever, As It Appeared in the City of Philadelphia, in the Year 1793*, Phila., 1794.—H. S. P.

Sachse, Julius Friedrich, *Letters Relating to the Settlement of Germantown in Pennsylvania 1683-1684. From the Könneken Manuscript in the Ministerial-Archiv of Lübeck. Reproduced in Facsimile.* Lübeck and Phila., 1903.—Early notice of negroes in Pa.—P. S. L.

Sandiford, R[alph], *The Mystery of Iniquity; in a brief Examination of the Practice of the Times, etc. Printed for the Author, Anno* 1730. 2d ed. with additions.—Sandiford was one of the earliest abolitionist writers in Pa. He was honest, but eccentric and vehement.—H. S. P.

Saunders, Prince, *An Address Delivered at Bethel Church, Philadelphia, . . . Before the Pennsylvania Augustine Society for the Education of People of Colour,* etc. Phila., 1818.—H. S. P.

Saunders, Prince, *A Memoir Presented to the American Convention for Promoting the Abolition of Slavery,* etc. Phila., 1818.—R. B.

A Serious Address to the Rulers of America, On the Inconsistency of their Conduct respecting Slavery, etc. Trenton, 1773.—R. B.

A Sermon Occasioned by the Destruction of Pennsylvania Hall, and Delivered . . . in the First Congregational Unitarian Church, by the Pastor, etc. Philadelphia., 1838.—Mob violence and anti-slavery.—H. S. P.

Seward, William, *Journal of A Voyage from Savannah to Philadelphia and from Philadelphia to England MDCCXL.* London, 1740.—Early religious work among the negroes.—R. B.

Sharp, Granville, *An Essay on Slavery, Proving from Scripture its Inconsistency with Humanity and Religion,* etc. Burlington, 1773.—By an eminent English abolitionist who corresponded with the abolition leaders in Pa. Remarks on manumission in Pa.—R. B.

Sketches of the Higher Classes of Colored Society in Philadelphia. By a Southerner. Phila., 1841.—Interesting and temperate. Apparently by one well informed and impartial. If this work can be fully trusted, it contains more information as to the social status of the negro in Phila. than any other book in the whole period.—H. S. P.

Slavery Clippings. 4 vols.—Newspaper clippings.—H. S. P.

Slavery not Forbidden by Scripture, Or A Defence of the West India Planters, From the Aspersions Thrown Out Against Them, By the Author of A Pamphlet, Entitled, "An Address to the Inhabitants," etc., by a West Indian. Phila., 1773.—Early anti-abolition tract.—R. B.

Sleigh, W. W., *Abolitionism Exposed! Proving that the Principles of Abolitionism Are Injurious to the Slaves Themselves,* 2d ed. Phila., 1838.—R. B.

Smith, Capt. J. S., *A Letter from, to the Revd Mr Hill on the State of the Negroe Slaves. To which are added An Introduction and Remarks on Free Negroes, etc. By the Editor.* London, 1786.—Occupation and conduct of the freedmen of Pa. —R. B.

A Statistical Inquiry into the Condition of the People of Colour of the City and Districts of Philadelphia. Phila., 1849.— Made under direction of Friends. Based on careful investigations.—H. S. P.

Statistics of the Colored People of Philadelphia taken by Benjamin C. Brown and published by order of the Board of Education of "The Pennsylvania Society for Promoting the Abolition of Slavery," etc. Phila., 1856.—H. S. P.

Sumner, Charles, *Letter of Sympathy to Passmore Williamson,* Aug. 11, 1855.—Uncatalogued. H. S. P.

Thomas, Gabriel, *An Historical and Geographical Account of the Province and Country of Pensilvania and West-New-Jersey in America, etc.* London, 1698. Lithographed for H. A. Brady, New York, 1848.—Early notice of negroes in Pa. Protest of Keithian Quakers against slavery.—Pea.

Thompson, John, The Life of, A Fugitive Slave; Containing His History of 25 Years in Bondage, and His Providential Escape, Written by Himself. Worcester, 1856.—Fled through Pa.—R. B.

Torrey, Jesse, Jr., *A Portraiture of Domestic Slavery, in the United States . . . including Memoirs of Facts . . . on Kidnapping.* Phila., 1817.—Of value if used cautiously.—R. B.

Tyson, J. R., *A Discourse before the Young Men's Colonization Society of Pennsylvania,* etc. Phila., 1834.—H. S. P.

Tyson, J. Washington, The Doctrines of the "Abolitionists" Refuted, in a Letter from, etc. Phila., 1840.—H. S. P.

The Visions of A Certain Thomas Say, Of the City of Phila-delphia, Which He Saw in a Trance, etc. Phila., 1774.—R. B.

Was ist Aufhebung der Sclaverei (Abolition)? Heraus-gegeben von der östlichen Abtheilung der pennsylvanischen Anti-Sclaverei-Gesellschaft.—To enlist support of Pennsylvania's German population.—H. S. P.

What Has Pennsylvania To Do With Slavery?—H. S. P.

What is Sauce for a Goose is also Sauce for a Gander . . . An Epitaph on a certain great man. Written by a departed spirit, etc. Phila., 1764.—Franklin said to have had a negro paramour. —R. B.

Whitefield, George, Journal of a Voyage From London to Gibraltar by, etc. 6th ed., Phila., 1740.—Early religious work among negroes.—R. B.

A Continuation Of the Reverend Mr. Whitefield's Journal From A few Days after his Arrival at Georgia, To His second Return thither from Pennsylvania. Phila., 1740. —R. B.

Three Letters from the Reverend Mr. G. Whitefield: etc. Phila., Printed and Sold by B. Franklin, etc., *MDCCXL.*—H. S. P.

Why Colored People in Philadelphia Are Excluded from the Street Cars. Phila., 1866.—Prejudice against negroes.—L. C. P.

Williamson, Passmore, Case of. Report of the Proceedings on the Writ of Habeas Corpus Issued by the Hon. John K. Kane, etc. Phila., 1856.—Fugitive slaves.—H. S. P.

Woolman, John, *Some Considerations On* the Keeping of *Negroes. Recommended to the Professors of Christianity of every Denomination,* etc. Phila., 1754.—H. S. P.

Woolman, John, *Considerations on Keeping Negroes,* etc. Part Second. Phila., 1762.—H. S. P.

Woolman, John, *The Works of. In two Parts.* Phila., *MDCCLXXIV.*—L. C.

A Journal of the Life, Gospel Labours, and Christian Experiences of That Faithful Minister of Jesus Christ, John Woolman, etc. Dublin, 1778.—Fr. Hist. Lib., Swarthmore, Pa. Woolman was the greatest of the early abolitionist apostles. His writings reflect his gentle, kindly, but vigorous character. As notable for their style as their content.

Yates, William, *Rights of Colored Men to Suffrage, Citizenship and Trial by Jury:* etc. Phila., 1838.—Careful discussion. —H. S. P.

IV.

PICTURES.

Pictures relating to slavery or the negro in Pennsylvania before 1800 are rare. Not the least valuable among the early ones are the rude wood-cuts inserted in the advertisements for runaway negroes or negroes for sale, in the colonial newspapers. Most of the formal illustrations in books are worthless.

The Election A Medley. Humbly Inscribed to Squire Lilliput Professor of Scurrillity.—Large engraved caricature showing group in front of the Court House, Phila. A negro man is seen following his master. There are two negro boys and a negro woman. The picture probably affords some indication of how slaves were dressed. About 1765.—H. S. P.

Colored prints by Charles Hunt and I. Harris.—Caricature extravagance of dress, and absurd imitation by negroes of doings of white people. Probably about 1825.—Museum of Independence Hall, Phila.

Numerous engravings, paintings, etc., of anti-slavery leaders, friends of the negro, etc.—"Anti-Slavery Repository" in the Colored Home, 44th Street and Girard Avenue, Phila.

INDEX.

African Hall, burned by incendi-
aries (1842), 164
African Methodist Episcopal
Church, 135
African Presbyterian Church,
ruined by mob (1834), 160
Alabama, suffrage in, 176 n.; asks
Pennsylvania to suppress anti-
slavery, 219 n.
Aldermen, forbidden to try cases
of fugitive slaves (1820), 117,
232
Allen, R., negro bishop of Philadelphia, 125, 136 n.
Almshouse, Philadelphia, negroes
in, 154
Alricks, Peter, uses negroes, 1;
his negroes confiscated by English, 2
American Anti-Slavery Society,
founded 1833, 208 n.
American Colonization Society,
commended by negroes (1830),
138
Anthony, negro of Governor
Printz, 1.
Antigua, negroes imported from, 9
Anti-slavery, increases race prejudice, 150; causes riots in eastern cities (1834), 160; causes
riot in Philadelphia (1838), 162;
contrasted with abolitionism,
206-209; meaning of, 208 n.;
beginning of, in Pennsylvania,
217; violence of, 218; anger
aroused by, in Pennsylvania,
219; hatred of, causes destruction of Pennsylvania Hall, 219;
suppression of, asked by southern states, 219; proposed suppression of, in Pennsylvania, by
law, 220; discountenanced by
some of the abolitionists, 220;
gains ground in Pennsylvania
(1839-1861), 221, 223, 244
Anti-slavery societies, founded,
208 n.; in Pennsylvania, 218;
records of, 262-264
Anti-slavery workers, threats made
against (1861), 247

Apprentices, negro, 101-107; terms
of indenture of, 105 n.; before
1780, 106
Apprentices, white, children bound
as, 102-103; numerous, 103; regulation of, by law (1762-1763,
1769-1770), 103-106; consent of,
necessary, when indentured, 103;
length of service of, 104; schooling of, 104; obligations to master, 105; marriages of, 105; punishment of, for running away,
105-106
Apprenticeship, 90, 101-107.
Arkansas, suffrage in, 176 n.
Arms, right to bear, connection of,
with right to vote, 174
Arson, by slaves, 47, 48 n.
Assembly, colonial, of Pennsylvania, imposes duties upon negroes
imported, 3-7; rejects petition
against hiring of negroes, 5; protests against enlistment of servants, 5; imposes duties to restrict
importation of negroes, 8, 9;
regulates but few incidents of
slavery, 20
Assessment books, 260
Association of Friends for the
Free Instruction of Adult Colored Persons, founded 1832,
132 n.
Association of negroes tries to gain
suffrage, 192
Atlee, Edwin P., issues anti-slavery pamphlet in Philadelphia,
217; attacks constitution of
United States, 217

Bakers, slaves employed as, 41;
negroes in business as, 125 n.
Baldwin, John, of Chester, frees
negroes (1731), 57
Baltimore, case of kidnapped negress in (1853), 242; policeman
from, fails to capture fugitive
slave, 244
Baptism of slaves, 20
Baptist church, negro, 135

Instruction, free, of white children, laws regarding (1802, 1804, 1809), 130
Insurrection of slaves, not feared in Pennsylvania, 48
Intercourse, sexual, between negroes and white people, forbidden (1725-1726), 29; decision of Chester County Court respecting (1698), 30; evidences of, 31, 196, 197
Intermarriage, of free negroes with white people, forbidden, 112; punishments for, 113; efforts to prevent, 194-196
Iron-masters, desire negro labor, 4 n.; own negroes, 13
Iron-works, negroes desired at, 15
Iron-workers, slaves employed as, 41

Jackson, Isaac, member of Friends' visiting committees, 75
Jails, fugitive slaves to be lodged in (1826), 233; debarred from (1847), 238; readmitted to (1852), 244
Jamaica, negroes imported into Pennsylvania from, 9
John, negro property-owner (1779), 125
Jones, Absalom, negro minister, 129 n.; helps to prepare resolution for negroes, 138
Jones, Henry, of Moyamensing, owns negroes (1688), 13 n.
Jones, Jonathan, visited by committees, regrets purchase of negro, 73 n.
Jury, trial by, negroes debarred from (1700-1780), 27, 110; for fugitive slaves, numerous petitions asking for, 235, 236
Justices of Courts of Quarter Sessions, assent to indentures of apprentices, 103; jurisdiction of, over negroes marrying white people, 113; forbidden to try cases of fugitive slaves (1820), 117, 232

Kalm, Peter, on effect of cold upon negroes in Pennsylvania, 10 n.; on death penalty for murder of slave, 36 n.; on good treatment of negroes, 38; declares negroes were refused religious teaching, 43
Kansas, trouble in, increases anti-slavery sentiment in Pennsylvania, 226
Keimer, Samuel, scheme to teach negroes to read, 128 n.
Keith, George, denounces slavery, 19; declaration of (1693), 21; issues first protest against slavery printed in America, 66
Keithian Quakers, advise masters to give negroes Christian education (1693), 43; protest of, 208
Kennett Square, Society of Progressive Friends founded at , (1853), 222
Kentucky, Court of Appeals of, decides that negroes are not citizens, 176 n.; asks Pennsylvania to suppress anti-slavery, 219 n.
Kidnapping of free negroes in Pennsylvania, 115-119, 211-212, 238, 242
"Killers of Moyamensing," attack negroes (1849), 164
King, Adam, of Georgetown, sells negro servants in Pennsylvania, 93 n.
Knowles, John, of Oxford, frees negro (1744), 57

Labor, slaves needed because of high price of, 6
Lancaster County, fugitive slave in, 240; Underground Railroad started in, 240
Langhorne, Jeremiah, Judge, of Bucks County, frees negroes (1742), 57; gives property to manumitted slaves, 121
Laws of Pennsylvania, editions of, 280